New
ENTERPRISE

B1

Teacher's Book

Jenny Dooley

Express Publishing

Published by Express Publishing

Liberty House, Greenham Business Park, Newbury,
Berkshire RG19 6HW, United Kingdom
Tel.: (0044) 1635 817 363
Fax: (0044) 1635 817 463
email: inquiries@expresspublishing.co.uk
www.expresspublishing.co.uk

First published 2019
Second impression 2019

Made in EU

ISBN978-4-7647-4137-9

Contents

Introduction to the Teacher

New Enterprise B1 is a modular course for young adults and adults studying British English at CEFR Level B1. It allows flexibility of approach, which makes it suitable for classes of all kinds, including large or mixed ability classes.

New Enterprise B1 consists of twelve units. Each unit consists of three lessons plus Culture sections, Reviews & Competences. The corresponding unit in the Workbook provides the option of additional practice.

COURSE COMPONENTS

Student's Book

The **Student's Book** is the main component of the course. Each unit is based on specific themes and the topics covered are of general interest. All units follow the same basic structure (see **Elements of the Coursebook**).

Workbook

The **Workbook** is in full colour and contains units corresponding to those in the Student's Book, with practice in Vocabulary, Grammar, Everyday English & Reading. There is a Revision Section every three units for students to revise the vocabulary and grammar taught. There is also a Skills Practice section for students to get more practice in Listening, Everyday English, Reading and Writing. All the exercises in the Workbook are marked with graded level of difficulty (*, **, ***).

Teacher's Book

The **Teacher's Book** contains step-by-step lesson plans and suggestions on how to present the material. It also includes answers to the exercises in the Student's Book, the audioscripts of all the listening material, suggested speaking and writing models, and evaluation sheets as well as the answers to the exercises in the Workbook and Grammar Book.

Class Audio CDs

The Class Audio CDs contain all the recorded material which accompanies the course. This includes the monologues/dialogues and texts in the Listening and Reading sections, Values, Presentation Skills, Public Speaking Skills & CLIL sections as well as the Pronunciation/Intonation sections in the Student's Book, and the material for all listening tasks in the Workbook.

IWB

The IWB contains all the material in the Student's Book, Teacher's Book, Workbook, Grammar Book and Audio CDs and aims to facilitate lessons in the classroom. It also contains grammar presentations of all the grammar structures in the Student's Book as well as **videos** closely linked to the texts in the course and activities for Ss to

further practise their English and expand their knowledge, as well as **games** for students to revise the vocabulary and grammar taught.

Digibook applications

The **Digi apps** contain all the material in the Student's Book, Workbook and Grammar Book and help students monitor their progress and improve their stats which are stored so that they can be accessed at any time.

Grammar Book

The Grammar Book contains clear, simple presentations of all grammar structures that appear in the course with a variety of graded exercises.

ELEMENTS OF THE COURSEBOOK

Each unit begins with a brief overview of what will be covered in the unit.

Each unit contains the following sections:

Vocabulary

Vocabulary is introduced in a functional and meaningful context. It is practised through a variety of exercises, such as picture-word association and completing set phrases in order to help students use everyday English correctly.

Reading

Each unit contains reading texts, such as: articles, blog entries, articles, emails, tweets, forum entries, adverts, etc. These allow skills, such as reading for gist, for specific information, for cohesion & coherence etc to be systematically practised.

Grammar

The grammar items taught in each unit are first presented in context, then highlighted and clarified by means of clear, concise theory boxes. Specific exercises and activities methodically reinforce learners' understanding and mastery of each item. Detailed explanations of all grammar points and exercises are in the Grammar Reference. The Workbook contains practice on each grammar structure presented within each unit.

Listening

Learners develop their listening skills through a variety of tasks which employ the vocabulary and grammar practised in the unit in realistic contexts. This reinforces learners' understanding of the language taught in the unit.

Speaking

Controlled speaking activities have been carefully designed to allow learners' guided practice before leading them to less structured speaking activities.

Everyday English

Functional dialogues set in everyday contexts familiarise students with natural language. The dialogues are followed by language boxes to help learners practise.

Pronunciation/Intonation

Pronunciation/Intonation activities help learners to recognise the various sounds of the English language, distinguish between them and reproduce them correctly.

Writing

There are writing activities throughout the units, based on realistic types and styles of writing, such as emails, letters, blogs, online forms, reviews, stories, articles, essays, news reports, etc. These progress from short paragraphs to full texts, allowing learners to gradually build up their writing skills.

Culture

Each unit is accompanied by a *Culture* section.

In each *Culture* section, learners are provided with cultural information about aspects of English-speaking countries that are thematically linked to the unit. Learners are given the chance to process the information they have learnt and compare it to the culture of their own country.

Study Skills

Brief tips, explanations and reminders at various points throughout each unit help learners to develop strategies which improve holistic learning skills and enable them to become autonomous learners of the English language.

Review

This section appears at the end of each unit, and reinforces students' understanding of the topics, vocabulary and structures that have been presented in the unit. A Competences marking scheme at the end of every *Review* section allows learners to evaluate their own progress and identify their strengths and weaknesses.

Values

This section aims to develop moral values learners need to have in our globalised world.

Public Speaking Skills

This section aims to help learners develop their public speaking skills, giving them guidance on how to become competent public speakers.

CLIL

The *CLIL* sections enable learners to link the themes of the units to an academic subject, thus helping them contextualise the language they have learnt by relating it to their own personal frame of reference. Lively and creative tasks stimulate learners and allow them to consolidate the language they have learnt throughout the units.

Each *CLIL* section is aimed to be taught after the corresponding *Values & Public Speaking Skills* sections.

Irregular Verbs

This provides students with a quick reference list for verb forms they might be unsure of at times.

SUGGESTED TEACHING TECHNIQUES

A Presenting new vocabulary

The new vocabulary in *New Enterprise B1* is frequently presented through pictures. *(See Student's Book, Unit 4, p. 30, Ex. 1.)*

Further techniques that you may use to introduce new vocabulary include:

- **Miming.** Mime the word you want to introduce. For instance, to present the verb sing, pretend you are singing and ask learners to guess the meaning of the word.
- **Synonyms, opposites, paraphrasing and giving definitions.** Examples:
  - present the word **strong** by giving a synonym: 'powerful'.
  - present the word **strong** by giving its opposite: 'weak'.
  - present the word **weekend** by paraphrasing it: 'Saturday and Sunday'.
  - present the word **famous** by giving its definition: 'very well-known (person or thing)'.
- **Example.** Use of examples places vocabulary into context and consequently makes understanding easier. For instance, introduce the words **city** and **town** by referring to a city and a town in the learners' country: 'Rome is a city, but Parma is a town.'
- **Sketching.** Draw a simple sketch of the word or words you want to explain on the board. For instance:

- **Use of L1.** In a monolingual class, you may explain vocabulary in the learners' native language. This method, though, should be employed in moderation.
- **Use of a dictionary.** In a multilingual class, learners may refer to a bilingual dictionary.

The choice of technique depends on the type of word or expression. For example, you may find it easier to describe an action verb through miming than through a synonym or a definition.

> **Note:** ✓ *Check these words* sections can be treated as follows: Go through the list of words after Ss have read the text and ask Ss to explain the words using the context they appear in. Ss can give examples, mime/ draw the meaning, or look up the meaning in their dictionaries.

B Choral & individual repetition

Repetition will ensure that learners are thoroughly familiar with the sound and pronunciation of the lexical items and structures being taught and confident in their ability to reproduce them.

Always ask learners to repeat chorally before you ask them to repeat individually. Repeating chorally will help learners feel confident enough to then perform the task on their own.

C Reading & Listening

You may ask learners to read and listen for a variety of purposes:

- **Reading for detail.** Ask learners to read for specific information. *(See Student's Book, Unit 1, p. 5, Ex. 5. Ss will have to read the text in order to do the task. They are looking for specific details in the text and not for general information.)*
- **Listening for detail.** Learners listen for specific information. *(See Student's Book, Unit 1, p. 8, Ex. 2.)*
- **Listening and reading for gist.** Ask learners to read and/or listen to get the gist of the dialogue or text being dealt with. *(See Student's Book, Unit 3, p. 20, Ex. 3. Tell Ss that in order to complete this task successfully, they do not need to understand every single detail in the text.)*

> **Note:** ▶ VIDEO
> Main texts in the Student's Book are accompanied by videos that are included in the digi applications and the IWB. The videos can be watched after learners have read the texts. Activities that accompany the videos can be done in class or assigned as HW.

D Speaking

- Speaking activities are initially controlled, allowing for guided practice in language/structures that have just been learnt. *(See Student's Book, Unit 1, p. 8, Ex. 1b.).*
- Ss are led to free speaking activities. *(See Student's Book, Unit 1, p. 8, Ex. 4, where Ss are provided with the necessary lexical items and structures and are asked to act out their dialogues.)*

E Writing

All writing tasks in *New Enterprise B1* have been carefully designed to closely guide learners to produce a successful piece of writing. They are fully analysed in the *Skills in Action* sections in the Student's Book with model texts and exercises that aim to help learners improve their writing skills.

- Make sure that Ss understand that they are writing for a purpose. Go through the writing task so that Ss are fully aware of why they are writing and who they are writing for. *(See Student's Book, Unit 4, p. 35, Ex. 9. Ss are asked to write an informal email.).*
- It would be well advised to actually complete the task orally in class before assigning it as written homework. Ss will then feel more confident with producing a complete piece of writing on their own.

F Assigning homework

When assigning homework, prepare learners as well as possible in advance. This will help them avoid errors and get maximum benefit from the task.

Commonly assigned tasks include:

Dictation – learners learn the spelling of particular words without memorising the text in which they appear;

Vocabulary – learners memorise the meaning of words and phrases or use the new words in sentences of their own;

Reading Aloud – assisted by the digi apps, learners practise at home in preparation for reading aloud in class;

Writing – after thorough preparation in class, learners are asked to produce a complete piece of writing.

G Correcting learners' work

All learners make errors – it is part of the learning process. The way you deal with errors depends on what the learners are doing.

- **Oral accuracy work:**
  Correct learners on the spot, either by providing the correct answer and allowing them to repeat, or by indicating the error but allowing learners to correct it. Alternatively, indicate the error and ask other Ss to provide the answer.
- **Oral fluency work:**
  Allow learners to finish the task without interrupting, but make a note of the errors made and correct them afterwards.

- **Written work:**
  Do not over-correct; focus on errors that are directly relevant to the point of the exercise. When giving feedback, you may write the most common errors on the board and get the class to attempt to correct them.

Remember that rewarding work and praising learners is of great importance. Praise effort as well as success.

H Class organisation

- **Open pairs**
  The class focuses its attention on two learners doing the set task together. Use this technique when you want your learners to offer an example of how a task is done. *(See Student's Book, Unit 1, p. 8, Ex. 1b.)*

- **Closed pairs**
  Pairs of learners work together on a task or activity while you move around offering assistance and suggestions. Explain the task clearly before beginning closed pairwork. *(See Student's Book, Unit 1, p. 8, Ex. 4b.)*

- **Stages of pairwork**
  - Put Ss in pairs.
  - Explain the task and set a time limit.
  - Rehearse the task in open pairs.
  - In closed pairs, get Ss to do the task.
  - Go around the class and help Ss.
  - Open pairs report back to the class.

- **Group work**
  Groups of three or more Ss work together on a task or activity. Class projects or role-play are most easily done in groups. Again, give Ss a solid understanding of the task in advance.

- **Rolling questions**
  Ask Ss one after the other to ask and answer questions based on the texts.

I Using L1 in class

Use L1 in moderation and only when necessary.

ABBREVIATIONS

Abbreviations used in the Student's and Teacher's Books.

T	teacher	p(p).	page(s)
S(s)	student(s)	e.g.	for example
HW	homework	i.e.	that is
L1	students' native language	etc	et cetera
		sb	somebody
Ex(s).	exercise(s)	sth	something

Key to symbols used in the Student's/Teacher's Books

 audio

 pairwork

 groupwork

 words to be explained using the context each appears in

ICT tasks to help learners develop research skills

Study Skills suggestions to help learners become autonomous

 suggestions to help learners develop their writing skills

 sections to develop Ss' critical thinking skills

 **Culture** texts to familiarise Ss with the culture of English-speaking countries and develop cross-cultural awareness

VALUES sections to help Ss develop critical thinking skills and values

CLIL sections that link the themes of the units to a subject from the core curriculum

In Character

Topic

In this unit, Ss will explore the topics of character, appearance, clothes and accessories.

1a	Reading & Vocabulary	4-5

Lesson objectives: To learn vocabulary for character & appearance, to listen and read for gist, to read for specific information (correcting sentences), to learn prepositional phrases, to practise words easily confused, to learn phrasal verbs with *look*, to describe a person

Vocabulary: Character *(bossy, calm, cheerful, kind, confident, jealous, gentle, clever, cruel, lazy, honest, curious, generous, reliable, friendly, patient, sensible, funny, brave, rude, sociable, serious, charming, careful)*; Appearance *(early/late twenties, middle-aged, elderly, early/late thirties, teenager, thick eyebrows, big ears, small round ears, a long nose, bottom lip fuller than top lip, a big forehead, a curved forehead, blue eyes, brown eyes)*; Nouns *(feature, earlobe, brain)*; Verbs *(judge, tend, brighten up)*; Phrasal verbs *(look)*; Adjectives *(popular, violent, chubby, bushy, arched, rectangular, hooked, adventurous, curved, famous)*

1b	Grammar in Use	6-7

Lesson objectives: To learn/revise the present simple – present continuous, to compare action verbs & stative verbs, to learn/revise stative verbs with continuous forms, to learn/revise relatives & defining/non-defining relative clauses

1c	Skills in Action	8-9

Lesson objectives: To learn vocabulary for clothes & accessories, to listen for specific information (multiple choice), to act out a dialogue and practise everyday English for deciding what to wear, to learn the pronunciation of diphthongs /eɪ/, /aɪ/, /ɔɪ/, to read for cohesion & coherence (word formation), to write an article

Vocabulary: Clothes & Accessories *(leather belt, evening dress, ankle socks, high-heeled shoes, polo-neck jumper, bow tie, skinny jeans, silk blouse, swimsuit, pullover, tracksuit, walking boots, waistcoat, raincoat, tailored suit, polo shirt, sweatshirt)*; Departments *(accessories, beachwear, sportswear, footwear, menswear, womenswear)*

Culture 1		10

Lesson objectives: To listen and read for gist, to read for specific information, to present the kilt, to write a short article on a traditional piece of clothing from one's country

Vocabulary: Nouns *(occasion, funeral, event, knee, cloth, pleat, pattern, hose, ghillie brogues, sporran, pouch, kilt pin)*; Verb *(hang)*; Phrasal verb *(date back)*; Preposition *(unlike)*

Review 1		11

Lesson objectives: To test/consolidate vocabulary and grammar learnt throughout the unit, to practise everyday English

Go through the objectives box and tell Ss that these are the topics, skills and activities this unit will cover.

1a

Vocabulary

1 **Aim** To present vocabulary related to character

- Put some examples of character adjectives on the board, e.g. friendly, clever, etc.
- Give Ss a one-minute time limit to come up with as many character adjectives as they can think of.
- Then ask Ss to compare their list with their partner's.
- Ask various Ss around the class to read from their lists.

Suggested Answer Key

bossy, brave, calm, cheerful, clever, confident, cruel, friendly, funny, generous, intelligent, jealous, lazy, negative, noisy, patient, rude, serious

2 a) **Aim** To practise vocabulary for character

- Go through the **Study Skills** box with your Ss. Advise Ss to use a printed or digital dictionary and explain that this will help them enrich their vocabulary.
- Ask Ss to go through the sentences, choose the correct words and then check their answers in their dictionaries.
- Check Ss' answers around the class.

Answer Key

1	bossy	7	generous
2	cheerful	8	patient
3	confident	9	sensible
4	gentle	10	rude
5	cruel	11	serious
6	curious	12	charming

- As an extension, ask Ss to make sentences using the other option, or ask Ss to list the adjectives in bold under the headings: POSITIVE – NEGATIVE.

b) **Aim** To practise character adjectives

Ask Ss to use the character adjectives in Ex. 2a to describe themselves and their friends, giving reasons.

Suggested Answer Key

I am a calm and kind person because I don't get angry easily and I like helping other people.
My friend Jane is a clever and curious person because she knows a lot of things and always wants to learn more.

3 **Aim** **To present/practise vocabulary for appearance**

- Ask Ss to look at the pictures and go through the list of vocabulary. Explain any unknown words Ss might have, either miming the meaning of the word or providing an example sentence. Alternatively, ask Ss to look up the meanings of any unknown words in the Word List or in their dictionaries.
- Elicit answers to the questions from Ss around the class.

Suggested Answer Key

Helen is a teenager with big ears, a long nose, a big forehead and brown eyes.

Mark is in his early twenties. He has got thick eyebrows, small round ears and brown eyes.

Ann is elderly with a big forehead, a bottom lip fuller than the top lip and brown eyes.

Sam is in his early thirties. He has got thick eyebrows, a long nose, a curved forehead and brown eyes.

Sue is in her late thirties. She has got a long nose, a bottom lip fuller than the top lip, a big forehead and brown eyes.

Amira is in her late twenties with thick eyebrows and brown eyes.

Listening & Reading

4 **a)** **Aim** **To listen and read for gist**

- Elicit Ss' guesses as to what someone's facial features may say about their character. Provide an example if Ss need help.
- Play the recording. Ss listen and follow the text in their books and find out if their guesses were correct.

Suggested Answer Key

I think thick eyebrows may mean you are confident. I think big eyes may mean you are friendly. I think small ears may mean you are patient. I think a small nose may mean you are generous. I think thin lips may mean you are cruel. I think a big forehead may mean you are intelligent.

b) **Aim** **To identify a text type**

- Ask Ss to study the text again and elicit where they think it is from, choosing from the options provided.
- Elicit what style is typical of the types of texts in the list, e.g. a newspaper article is usually on a serious topic with mostly factual information and some opinion; a personal blog usually contains information about the person who writes it; a light-

hearted magazine can contain gossip, news, tips on fashion, etc.
- Then check Ss' answers around the class.

Suggested Answer Key

I think the text is from a light-hearted magazine.

5 **Aim** **To read for key information (sentence correction)**

- Ask Ss to read the sentences and then read the text again and correct them.
- Check Ss' answers.
- Then give Ss time to explain the words in bold by using the Word List or their dictionaries to help them/elicit explanations from Ss around the class.

Answer Key

1   *A person with thick dark eyebrows is **sociable**./A person with **bushy** eyebrows is bossy.*
2   *Blue-eyed people are **calm**./**Brown-eyed** people are confident.*
3   *People with rectangular ears are **honest and hard-working**./People with **big** ears are cruel.*
4   *People with hooked noses are **confident**./People with **long** noses are patient.*
5   *People with lips the same size are **fair**./People with a **fuller top lip** are rude.*
6   *A bright happy person often has a **curved** forehead./A **clever** person often has a big forehead.*

Suggested Answer Key

judge (v): *to form an opinion about sth/sb*
popular (adj): *being liked by many people*
feature (n): *a part of the face [facial features]*
tend [to] (v): *to be likely to have sth/behave in a certain way*
adventurous (adj): *willing to try new things*
curved (adj): *having a rounded shape*
brighten up (v): *to make happier*

- Give Ss time to look up the meanings of the words in the **Check these words** box in the Word List.
- Play the video for Ss and elicit their comments.

6 **Aim** **To consolidate new vocabulary**

- Explain the task and give Ss time to complete the phrases using the words in the list.
- Then check Ss' answers by having Ss use the phrases in sentences of their own.

NOTE: Explain to Ss that certain words collocate in English. Ss can look in their dictionaries for words that collocate and have a Collocations section in their

notebooks. This will help them expand their vocabulary. Ss can make sentences using the collocations and try to use them as often as they can.

e.g. easy

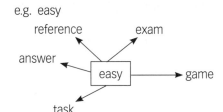

Answer Key

1	ancient	4	eye	7	curved
2	chubby	5	round		
3	thick	6	bottom		

Suggested Answer Key

*Origami is the **ancient art** of paper folding.*
*Babies often have **chubby cheeks**.*
*My dad has got **thick eyebrows**.*
*Brown is a common **eye colour**.*
*Mickey Mouse has got big **round ears**.*
*Sue's **bottom lip** trembles when she is going to cry.*
*James has got a **curved forehead**.*

7 **Aim** To consolidate prepositional phrases from a text

- Give Ss time to read the gapped sentences and fill the gaps with the correct prepositions.
- Then check Ss' answers.

NOTE: Ask Ss to create a Prepositions section in their notebooks and list all prepositional phrases they come across. Ss can revise them regularly.

Answer Key

1	to	3	to	5	about
2	with	4	of	6	to

8 **Aim** To understand words easily confused

- Explain the task and give Ss time to use their dictionaries to help them complete it.
- Check Ss' answers.

Answer Key

1	famous	3	famous
2	popular	4	popular

9 **Aim** To learn phrasal verbs with *look*

- Ask Ss to read the phrasal verbs box. Make sure that Ss understand the definitions.
- Then give Ss time to complete the task and check their answers.

- Tell Ss to create a Phrasal Verbs section at the back of their notebooks and list all phrasal verbs they come across and include their definitions. Ss can revise this list from time to time.

Answer Key

1	up	3	forward to
2	after	4	for

Speaking

10 **Aim** THINK To develop critical thinking skills; to describe a person and compare their character with the information in the text

- Explain the task and ask Ss to work in pairs and describe a person to their partner. They then compare their character with the character the text says their features match and say whether this is true or not.
- Ss take turns to complete the activity. Monitor the activity around the class and then ask some Ss to share their answers with the class.

Suggested Answer Key

My friend Anna has got thick eyebrows, round ears, a long nose and blue eyes. According to the text this means she is sociable, reliable, patient and calm. She is truly all these things and a really good friend.

1b Grammar in Use

1 **Aim** To present/revise the present simple and the present continuous

- Ask Ss to read the dialogue and identify the tenses in bold. Elicit how these tenses are formed.
- Read out the list of uses and have Ss say which example in bold matches which use.
- Refer Ss to the **Grammar Reference** section for detailed information.
- Then direct Ss' attention to the adverbs of frequency in the dialogue and elicit how we use them in a sentence.

Answer Key

Present simple: *works, comes, starts*
Present continuous: *'m starting, 'm doing, is showing*

*We form the present simple with the base form of the verb. 3rd person affirmative is usually formed adding **-s** to the base form of the verb. We use **do/does** to form the negative and interrogative forms.*
*We form the present continuous with the verb **to be** and the **-ing** form of the main verb.*

We use the present simple for:
- *habits/routines/repeated actions (comes)*
- *timetables/schedules (future meaning) starts*
- *permanent states (works)*

We use the present continuous for:
- *actions happening at the time of speaking (is showing)*
- *fixed arrangements in the near future ('m starting)*
- *temporary situations ('m doing)*

*Adverbs of frequency go before the main verb but after the verb 'to be'. E.g. She **often comes** over ... it**'s never** slow!*

2 (Aim) To compare action verbs and stative verbs

- Ask Ss to read the theory box and then direct their attention to the highlighted verbs in the dialogue.
- Elicit whether they have continuous forms and why [not].
- Refer Ss to the **Grammar Reference** section for more information on stative verbs.

Answer Key

The verbs 'want' and 'have' (own) do not have a continuous form because they are both stative verbs.

3 (Aim) To practise the present simple and the present continuous

- Explain the task and give Ss time to complete it.
- Then check Ss' answers.

Answer Key

1 *works (permanent state)*
2 *gets (routine)*
3 *is directing (action happening at the time of speaking)*
4 *is staying (temporary situation)*
5 *is flying (fixed arrangement in near future)*
6 *leaves (timetable – future meaning)*
7 *loves (stative verb)*
8 *dislikes (stative verb)*

Background Information

Morocco is a country in North Africa. It has a long coastline and large areas of desert. Its capital city is Rabat and it has a population of 33.8 million people.

4 (Aim) To learn stative verbs with continuous forms

- Ask Ss to read the theory box. Then direct their attention to the underlined verbs in the dialogue and elicit how the meaning differs.
- Refer Ss to the **Grammar Reference** section for more information.
- Give Ss time to complete the task and then elicit answers from Ss around the class.

Answer Key

'm thinking = am considering
think = believe

5 (Aim) To practise stative verbs and their continuous forms

- Explain the task and give Ss time to complete it.
- Check Ss' answers.

Answer Key

1 *is seeing (is visiting)*
2 *see (view with my eyes)*
3 *looks (seems)*
4 *are looking (are reading)*
5 *is tasting (is sampling)*
6 *tastes (has the flavour of)*
7 *is (fact)*
8 *are being (are behaving)*

6 (Aim) To practise the present simple and the present continuous

- Explain the task and give Ss time to complete it.
- Check Ss' answers.

Answer Key

1 *is putting (fixed future arrangement)*
2 *starts (timetable – future meaning)*
3 *am trying (action happening at the time of speaking)*
4 *know (stative verb)*
5 *works (permanent state)*
6 *teaches (routine)*
7 *doesn't like (stative verb)*
8 *need (stative verb)*
9 *don't have (stative verb)*
10 *Are you getting (temporary situation)*
11 *believe (stative verb)*
12 *is appearing (fixed future arrangement – stative verb with a continuous form)*

Background Information

Snow White is a German fairy tale from the Brothers Grimm. It was published in 1812 and features magical elements such as a magic mirror, a poisoned apple and a glass coffin. The characters include Prince Charming, the Evil Queen and the seven dwarfs. It is often seen in pantomime.

7 **Aim** To learn/revise relatives

- Ask Ss to look at the words in bold in the sentences and identify which ones are used for people, things, time or place and which shows possession. Then elicit an example from the dialogue on p. 6.
- Refer Ss to the **Grammar Reference** section for more information.

Answer Key

1 people   3 possession   5 time
2 things   4 place

8 **Aim** To learn/revise/practise defining/non-defining relative clauses

- Go through the theory box with Ss. Refer Ss to the **Grammar Reference** section for more information. Use the examples to help Ss understand the difference between defining/non-defining sentences.
- Then give them time to fill in the correct relative pronouns in the sentences and put commas where necessary.
- Check Ss' answers and elicit which are defining and which are non-defining relative clauses.

Answer Key

1 who/that (defining)
2 where (defining)
3 which/that (defining)
4 My cousin Harry, whose uncle is a physicist, plans to get a science degree. (non-defining)
5 whose (defining)
6 when (defining)
7 Mr Bloggs, who is a reliable builder, did an excellent job on our house. (non-defining)
8 Sandra is curious by nature, which means that she enjoys exploring new places. (non-defining)

9 **Aim** To practise relative clauses

- Explain the task and read out the example.
- Give Ss time to complete the task and then check Ss' answers.

Answer Key

2 James enjoys sailing in summer when the weather is good.
3 Claire is a model who has been in lots of fashion shows.
4 The Wilsons live in a big house which is near the park.
5 Sheila is wearing a nice dress which fits her perfectly.
6 Steven is a lawyer whose office is in Baker Street./ Steven, whose office is in Baker Street, is a lawyer.
7 Alfie works in a shop where they sell men's clothes.

Speaking

10 **Aim** To practise relatives using personal examples

- Explain the task and give Ss time to complete it using personal examples.
- Elicit answers from Ss around the class.

Suggested Answer Key

1 … who talk loudly.
2 … whose children behave rudely to others.
3 … which have a lot of action.
4 … when I can't get out of bed in the morning.
5 … where there are big crowds.

1c Skills in Action

Vocabulary

1 a) **Aim** To present vocabulary for clothes & accessories

- Read out the list of departments in the store directory and then ask Ss to read the list of clothes and accessories.
- Give Ss time to list the items under the correct departments.
- Check Ss' answers on the board.

Answer Key

ACCESSORIES: leather belt, ankle socks, bow tie
BEACHWEAR: swimsuit
SPORTSWEAR: tracksuit, sweatshirt
FOOTWEAR: high-heeled shoes, walking boots
MENSWEAR: polo-neck jumper, skinny jeans, pullover, waistcoat, raincoat, tailored suit, polo shirt, sweatshirt
WOMENSWEAR: evening dress, polo-neck jumper, skinny jeans, silk blouse, pullover, raincoat, polo shirt, sweatshirt

b) **Aim** **To ask for information; to practise vocabulary for clothes & accessories**

- Explain the task and ask two Ss to read out the example exchange. Have Ss work in closed pairs and act out similar exchanges for the clothes and accessories in Ex. 1a.
- Monitor the activity around the class and then have some pairs act out their exchanges in front of the rest of the class.

Suggested Answer Key

A: Excuse me. Where can I find evening dresses?
B: In the womenswear department on the ground floor.

A: Excuse me. Where can I find high-heeled shoes?
B: In the footwear department on the second floor.

A: Excuse me. Where can I find polo-neck jumpers?
B: In the menswear department on the first floor. / In the womenswear department on the ground floor.

A: Excuse me. Where can I find swimsuits?
B: In the beachwear department on the fourth floor.

A: Excuse me. Where can I find a tracksuit?
B: In the sportswear department on the third floor. etc

Listening

2 **Aim** **To listen for specific information (multiple choice)**

- Ask Ss to read the questions and the answer choices and underline the key words.
- Then play the recording twice. Ss listen and choose their answers.
- Check Ss' answers. You can play the recording with pauses for Ss to check their answers.

Answer Key

1   D   *2   C*   *3   A*

Everyday English

3 a) **Aim** **To read for cohesion and coherence (missing words); to identify relationship**

- Ask Ss to read the dialogue and complete the task by completing the gaps with the verbs in the list in the correct tense.
- Elicit who the speakers might be.

Answer Key

The speakers are a couple – probably a husband and wife.

b) **Aim** **To listen for cohesion & coherence**

Play the recording for Ss to listen and check their answers to Ex. 3a.

Answer Key

1 match	*3 fit*	*5 prefer*
2 suits	*4 goes with*	*6 look*

4 **Aim** **To role-play a dialogue deciding what to wear**

- Explain the task and ask Ss to act out a similar dialogue to the one in Ex. 3 in closed pairs using the prompts and the language in the box to help them.
- Write this diagram on the board for Ss to follow.

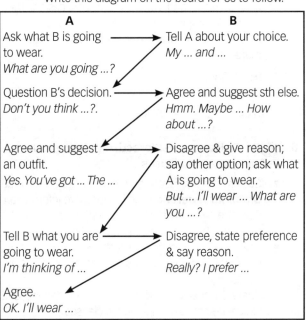

- Monitor the activity around the class and offer assistance as necessary.
- Then ask some pairs to act out their dialogues in front of the class.
- Have Ss use a recording device to record themselves.

Suggested Answer Key

A: What are you going to wear to our cousin's barbecue?
B: My new dress and my high-heeled shoes.
A: Don't you think a dress and high-heeled shoes are a bit too much to wear to a barbecue?
B: Hmm. Maybe you're right. How about jeans then?
A: Yes. You've got lots of nice jeans. The black ones really suit you.
B: But I don't like them so much. I'll wear my blue ones. What are you going to wear?
A: I'm thinking of wearing my jeans with a white shirt.
B: Really? I prefer your blue shirt. It really suits you.
A: OK. I'll wear that then.

A: *What are you going to wear for the cycling trip?*
B: *My jeans and trainers.*
A: *Don't you think jeans will be a bit uncomfortable on a cycling trip?*
B: *Hmm. Maybe you're right. How about shorts then?*
A: *Yes. You've got lots of nice shorts. The white ones really suit you.*
B: *But they aren't clean. I'll wear my blue ones. What are you going to wear?*
A: *I'm thinking of wearing shorts and my blue T-shirt.*
B: *Really? I prefer your green T-shirt. It really suits you.*
A: *OK. I'll wear that then.*

A: *What are you going to wear to the presentation at work?*
B: *My jeans and a green blouse.*
A: *Don't you think jeans are a bit too casual to wear to a presentation?*
B: *Hmm. Maybe you're right. How about trousers then?*
A: *Yes. You've got lots of nice trousers. The black ones really suit you.*
B: *But they aren't very comfortable. I'll wear my grey ones. What are you going to wear?*
A: *I'm thinking of wearing black trousers with a white shirt.*
B: *Really? I prefer your blue trousers. They really suit you.*
A: *OK. I'll wear those then.*

Pronunciation

5 **Aim** **To learn the pronunciation of diphthongs**
/eɪ/, /aɪ/, /ɔɪ/

- Play the recording. Ss listen and repeat chorally and/or individually.
- Elicit other words with the same sounds from Ss around the class.

Answer Key

/eɪ/ *day, play, weigh*
/aɪ/ *eye, sky, guy*
/ɔɪ/ *toy, employ*

Reading & Writing

6 **Aim** **To analyse a rubric**

Ask Ss to read the task and then answer the questions. Elicit answers from Ss around the class.

Answer Key

1 *I am going to write an article for a magazine.*
2 *I should write about a person I greatly admire and give reasons why they are inspiring to me. My piece of writing should be 120-150 words.*

7 **Aim** **To read for cohesion and coherence; to expand on vocabulary (word formation)**

- Go through the theory box with Ss and then give Ss time to read the article and complete the task by forming adjectives from the words in brackets.
- Check Ss' answers on the board.

Answer Key

1 *famous*	3 *attractive*	5 *acceptable*
2 *successful*	4 *responsible*	

- You can ask Ss to start a Word Formation section in their notebooks and list words under the following headings. Ss can add words using their dictionaries to check the derivatives. Ss can revise regularly.

abstract noun	person noun	adjective	adverb
fame	—	*famous*	*famously*

8 **Aim** **To introduce/practise linking ideas**

- Go through the **Writing Tip** with Ss. Focus Ss' attention on punctuation in the examples.
- Give Ss time to join the sentences using the linking words in brackets.
- Check Ss' answers.

Suggested Answer Key

1 *Roger is friendly and he is caring as well.*
2 *John suffers from a disease. However, he is a champion swimmer.*
3 *Fran looks after old people and also cares for stray animals.*
4 *Although Becky is very young, she has a successful career.*
5 *Hugo usually has a lot of energy but he gets tired sometimes.*

Writing

9 a) **Aim** **To prepare for a writing task**

Ask Ss to reread the task in Ex. 6 and then think about an inspiring person they know of and make notes under the headings in their notebooks.

Suggested Answer Key

Name: *Steve Brown*
Where from: *Great Britain*
What famous for: *well-known athlete from wheelchair rugby*
Achievements: *accident at the age of 23, Steve is one of the best wheelchair rugby players in the UK and Team GB captain in the 2012 Paralympics*
Appearance: *fit and attractive with short blond hair and blue eyes*

Character: cheerful and confident
Why inspiring: he doesn't give up and he follows his dreams

b) (Aim) To write an article

- Give Ss time to write their articles using their notes in Ex. 9a and following the plan. Remind Ss to give their article a title.
- Ask various Ss to share their answers with the class.
- Alternatively, assign the task as HW and check Ss' answers in the next lesson.

Suggested Answer Key

A Great Role Model

The person I really admire is British Paralympian and TV presenter Steve Brown. He's a well-known athlete from wheelchair rugby. However, being unable to walk doesn't stop him from having a successful career.

Starting after an accident at the age of 23, Steve is one of the best wheelchair rugby players in the UK and Team GB captain in the 2012 Paralympics.

Steve is fit and attractive with short blond hair and blue eyes. He is always cheerful and confident and he helps other people in wheelchairs build their confidence too. Steve inspires me because he doesn't give up and he follows his dreams. As well as playing wheelchair rugby, he now also works as a sports commentator and a wildlife presenter, as he loves nature.

Values

Ask Ss to think about the quotation. Then initiate a class discussion about the meaning of the quotation and encourage Ss to participate. You can ask Ss to research for similar quotations and present them in the next lesson.

Suggested Answer

A: I think the quotation means that being kind is a universal language that everyone understands.
B: I agree. Showing kindness is the best way to deal with everyone.

Culture 1

Reading & Listening

1 (Aim) To introduce the topic and listen and read for specific information

- Read out the question and elicit Ss' guesses in answer to it.
- Then play the recording. Ss listen to and read the text and find out.

Answer Key

Scottish men wear kilts on traditional and formal occasions.

2 (Aim) To consolidate new vocabulary

- Ask Ss to look at the picture and the highlighted words and then read the text again and match the words to the numbers.
- The give Ss time to look up the words in bold in the Word List or in their dictionaries and elicit explanations from Ss around the class.

Answer Key

1 sporran
2 kilt pin
3 pleats
4 hose
5 ghillie brogues

Suggested Answer Key

occasion (n): a special event
event (n): something important that happens
cloth (n): material used to make clothing, etc
pattern (n): a repeated design
pouch (n): a small soft bag
unlike (prep): not the same as

- Give Ss time to look up the meanings of the words in the **Check these words** box in the Word List.
- Play the video for Ss and elicit their comments.

Speaking & Writing

3 (Aim) To consolidate new vocabulary

Direct Ss' attention to the photo and then ask various Ss to present the kilt to the class using their answers in Ex. 2 as necessary.

Suggested Answer Key

The kilt is a traditional piece of clothing from Scotland. It is made of a thick high quality wool cloth called twill. The Scottish wear it with a small pouch called a sporran, a kilt pin that holds the kilt together, socks called hose and shoes called ghillie brogues.

4 (Aim) ICT To develop research skills; to write a short article about a traditional piece of clothing from one's country

- Explain the task and give Ss time to research online and collect information about a traditional piece of clothing from their country and then make notes under the headings.
- Give Ss time to use their notes to write a short article for an online travel website.
- Alternatively, assign the task as HW and ask Ss to share their articles in the next lesson.

Suggested Answer Key

Name and where/when it is from: *sari, India and Asia*

Description: *large piece of silk or cotton cloth wrapped around the body and worn over the shoulder, often worn with a short top called a choli and an underskirt called a parkar*

Present popularity: *women wear it every day in some countries such as Bangladesh and Sri Lanka and women in other countries such as Pakistan wear it for special occasions, e.g. weddings, formal events*

A sari is a piece of clothing that women from India and Asia wear. It is a large piece of silk or cotton cloth wrapped around the body and worn over the shoulder. Women often wear it with a short top called a choli and an underskirt called a parkar. Women wear it every day in some countries such as Bangladesh and Sri Lanka and women in other countries such as Pakistan wear it for special occasions such as weddings and formal events.

Review 1

Vocabulary

1 **Aim** **To consolidate vocabulary from the unit**

- Explain the task.
- Give Ss time to complete it.
- Check Ss' answers.

Answer Key

1 b   2 d   3 f   4 c   5 a   6 e

2 **Aim** **To consolidate vocabulary from the unit**

- Explain the task.
- Give Ss time to complete it.
- Check Ss' answers.

Answer Key

1 raincoat	3 polo-neck	5 suit
2 fit	4 Skinny	6 walking

3 **Aim** **To practise prepositional phrases and phrasal verbs**

- Explain the task.
- Give Ss time to complete it.
- Check Ss' answers.

Answer Key

1 after	3 of	5 up
2 to	4 for	6 to

Grammar

4 **Aim** **To practise the present simple and the present continuous**

- Explain the task.
- Give Ss time to complete it.
- Check Ss' answers.

Answer Key

1 enjoy	5 does your plane leave
2 are getting	6 Is your daughter
3 doesn't wear	studying
4 isn't going	

5 **Aim** **To practise relative pronouns**

- Explain the task.
- Give Ss time to complete it.
- Check Ss' answers.

Answer Key

1 where	3 whose	5 who
2 which	4 when	

Everyday English

6 **Aim** **To match exchanges**

- Explain the task.
- Give Ss time to complete it.
- Check Ss' answers.

Answer Key

1 d   2 e   3 a   4 c   5 b

Competences

Ask Ss to assess their own performance in the unit by ticking the items according to how competent they feel for each of the listed activities.

2 Reading Time

<table>
<tr><td colspan="3">Topic</td></tr>
<tr><td colspan="3">In this unit, Ss will explore the topics of types of books and feelings.</td></tr>
<tr><td>2a</td><td>Reading & Vocabulary</td><td>12-13</td></tr>
<tr><td colspan="3">Lesson objectives: To learn vocabulary for types of books, to read for gist, to listen and read for gist, to read for key information (multiple matching), to learn prepositional phrases, to practise words easily confused, to learn phrasal verbs with break, to design and talk about a book cover, to write about a book
Vocabulary: Types of books (thriller, science fiction, crime, horror, textbook, biography, fantasy, travel, romance, mystery, health, science, comedy, history, action & adventure); Adjectives describing books (amusing, interesting, full of action, educational, complicated, confusing, serious, easy to read, exciting, impossible to put down, scary, silly, realistic, powerful, full of imagination, dull, difficult to read, unbelievable, original, clever); Nouns (throne, epic, spaceship, bestseller); Verbs (rule, break, look, see, watch); Phrasal verbs (settle down, break down/into/out/up); Adjectives (missing, main, depressed, unlikely); Adverb (totally); Phrase (secret code)</td></tr>
<tr><td>2b</td><td>Grammar in Use</td><td>14-15</td></tr>
<tr><td colspan="3">Lesson objectives: To learn/revise the past simple and the past continuous, to learn/revise used to/would</td></tr>
<tr><td>2c</td><td>Skills in Action</td><td>16-17</td></tr>
<tr><td colspan="3">Lesson objectives: To learn vocabulary for feelings, to listen for gist, to act out a dialogue and practise everyday English for narrating an event and expressing sympathy, to learn the intonation in interjections, to read for cohesion & coherence (time words), to write a story
Vocabulary: Feelings (relieved, embarrassed, miserable, confused, nervous, disappointed, bored, annoyed, amazed, scared)</td></tr>
<tr><td colspan="2">Culture 2</td><td>18</td></tr>
<tr><td colspan="3">Lesson objectives: To read for gist, to listen and read for cohesion and coherence (multiple choice cloze), to talk about a famous book character, to present a famous book character
Vocabulary: Nouns (collection, detective, intelligence, moustache, circumstances, tragedy); Verbs (rush, unlock, ignore); Adjectives (popular, fine, proper); Phrase (a link in the chain)</td></tr>
<tr><td colspan="2">Review 2</td><td>19</td></tr>
<tr><td colspan="3">Lesson objectives: To test/consolidate vocabulary and grammar learnt throughout the unit, to practise everyday English</td></tr>
</table>

Go through the objectives box and tell Ss that these are the topics, skills and activities this unit will cover.

2a

Vocabulary

1 **Aim** To present vocabulary related to types of books

- Ask Ss to read out the words in the list. Explain/Elicit the meanings of any unknown vocabulary. Explain that fiction is literature created from imagination whereas non-fiction is literature based on fact.
- Give Ss time to consider their answers and then ask various Ss to tell the class which of the types of books are fiction/non-fiction.

Answer Key

Fiction: *thriller, science fiction, crime, horror, fantasy, romance, mystery, comedy, action & adventure*
Non-fiction: *textbook, biography, travel, health, science, history*

2 **Aim** To rank items in order of preference

- Ask Ss to look at the fiction books in Ex. 1 and give them time to rank them in order of personal preference.
- Go through the list of adjectives and explain/elicit the meanings of any unknown words.
- Ask two Ss to read out the example and then ask Ss to compare their list with their partner's, using the adjectives in the list and following the example.
- Monitor the activity around the class.
- Ask some pairs to tell the class.

Suggested Answer Key

A: I like thrillers most of all. They're clever.
B: Oh, really? I prefer comedy books. They're easy to read and amusing.
A: Well, I can't stand science fiction books. I find them complicated and confusing. etc

Listening & Reading

3 **Aim** To read for gist

Ask Ss to read the descriptions and elicit which types of books the people like reading from Ss around the class.

Suggested Answer Key

1 *Jake likes action & adventure books.*
2 *Patsy likes comedies.*
3 *Sam likes science fiction books.*
4 *Aidan likes reading fantasy stories.*

4 **Aim** To listen and read for gist

- Ask Ss to read the titles of the books in the text and elicit what type of story each one suggests from Ss around the class.
- Play the recording. Ss listen and check.

Answer Key

A suggests a fantasy story.
B suggests a science fiction story.
C suggests a crime story.
D suggests an action & adventure story.
E suggests a comedy.

5 **Aim** To read for key information (multiple matching)

- Read out the **Study Skills** box and tell Ss that this tip will help them to complete the task successfully.
- Ask Ss to read the descriptions of the people in Ex. 3 and the descriptions of the books in Ex. 4 again and give them time to complete the task.
- Check Ss' answers. Ss justify their answers.
- Then give Ss time to explain the words in bold by using the Word List or their dictionaries to help them. Elicit explanations from Ss around the class.

Answer Key

1 D (move fast – action, excitement; popular/classics – was bestseller)
2 E (ordinary people – two boys; everyday problems – never grew up, parents broke up, friendship; teach about life – help fix life)
3 B (amusing – funny, strange lands – Mars; interesting main character – first Martian; wants to learn – educational)
4 A (longer – 694 pages, exciting storyline – ancient families ... the land, thrilling read; imaginary worlds – the Seven Kingdoms of Westeros)

Suggested Answer Key

settle down (phr v): *to get comfortable*
totally (adv): *completely*
missing (adj): *not being able to be found*
break (v): *to solve sth (e.g. a code)*
bestseller (n): *a book that sells a lot*
depressed (adj): *being very unhappy*

- Give Ss time to look up the meanings of the words in the **Check these words** box in the Word List.
- Play the video for Ss and elicit their comments.

Background Information

George R R Martin (b. 1948) is an American writer best known for his epic fantasy series *A Song of Ice and Fire*, which the *Game of Thrones* TV series is based on. The first volume is called *A Game of Thrones (1996)*.

Andy Weir (b. 1972) is an American science-fiction writer. His first novel *The Martian* (2011) was made into a film. He has written many other novels and short stories including *The Egg* (2009) and *Artemis* (2017).

Jo Nesbø (b. 1960) is a Norwegian writer and musician. He is best known for writing crime novels with the character Harry Hole. Some of his novels are *The Bat* (2012), *Nemesis* (2008) , *The Snowman* (2010), *Phantom*, (2012) and *The Thirst* (2017).

Dan Brown (b. 1964) is an American author best known for his thrillers featuring Robert Langdon. A number of his books have been made into films. His most famous works include *Angels & Demons* (2000), *The Da Vinci Code* (2003), *The Lost Symbol* (2009) and *Inferno* (2013).

Nick Hornby (b. 1957) is an English writer and screenwriter. He has written a number of bestselling novels and award-winning screenplays. These include: *High Fidelity* (1995), *Fever Pitch* (1997), *About a Boy* (1998), and *Brooklyn* (2015).

6 **Aim** To consolidate prepositional phrases

- Give Ss time to read the gapped sentences and fill the gaps with the correct prepositions.
- Then check Ss' answers.

NOTE: Ask Ss to add the prepositional phrases to the Prepositions section in their notebook. Ss can revise regularly.

Answer Key

1	by	3	at	5	at
2	about	4	as	6	about

7 **Aim** To consolidate collocations

- Explain the task and give Ss time to complete the phrases using the words in the list.
- Then check Ss' answers by having Ss use the phrases in sentences of their own.

NOTE: Ask the Ss to add the collocations to the Collocations list in their notebooks.

Answer Key

1	stay	4	build	7	break
2	arrives	5	wear	8	take
3	falls	6	solve		

Suggested Answer Key

*The character did his best to **stay alive**.*
*Until **help arrived**, the character was on her own.*
*I love it when **snow falls** in winter.*
*In winter we always **build a snowman** when it snows.*
*We usually make our snowman **wear a scarf** and put a carrot for a nose.*
*Detectives can **solve crimes**.*
*I am not very good at **breaking codes** as I don't know much about computer programming.*
*I convinced my friend to **take a chance** and read a fantasy story.*

8 **Aim** To understand words easily confused

- Explain the task and give Ss time to use their dictionaries (digital or printed) to help them complete it.
- Check Ss' answers.

Answer Key

1	looked	2	saw	3	watch

9 **Aim** To learn phrasal verbs with *break*

- Ask Ss to read the phrasal verbs box and make sure that Ss understand the definitions.
- Then give Ss time to complete the task and check their answers.
- Tell Ss to add the phrasal verbs to the section at the back of their notebooks and include their definitions. Remind Ss to revise this list from time to time.

Answer Key

1	out	3	down	5	up
2	up	4	into		

Speaking & Writing

10 a) **Aim** THINK To develop creative skills; to design a book cover

- Explain the task and give Ss time to work in small groups and design a book cover for a book from their own imagination.
- Ask various Ss around the class to share their answers with the class.

Suggested Answers

Our book will be a fantasy one. The title will be Nowhere *and it will show a glass castle up near a cliff.*

b) **Aim** To write a short paragraph about a book

- Explain the task and give Ss time to write a short paragraph about their book following the examples in the text.
- Ask various Ss to share their answers with the class.

Suggested Answer Key

This novel is about the magical land of Nowhere and Princess Daisy. She must stay alive and solve the mystery of who killed her father before she takes the throne. She has her magical friends to help her but can she trust them?

2b Grammar in Use

1 **Aim** To present/revise the past simple and the past continuous

- Ask Ss to read the story and identify the past simple and past continuous forms used. Elicit how these tenses are formed.
- Read out the list of uses and have Ss say which tense matches which use.
- Refer Ss to the **Grammar Reference** section for detailed information.

Answer Key

*We form the past simple of regular verbs with the base form of the main verb + **-ed**. Irregular verbs have got their own forms.*
*We form the past continuous with was/were + the **-ing** form of the main verb.*

We use the past simple for:

- *actions that happened at a definite time in the past (stated or implied) – changed, made, had, felt*
- *actions that happened one after the other in the past – went, got, crashed*

We use the past continuous for:

- *an action in progress at a specific time in the past – were sailing*
- *two or more actions in progress at the same time in the past – were helping, were talking*
- *a past action in progress when another action interrupted it (the interrupting action is in the past simple) was trying, shouted*
- *background information in a story – was blowing*

2 **Aim** To practise the past simple and the past continuous

- Explain the task and give Ss time to complete it.
- Check Ss' answers.

Answer Key

1 were you, fell, took
2 Was it snowing, was snowing, didn't stop
3 Did you see, was going
4 did Susie look, heard, wasn't
5 were you doing, were searching, was waiting

3 Aim To practise the past simple and the past continuous

- Explain the task and give Ss time to complete it.
- Then check Ss' answers.
- Elicit answers to the questions from Ss around the class.

Answer Key

1	was	7	was taking
2	wasn't raining	8	was going
3	was shining	9	pulled
4	was raining	10	drove
5	was moving	11	felt
6	heard	12	wanted

Suggested Answer Key

A: What was the weather like at first?
B: The sun was shining.
A: What did Paul do when it started raining?
B: He went under a tree.
A: What did he hear?
B: He heard a shout for help.
A: Who was asking for help?
B: A man.
A: What did Paul do when he saw the man in the river?
B: He jumped in, grabbed his arm and pulled him to the river bank.
A: Where did Paul take the man?
B: To hospital.
A: What did the doctors say?
B: They said he was fine.
A: What did Paul want?
B: He wanted to go home and have a hot shower.

4 Aim To practise linking ideas

- Explain the task and read out the example.
- Give Ss time to complete the task and then elicit answers from Ss around the class.

Answer Key

2 a   3 e   4 d   5 b

Aidan was watching TV while his brother was getting dressed.
I was having a bath when my doorbell rang.
I heard a noise in the garden so I went to see what it was.

Amy went to bed early last night because she was very tired.

5 Aim To practise avoiding repetition

- Read out the box and explain that this tip will help Ss to complete the task successfully.
- Explain the task and give Ss time to complete it.
- Then check Ss' answers.

Answer Key

1 He was running down the street carrying a big box.
2 They were standing on the beach admiring the view.
3 Olivia was sitting in front of the TV eating her dinner.
4 Max was sitting in the garden reading a book.
5 Jenny and Ann were drinking coffee talking about their summer plans.

6 Aim To present/revise used to/would

- Ask Ss to read the box.
- Then direct Ss' attention to the underlined verbs in the text on p. 14 and elicit answers to the questions.
- Refer Ss to the **Grammar Reference** section for more information.

Answer Key

1 The first underlined verb ('used to be') is talking about a past state. The second ('would meet') is talking about a past habit.
2 No. **Would** cannot be used to talk about a past state.
3 Yes. **Used to** and **would** can both be used to talk about a past habit.

7 Aim To practise used to/would

- Explain the task and give Ss time to complete it.
- Check Ss' answers around the class.

Answer Key

1	used to/would	5	used to
2	used to	6	used to/would
3	used to/would	7	used to
4	used to	8	used to/would

Speaking

8 Aim To practise using used to/would

- Explain the task. Ask Ss to read the ideas and then talk in pairs about their past states/habits using used to.
- Monitor the activity around the class and then ask some Ss to share their answers with the rest of the class.

Suggested Answer Key

I didn't use to play basketball when I was ten years old.
I used to play video games when I was ten years old.
I didn't use to go scuba diving when I was ten years old.
I used to read comics when I was ten years old.
I didn't use to chat online when I was ten years old.
I didn't use to watch films online when I was ten years old.
I used to hang out with my friends when I was ten years old.
I used to share a room with my brother when I was ten years old.

9 (Aim) To practise sentence transformations

- Explain the task and give Ss time to complete it following the directions.
- Check Ss' answers.

Answer Key

1 used to have
2 was watching TV
3 would always visit
4 you use to read
5 took the ship an hour

10 (Aim) To practise past tenses through a chain story

- Explain the task and read out the scenario and the two examples.
- Then have Ss around the class continue the chain story using past tenses.

Suggested Answer Key

Tim couldn't see his face because it was too dark.
He crossed the street.
The man crossed the street, too.
Tim walked along the pavement.
The man followed him.
Tim stopped and turned around.
The man started laughing.
Tim recognised the laugh.
It was his uncle.

2c Skills in Action

Vocabulary

1 (Aim) To present vocabulary for feelings

- Ask Ss to look up the meanings of the adjectives in the list in the Word List.
- Then explain the task and read out the example.
- Have Ss complete the task and elicit answers from various Ss.

Answer Key

2 Ann felt bored.
3 Kate felt nervous.
4 Jake felt amazed.
5 Liz felt miserable.
6 Sue felt confused.
7 Tim felt annoyed.
8 Kelly felt disappointed.
9 Bob felt scared.
10 Steve felt relieved.

Listening

2 a) (Aim) To describe events in a story

- Read out the **Study Skills** box and tell Ss this tip will help them to complete the task successfully.
- Ask Ss to work in pairs and complete the task, following the directions.
- Then ask various pairs to share their answers with the class.

Suggested Answer Key

The story took place in the mountains in winter. Two girls were involved in the story. They could be mother and daughter, sisters or friends.
The girls were walking in the snowy mountains.
Suddenly, there was an avalanche.
They got behind a tree and hugged each other.
A helicopter rescued them.
The girls felt happy when they started their hike. They felt scared when they saw the avalanche. In the end, they felt relieved to be safe.

b) (Aim) To listen for sequence of events

- Play the recording. Ss listen and compare their story to the recording.
- Check Ss' answers.

Suggested Answer Key

The story says it is early spring – we thought it was winter. The girls were sisters – we thought that, too. We thought they got behind the tree together, but actually Harriet pulled Patsy behind it, saving her. The other events are the same except the girls called the helicopter on their mobile phone and we didn't mention that.

Everyday English

3 (Aim) To read for cohesion and coherence (missing verb tenses)

- Ask Ss to read the dialogue and complete the task by putting the verbs in brackets into the correct tense.
- Check Ss' answers.

Answer Key

1 was hiking
2 changed
3 was blowing
4 was pouring
5 found
6 could not/couldn't
7 stayed

22

4 **Aim** **To role-play a dialogue narrating an event; to express sympathy**

- Explain the task and ask Ss to act out a similar dialogue to the one in Ex. 3 in closed pairs using the prompts and the language in the box to help them.
- Write this diagram on the board for Ss to follow.

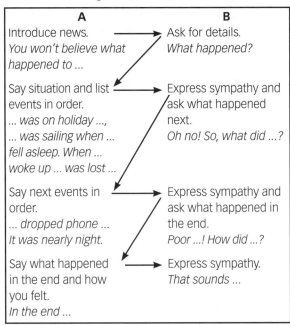

A	**B**
Introduce news. *You won't believe what happened to ...*	Ask for details. *What happened?*
Say situation and list events in order. *... was on holiday ...,* *... was sailing when ...* *fell asleep. When ...* *woke up ... was lost ...*	Express sympathy and ask what happened next. *Oh no! So, what did ...?*
Say next events in order. *... dropped phone ...* *It was nearly night.*	Express sympathy and ask what happened in the end. *Poor ...! How did ...?*
Say what happened in the end and how you felt. *In the end ...*	Express sympathy. *That sounds ...*

- Monitor the activity around the class and offer assistance as necessary.
- Then ask some pairs to act out their dialogues in front of the class.

Suggested Answer Key

A: *You won't believe what happened to Liam!*
B: *What happened?*
A: *He was on holiday abroad. He was sailing when he fell asleep in the sun. When he woke up, he was lost at sea.*
B: *Oh, no! So, what did he do?*
A: *Well, he dropped his phone into the sea so he couldn't call for help and it was nearly night.*
B: *Poor Liam! How did he get back?*
A: *He saw another boat and it came and rescued him.*
B: *That sounds terrible!*

Intonation

5 **Aim** **To learn the intonation in interjections**

- Explain that interjections are parts of speech we use to express emotions.
- Play the recording. Ss listen and match the interjections to how the person feels.
- Check Ss' answers.
- Then play the recording again with pauses for Ss to repeat chorally and/or individually.

Answer Key

| 1 | b | 2 | a | 3 | a | 4 | b | 5 | a |

Reading & Writing

6 **Aim** **To read for cohesion and coherence (time words)**

- Give Ss time to read the story and complete the task by choosing the correct time words.
- Check Ss' answers.

Answer Key

1	when	4	A short while later
2	before	5	soon
3	until		

Prepositions of movement: *through, from ... to, into*

7 **Aim** **To practise word formation**

- Read out the theory box and elicit examples in the story in Ex. 6.
- Then give Ss time to complete the task and check Ss' answers.

Answer Key

Examples: *relaxing, terrified, relieved*

1	amazing	3	worried
2	exhausted	4	terrifying

8 **Aim** **To introduce/practise techniques for ending a story**

- Read out the ***Writing Tip***. Elicit how the writer has ended the story.
- Elicit suggestions for another ending using the other technique from the ***Writing Tip*** box from Ss around the class.

Answer Key

The writer has ended the story by using direct speech.

Suggested Answer Key

Kate drove off and they were soon home relieved to be safe. Wasn't that a lucky escape?

Writing

9 **Aim** **To prepare for a writing task**

Ask Ss to read the task and look at the pictures and decide on a plot. Ask various Ss to tell the class.

Suggested Answer Key

Mark and Paul were walking along the beach carrying their surfboards. Mark was surfing. Paul saw a shark and shouted to him to get out of the water. Mark made it out just in time.

10 a) (**Aim**) **To keep notes**

Ask Ss to read the rubric in Ex. 9 again and play the recording. Ss keep notes.

b) (**Aim**) **To write a story**

- Give Ss time to write their stories using their notes in Ex. 10a and following the plan.
- Ask various Ss to share their answers with the class.
- Alternatively, assign the task as HW and check Ss' answers in the next lesson.

Suggested Answer Key

Almost Lunch!

Mark and Paul were walking along the beach carrying their surfboards. The sun was shining and the waves were crashing on the beach. It was a perfect day for surfing.

While Paul was cleaning his board, Mark went surfing. Paul was relaxing on the beach when he saw a dark shape in the water moving towards Mark. It was a shark!

Paul jumped up and shouted to Mark to get out of the water. Mark was riding a wave and at first, he didn't hear him. Paul started waving his hands and shouting louder. Mark saw him and paddled as fast as he could. Paul ran to meet him and pulled him out of the water just in time.

As they watched the shark swim away, they both felt relieved. "I was almost that shark's lunch!" said Mark.

Values

Ask Ss to think about the quotation. Then initiate a class discussion about the meaning of the quotation and encourage Ss to participate. You can ask Ss to research for similar quotations and present them in the next lesson.

Suggested Answer

A: I think the quotation means that imagination helps us get very far in life.

B: I don't quite agree. I think it means more than that. I think it means that your imagination allows you to be free.

Culture 2

Reading & Listening

1 (**Aim**) **To introduce the topic and read for specific information**

- Ask Ss to look at the picture. Read out the questions in the rubric and then give Ss time to read the text and find out.
- Elicit answers from Ss around the class.

Answer Key

The character is Hercule Poirot. Agatha Christie created him. He works with Captain Hastings.

2 a) (**Aim**) **To read for cohesion and coherence (multiple choice cloze)**

Ask Ss to do the task. Point out that Ss need to look at the words before/after each gap as they will help them do the task.

b) (**Aim**) **To listen for confirmation**

- Play the recording. Ss listen and check their answers to Ex. 2a.
- Give Ss time to look up the meanings of the words in the **Check these words** box in the Word List.
- Play the video for Ss and elicit their comments.

Answer Key

| 1 C | 2 A | 3 D | 4 B | 5 C |

3 (**Aim**) **To consolidate new vocabulary**

Direct Ss' attention to the words in bold in the text and then give Ss time to match them to the synonyms in the list using their dictionaries as necessary.

Answer Key

popular *= well-liked*
finest *= most stylish*
rushes *= moves quickly*
unlocked *= opened*
proper *= correct*
ignore *= not pay attention to*

Speaking & Writing

4 (**Aim**) (THINK) **To develop critical thinking skills**

Give Ss time to consider their answers to the question and then ask various Ss around the class to share their answers with the rest of the class.

Suggested Answer Key

I think Hercule Poirot is a popular character because he is very clever and his intelligence is impressive to readers. I think he is also popular because his character is a little strange. I think reading about a short well-dressed Belgian detective with a moustache and funny eating habits who solves mysteries is interesting to a lot of people.

5 **Aim** **ICT** To develop research skills; to write/ present a short text about a book character

- Explain the task and give Ss time to research online and collect information about a book character and then make notes under the headings.
- Give Ss time to use their notes to present their character to the class.
- Alternatively, assign the task as HW and ask Ss to present their characters in the next lesson.

Suggested Answer Key

Who he/she is: *Miss Marple*
Where he/she appears: *in crime fiction novels by Agatha Christie*
Why he/she is a great character: *She is a kind, little, old lady famous for her intelligence and her stories of St. Mary Mead, the village where she lives. She always links a crime to a story from her village through a comment by one of the people involved or in some other way.*

Miss Marple appears in crime fiction novels by Agatha Christie. She is a kind, little, old lady famous for her intelligence and her stories of St. Mary Mead, the village where she lives. She always links a crime to a story from her village through a comment by one of the people involved or in some other way.

Review 2

Vocabulary

1 **Aim** To consolidate vocabulary from the unit

- Explain the task.
- Give Ss time to complete it.
- Check Ss' answers.

Answer Key

1 non-fiction	4 saw
2 adventure	5 amusing
3 bestseller	

2 **Aim** To consolidate vocabulary from the unit

- Explain the task.
- Give Ss time to complete it.
- Check Ss' answers.

Answer Key

1 stayed	5 disappointed
2 took	6 embarrassed
3 solved	7 relieved
4 confusing	8 annoyed

3 **Aim** To practise prepositional phrases and phrasal verbs

- Explain the task.
- Give Ss time to complete it.
- Check Ss' answers.

Answer Key

1 up	3 down	5 as
2 by	4 about	

Grammar

4 **Aim** To practise the past simple and the past continuous

- Explain the task.
- Give Ss time to complete it.
- Check Ss' answers.

Answer Key

1 was booking	4 was shining
2 were you doing	5 closed
3 didn't hear	6 were walking

5 **Aim** To practise *used to/would*

- Explain the task.
- Give Ss time to complete it.
- Check Ss' answers.

Answer Key

1 used to	4 used to
2 used to/would	5 used to/would
3 used to	

Everyday English

6 **Aim** To match exchanges

- Explain the task.
- Give Ss time to complete it.
- Check Ss' answers.

Answer Key

1 c	2 d	3 e	4 a	5 b

Competences

Ask Ss to assess their own performance in the unit by ticking the items according to how competent they feel for each of the listed activities.

3 All around the world

Topic
In this unit, Ss will explore the topic of travel and means of transport.

3a Reading & Vocabulary	20-21

Lesson objectives: To learn vocabulary for means of transport, to read for gist, to listen for specific information, to read for specific information (T/F/DS statements), to learn prepositional phrases, to practise words easily confused, to learn phrasal verbs with *run*, to talk about a visit to a place, to write a comment on a blog

Vocabulary: Means of transport *(reindeer sled, Monte toboggan, rainforest zip-line tour, reed boats, bamboo train, classic cars)*; Nouns *(ride, platform, wheel, railway track, uniform, travel, journey, trip)*; Verbs *(shine, whizz)*; Phrasal verbs *(come across, set up, run into/after/out of/over)*; Adjectives *(early, foreign)*

3b Grammar in Use	22-23

Lesson objectives: To learn/revise the present perfect and the present perfect continuous, to learn/revise the *past perfect* and the past perfect continuous, to learn/revise the definite article *(the)*

3c Skills in Action	24-25

Lesson objectives: To learn vocabulary for parts of an airport, to listen for specific information (gap fill), to read for cohesion & coherence (missing sentences), to act out a dialogue and practise everyday English for reporting lost luggage, to learn the pronunciation of silent letters, to read for cohesion & coherence (word formation), to write an article describing a journey

Vocabulary: Parts of an airport *(departures, arrivals, check-in, passport control, information, baggage reclaim, duty-free, customs)*

Culture 3	26

Lesson objectives: To scan a text, to listen and read for specific information (sentence completion), to talk and write about a symbol of one's country/capital city

Vocabulary: Nouns *(underground railway, line, diamond, curve, symbol)*; Verb *(change)*, Adjectives *(confusing, straight, bold, amusing)*; Phrase *(at the bottom of)*

Review 3	27

Lesson objectives: To test/consolidate vocabulary and grammar learnt throughout the unit, to practise everyday English

Go through the objectives box and tell Ss that these are the topics, skills and activities this unit will cover.

3a

Vocabulary

1 **Aim** To generate vocabulary for means of transport

- Ask Ss around the class to name different means of transport we use while on holiday. Write them on the board under each category.
- Ask individual Ss which their favourite means of transport is and why.

Suggested Answer Key

by air: plane, helicopter
by rail: train
by road: coach, bus, car, motorbike, scooter, rickshaw, taxi, quad bike
by water: boat, ship, gondola, ferry

My favourite means of transport while on holiday is a plane because I get excited on the journey to a faraway place. It's comfortable and safe, too.

2 a) **Aim** To present vocabulary related to unusual means of transport

- Ask Ss to look at photos 1-6 and read the list of countries and decide in pairs which form of transport they think comes from which country.
- Ask various Ss to tell the class.

Ss' own answers

b) **Aim** To listen for specific information

Play the recording. Ss listen and find out if their guesses were correct.

Answer Key

1	Finland	4	Peru
2	Portugal	5	Cambodia
3	Costa Rica	6	Cuba

Reading & Listening

3 **Aim** To introduce the topic of a text and listen and read for gist

- Ask Ss to skim the text quickly and elicit which photos each one relates to.
- Play the recording. Ss listen to and read the text to check.

Answer Key

A 6	B 5	C 3	D 2

4 **Aim** To read for specific information (T/F/DS statements)

- Ask Ss to read the statements and then give them time to read the text again and mark them accordingly.
- Check Ss' answers and then give Ss time to look up the meanings of the words in bold in the Word List or in their dictionaries and elicit definitions from Ss around the class.

Answer Key

1 T *(a 1950s American car)*
2 DS
3 DS
4 F *(wasn't very comfortable)*
5 T *(I spent ... the trees!)*
6 F *(We're about ... tourist)*

- Elicit meaning of bolded words. Alternatively, give Ss time to look up the meanings of the words in the **Check these words** box in the Word List or their dictionaries.

Suggested answer key

early (adj): *near the beginning of sth*
shine (v): *to sparkle*
foreign (adj): *coming from a country that is not yours*
come across (phr v): *to meet by chance*
set up (phr v): *to establish a business*
whizz (v): *to move fast*
uniform (n): *a special set of clothes worn when doing some jobs*

- Play the video for Ss and elicit their comments.

Background Information

Portugal (the Portuguese Republic) is a country in Southern Europe bordering Spain and the Atlantic Ocean. The capital city is Lisbon and the population is 10.4 million people. It is a popular tourist destination.

Cuba (the Republic of Cuba) is a Latin American island country in the north Caribbean. The capital city is Havana and the people speak Spanish. The population is 11 million.

Finland (the Republic of Finland) is a Scandinavian country between Norway, Sweden and Russia. The capital city is Helsinki and the population is 5.5 million people.

Peru (the republic of Peru) is a country on the west coast of South America. The capital city is Lima and the population is 32 million people. The people speak Spanish.

Background Information

Costa Rica (the Republic of Costa Rica) is a country in Central America. The capital city is San José and the population is 4.9 million people. The people speak Spanish.

Cambodia (The Kingdom of Cambodia) is a country in Southeast Asia. The capital city is Phnom Penh and it has a population of 15.2 million people. It was previously the Khmer Empire and it borders Thailand, Laos and Vietnam.

5 **Aim** To consolidate new vocabulary

- Give Ss time to read the words in the list and the paragraph and replace the bold words with their opposites using their dictionaries to help them if necessary.
- Check Ss' answers around the class.

Suggested Answer Key

1 long	6	fast
2 modern	7	hot
3 wide	8	amazing
4 comfortable	9	cheap
5 huge		

6 **Aim** To consolidate new vocabulary & practise collocations

- Ask Ss to choose the correct verbs to match the items a and b.
- Check Ss' answers and then give Ss time to use the collocations in sentences.
- Ask various Ss around the class to share their sentences with the rest of the class.

Answer Key

1	a go	b have
2	a take	b go
3	a go	b do
4	a do	b go
5	a make	b go
6	a take	b go

Suggested Answer Key

*I would like to **go on holiday** tomorrow.*
*Are you going to **have a holiday** this year?*
*Let's **take a trip** this weekend.*
*Where would you like to **go on a trip**?*
*Mary loves **going shopping**.*
*I have to go to the supermarket later to **do some shopping**.*

Do you usually **do some sightseeing** when you are on holiday?

Let's **go sightseeing** in Paris.

Tom is **making a journey** to Wales to see his mum.

I'd like to **go on a journey** across Australia.

Have you ever **taken a ride** on a camel?

I'm **going for a ride** on my bike later.

7 **Aim** To consolidate prepositional phrases from a text

- Give Ss time to read the gapped phrases and fill in the gaps with the correct prepositions.
- Then check Ss' answers.

Answer Key

1	in (BUT: by car)	4	by
2	on	5	at
3	by	6	in

8 **Aim** To understand words easily confused

- Explain the task and give Ss time to use their dictionaries to help them complete it.
- Check Ss' answers.

Answer Key

1 travel   2 trip   3 journey

9 **Aim** To learn phrasal verbs with *run*

- Tell Ss to add the phrasal verbs to the Phrasal Verbs list at the back of their notebooks and include the definitions. Tell Ss to revise this list from time to time and to add to it every time they come across a new phrasal verb.
- Ask Ss to read the phrasal verbs box and make sure that they understand the definitions.
- Give Ss time to complete the task, then check their answers.
- Then ask various Ss around the class to make up a short story using the phrasal verbs and share it with the class.

Answer Key

1 over   2 after   3 out of   4 into

Suggested Answer Key

Yesterday, I **ran into** an old school friend, Tom. He was walking his dog and I had **run out of** milk so I was on my way to the shops. We were chatting when a cat walked past and his dog got off its lead and **ran after** it. He dashed into the road and almost got **run over** by a car. It was very scary.

Speaking & Writing

10 **Aim** **THINK** To talk about an unusual form of transport

- Give Ss time to consider their answers and talk in pairs about either the reindeer sled or the reed boats and tell their partner about travelling on one.
- Then ask various Ss to tell the class.

Suggested Answer Key

Last year, I went to Finland and I got the chance to ride a reindeer sled. It was a fantastic experience and lots of fun. We sat in the sled with warm blankets on us and the reindeer pulled us along.

11 **Aim** To write a comment on a blog

- Ask Ss to use their answers from Ex. 10 and the texts in Ex. 3 to help them write a comment to post on Vince's blog about an unusual means of transport.
- Then ask various Ss to read their comment to the class.

Suggested Answer Key

Lisa Lewis: *Great stories, guys! Last year, I went to Finland and I got the chance to ride a reindeer sled. It was a fantastic experience and lots of fun. We sat in the sled with warm blankets on us and the reindeer pulled us along.*

3b Grammar in Use

1 **Aim** To learn/revise the present perfect and the present perfect continuous

- Ask Ss to read the tweets and identify the tenses. Elicit how we form the perfect tenses and then elicit which tense we use for each of the situations presented.
- Refer Ss to the **Grammar Reference** section for detailed information.

Answer Key

past simple: *we won*

present perfect: *Have you ever visited, We've had, who've booked, who've already flown, storm's left, Kauai has already started*

present perfect continuous: *we've been showing, that's been travelling, have been happening, we've been cleaning up*

We form the present perfect with **have/has (not) + past participle**.

We form the present perfect continuous with **have/has (not) + been + main verb with -ing**.

We use the present perfect for:

- *actions that happened at an unstated time in the past*
- *actions that started in the past and continue up to the present*
- *to talk about a past action that has a visible result in the present.*

We use the present perfect continuous:
- *to put emphasis on the duration of an action that started in the past and continues up to the present*
- *for actions that started in the past and lasted for some time and whose results are visible in the present.*

We use the past simple:
- *for actions that happened in the past at a specific time.*

Background Information

Kauai is the fourth largest and the oldest of the Hawaiian Islands. It is called the Garden Isle and it is 5 million years old. About 67,000 people live there. It has got a tropical climate and it is a popular film location and tourist destination.

Hawaii is the 50th state of the USA and it is an archipelago of hundreds of islands in the Pacific Ocean spread over 2,400 km. The biggest island is also called Hawaii. It is a popular destination for tourists, surfers, biologists and volcanologists.

2 **Aim** To practise the present perfect and the present perfect continuous

- Explain the task. Ss complete the task.
- Check Ss' answers.

Answer Key

1. *has flown, before (emphasis on numbers)*
2. *ever, landed (personal experience)*
3. *received, yet (action started in past – evidence in present)*
4. *risen, since (action started in past connected to present)*
5. *been waiting, for (emphasis on duration of action that started in past and continues up to present)*
6. *visited so far (emphasis on number)*
7. *already, frozen (action started in past and whose result is visible in present)*
8. *been travelling, since (past action of certain duration having visible results in present)*
9. *just, arrived (a recently completed action)*
10. *been reading, since (action started in past and continues up to present – emphasis on duration)*

Background Information

El Salvador (the Republic of El Salvador) is a country in Central America. It is the smallest and most populated country in the region. The capital is San Salvador and the population is 6.3 million people.

3 **Aim** To practise *been/gone*

- Explain that *been* is the past participle of *be* and *gone* is the past participle of *go*. Elicit that we use *have been* to say that sb was somewhere but they aren't anymore and *have gone* to say that sb has gone somewhere and they are still there.
- Explain the task and give Ss time to complete it.
- Check Ss' answers.

Answer Key

1	*been*	3	*been*	5	*been*
2	*gone*	4	*gone*		

Background Information

Dubai is the largest city in the UAE and one of the emirates that make up the country.

Spain (The Kingdom of Spain) is a country in southwestern Europe. 45 million people live there and the capital city is Madrid. The people speak Spanish and they have a king and a prime minister.

4 **Aim** To practise the present perfect through role play

- Explain the task and ask Ss to read the dialogue. Ss work in pairs and act out similar dialogues using the notes.
- Monitor the activity around the class and then choose various pairs to act out dialogues in front of the class for three more situations.

Suggested Answer Key

A: *Have you ever been in a helicopter?*
B: *Yes, I have.*
A: *When was that?*
B: *Two weeks ago.*
A: *What was it like?*
B: *It was exciting.*

A: *Have you ever gone out in a thunderstorm?*
B: *Yes, many times.*
A: *When was the last time?*
B: *Last autumn.*
A: *What was it like?*
B: *It was thrilling.*

A: *Have you ever driven a car?*
B: *Yes, I have.*
A: *When was that?*
B: *A month ago.*
A: *What was it like?*
B: *It was difficult.*

- *ride/a quad bike – yesterday/strange*
- *go on/package holiday – last June/interesting*
- *hire/rickshaw – never*

A: *Have you ever ridden a quad bike?*
B: *Yes, I have.*
A: *When was that?*
B: *Yesterday.*
A: *What was it like?*
B: *It was strange!*

A: *Have you ever gone on a package holiday?*
B: *Yes, I have.*
A: *When was that?*
B: *It was last June.*
A: *What was it like?*
B: *Interesting.*

A: *Have you ever hired a rickshaw?*
B: *No, I haven't. I've never hired a rickshaw.*

5 (Aim) To present the past perfect and the past perfect continuous

- Write on the board: *Sam **had gone** to the market before Kate arrived.* Elicit tenses *(had gone – past perfect; arrived – past simple)* Elicit that we form the past perfect with *had (not) + the past participle of the main verb*.
- Explain/Elicit that we use this tense to talk about an action that happened in the past before another past action.
- Write on the board: *We **had been waiting** for an hour before the plane landed.*
- Explain that *had been waiting* is the past perfect continuous. Elicit how the tense is used *(to put emphasis on the duration of an action that happened before another past action)* and how it is formed *(had + been + main verb + -ing form)*.
- Ask Ss to read the theory. Refer Ss to the **Grammar Reference** section for more information.

- Elicit examples from the tweets on p. 22.

Answer Key

We form the past perfect with had (not) + past participle. – it had passed
We form the past perfect continuous with had (not) + been + verb + -ing. – they'd been calling

6 (Aim) To practise the past perfect and the past perfect continuous

Explain the task and give Ss time to complete it and then check their answers around the class.

Answer Key

1 *had shown (action that happened before another past action)*
2 *hadn't left (action that happened before another past action)*
3 *had been travelling (emphasis on duration of an action that happened before another past action)*
4 *had been walking (action that lasted for some time in the past and whose result was visible in the past)*
5 *had you been saving up (emphasis on duration of an action that happened before another past action)*
6 *had broken (action that finished in the past whose result was visible in the past)*

Speaking

7 (Aim) To practise the past perfect and the past perfect continuous

- Explain the task and read out the example exchange.
- Have Ss complete the task in pairs.
- Monitor the activity around the class and then ask some pairs to act out their exchanges in front of the rest of the class.

Suggested Answer Key

A: *Why was Mary upset?*
B: *She had missed her flight.*

A: *Why were you on foot?*
B: *My car had broken down.*

A: *Why were Kelly's legs sore?*
B: *She had been cycling all day.*

A: *Why were John's parents late?*
B: *The snow had delayed them.*

8 (Aim) To practise the present/past perfect and the present/past perfect continuous through sentence transformations

- Explain the task.
- Give Ss time to complete the task by completing the second sentences using the words in bold.

Answer Key

1 *haven't been fishing since*
2 *first time she has eaten*
3 *it been since he went*
4 *hadn't eaten out for*
5 *had been raining*

9 **Aim** To revise/present the definite article *(the)*

- Explain that we use *the* with nouns when talking about something specific or something that has already been mentioned. *(I caught a train home. The train was late.)*
- Elicit other uses of *the*. We use *the*: with the names of rivers *(the River Thames)*, groups of islands *(the Balearic Islands)*, mountain ranges *(the Himalayas)*, deserts *(the Gobi Desert)*, oceans *(the Atlantic Ocean)*; countries when they include words such as States, Kingdom, Republic *(the United Kingdom)*; with the names of musical instruments *(the piano)*; families *(the Jones)* and nationalities ending in *-sh*, *-ch* or *-ese* *(the Chinese)*; with the words *morning*, *afternoon* and *evening*; with superlative forms.
- Explain that we do not use *the* with uncountable and plural nouns when talking about something in general. *(Cars are everywhere.)*
- Elicit other cases where we don't use *the*: with proper names, months and days of the week *(Lisa's birthday is in March.)*; with languages *(He speaks Dutch.)*; with the names of countries *(France)*, streets *(Main Street)*, parks *(Hyde Park)*, cities *(Paris)*, mountains *(Everest)*, individual islands *(Ibiza)*, lakes *(Lake Baikal)* and continents *(Asia)*.
- Refer Ss to the **Grammar Reference** section for more details.
- Explain the task and give Ss time to complete it.
- Check Ss' answers around the class.

Answer Key

1	–, –, –	Heathrow
2	the, the	Yes
3	the, –, –	Tower Bridge
4	the, the, the, the	The Alps
5	the, -	six months
6	the, the	No – in the Atlantic Ocean
7	the, the, –, –	November

Background Information

Heathrow is a major international airport in London, UK. It is the busiest airport in the UK and in Europe, and in 2017, it handled 78 million passengers. It is located 23 km west of Central London. It has two runways and four terminals. It covers an area of 12.27 km².

Gatwick is a major international airport in London, UK. It is the second busiest airport in the UK. It is located 47.5 km south of Central London. It has two terminals and one runway.

Background Information

Times Square is a major intersection and tourist destination in Midtown Manhattan in New York. It is a busy pedestrian area and is also called 'the Crossroads of the World'. 50 million people visit it every year. It used to be called Longacre Square but they renamed it after the *New York Times* newspaper made its headquarters there in 1904.

The River Thames is a 246 km long river that runs through London. The London Eye, Big Ben, the Houses of Parliament and the Tower of London are along its banks. You can cross the river by bridges or a cable car.

Tower Bridge is a moveable suspension bridge over the River Thames in London. It was built between 1886 and 1894. It has two bridge towers and it has become a symbol of London. It is used by pedestrians and vehicles. The bridge opens to let ships pass under. It is 244 metres long and 65 metres high.

Brooklyn Bridge is a suspension bridge over the East River in New York. It was built between 1869 and 1883. It is the oldest bridge in the USA. It has become a symbol of New York. It is used by pedestrians and vehicles. It is 1,825 metres long and 84.3 metres high.

The Alps is the highest and biggest mountain range in Europe. It is 1,200 km long and stretches across France, Switzerland, Italy, Monaco, Austria, Germany and Slovenia. The highest mountain in the Alps is Mont Blanc at 4,810 metres.

The Andes is the highest and biggest mountain range in South America and the longest mountain range in the world. It is 7,000 km long and stretches across Venezuela, Colombia, Ecuador, Peru, Bolivia, Chile and Argentina. The highest mountain in the Andes is Aconcagua at 6,961 metres.

The Canary Islands are a group of islands in the Atlantic Ocean belonging to Spain. They are located 100 km west of Morocco. There are seven main islands (Tenerife, Fuerteventura, Gran Canaria, Lanzarote, La Palma, La Gomera and El Hierro) and a number of smaller islands. They are a popular tourist destination.

The Pacific Ocean is the largest and deepest ocean. It covers 165,250,000 km² which is 46% of the Earth's water surface. It stretches from the Arctic to the Antarctic and from Asia and Australia to America.

3c Skills in Action

Vocabulary

1 **a)** **Aim** **To present vocabulary for parts of an airport**

- Ask Ss to read the signs and then match them to what passengers do there using the Word List or their dictionaries to help them as necessary.
- Check Ss' answers.

Answer Key

1 g	3 a	5 c	7 f
2 e	4 b	6 h	8 d

b) **Aim** **To consolidate new vocabulary**

- Explain the task and read out the example exchange. Have Ss complete the task in pairs using the words in the list.
- Monitor the activity around the class and then ask some pairs to act out their exchanges in front of the class.

Suggested Answer Key

A: *How much is this perfume?*
B: *You're at duty-free.*

A: *I can't wait for my mum's plane to land.*
B: *You're at arrivals.*

A: *When do we fly out?*
B: *You're at departures.*

A: *When's the next flight to Malaga?*
B: *You're at information.*

A: *Here's your boarding pass. You board at Gate 23A.*
B: *You're at check-in.*

Listening

2 **Aim** **To listen for specific information (gap fill)**

- Read out the ***Study Skills*** box and tell Ss this tip will help them to complete the task successfully.
- Ask Ss to read the gapped boarding pass and try to predict the missing words.
- Play the recording. Ss listen and fill in the gaps.
- Check Ss' answers.

Answer Key

1 AG533	3 24A	5 7:30
2 New York	4 23	

Everyday English

3 **a)** **Aim** **To test cohesion & coherence (missing sentences)**

Ask Ss to read sentences a-f and then give Ss time to read the dialogue and complete the gaps with the missing sentences.

b) **Aim** **To listen and read for specific information**

Play the recording. Tell Ss to follow the dialogue in their books and check their answers in Ex. 3a.

Answer Key

1 f	2 d	3 e	4 a	5 c	6 b

4 **Aim** **To role-play a dialogue reporting lost luggage**

- Explain the task and ask Ss to act out a similar dialogue to the one in Ex. 3 in pairs using the prompts.
- Write this diagram on the board for Ss to follow.

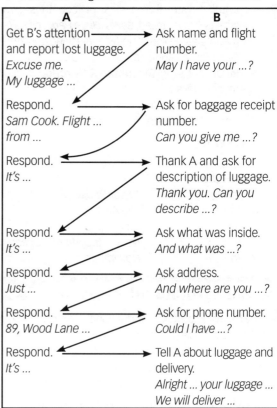

- Monitor the activity around the class and offer assistance as necessary.
- Then ask some pairs to act out their dialogues in front of the class.

3

Suggested Answer Key

A: Excuse me. My luggage never came out at baggage reclaim.

B: May I have your name and flight number, please?

A: Sam Cook. Flight EX147 from Glasgow.

B: Can you give me your baggage receipt number?

A: It's ML 45 87 66.

B: Thank you. Can you describe your luggage?

A: It's two small blue suitcases.

B: And what was in them?

A: Just clothes and papers.

B: And where are you staying?

A: 89, Wood Lane, London E12 6PQ.

B: Could I have a contact number?

A: It's 733 456 1290.

B: Alright, Mr Cook, your luggage was put on a later flight. We will deliver it to you before 7 pm.

Pronunciation

5 **Aim** **To identify silent letters**

- Play the recording. Ss listen and underline the silent letters, i.e. the ones they do not hear.
- Check their answers.
- Play the recording again with pauses for Ss to repeat chorally and/or individually.

Answer Key

1	inter<u>e</u>sting	3	saf<u>e</u>ty	5	foreign
2	autum<u>n</u>	4	<u>w</u>hole	6	Wed<u>n</u>esday

Reading & Writing

6 **Aim** **To analyse a rubric**

- Ask Ss to read the task and then give them time to complete the sentences.
- Check Ss' answers around the class.

Answer Key

1 I should write an article for an international travel magazine.

2 I should write about a journey I've never forgotten in 120-150 words.

7 **Aim** **To read for cohesion & coherence (word formation)**

- Read out the theory box and tell Ss this information will help them to complete the task successfully.
- Ask Ss to read the article and fill in the gaps using adjectives derived from the words in brackets.
- Check Ss' answers on the board.

Answer Key

1	fantastic	5	amazing
2	attractive	6	accessible
3	tasty	7	wonderful
4	friendly		

Background Information

Scotland is a country in Great Britain. It is to the north of England and it is part of the United Kingdom. 5.4 million people live there. The capital city is Edinburgh but the largest city is Glasgow. Scotland has its own parliament and the people speak English and Scottish Gaelic.

Mallaig is a main port on the west coast of the Highlands of Scotland. It was founded in the 1840s. it is a popular holiday destination and filming location.

Ben Nevis is the highest mountain in Great Britain. It is in Scotland in the Grampian Mountains and it is 1,345 metres high.

Background Information

Fort William is a town in the Scottish Highlands in the west of Scotland. It is a major tourist destination for people who like walking and hiking because it is near Ben Nevis. Over 10,000 people live there.

Glenfinnan Viaduct is a railway bridge that crosses a valley and the River Finnan in the West Highlands of Scotland. It was built in 1897 and opened in 1901. it has appeared in many films. It is made of concrete and is 380 metres long.

The River Finnan is a river in the West Highlands of Scotland. It runs through Glenfinnan, which is a forested valley.

8 **Aim** **To practise using the senses in descriptions**

- Read out the *Writing Tip* box and then explain the task.
- Go through the phrases in the list and explain/elicit the meaning of any unknown words.
- Give Ss time to complete the descriptions and then check Ss' answers.

Answer Key

	A		B
1	clear blue sea	4	tall green trees
2	sea birds' cries	5	only sound
3	sweet smell	6	perfume of

Writing

9 Aim To brainstorm for ideas; to prepare for a writing task

Ask Ss to copy the spidergram into their notebooks. Then ask them to complete it by thinking about the best journey they have ever taken.

Suggested Answer Key

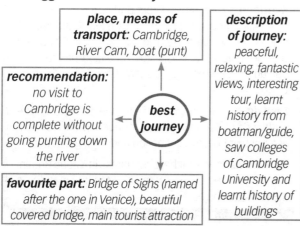

place, means of transport: Cambridge, River Cam, boat (punt)

description of journey: peaceful, relaxing, fantastic views, interesting tour, learnt history from boatman/guide, saw colleges of Cambridge University and learnt history of buildings

recommendation: no visit to Cambridge is complete without going punting down the river

best journey

favourite part: Bridge of Sighs (named after the one in Venice), beautiful covered bridge, main tourist attraction

10 Aim To write an article about a journey

- Ask Ss to read the rubric in Ex. 6 again and then give them time to write their article using their answers in Ex. 9 and following the plan.
- Ask various Ss to share their answers with the class.
- Alternatively, assign the task as HW and check Ss' answers in the next lesson.

Suggested Answer key

A Journey I've Never Forgotten

Last summer, I travelled along the River Cam in Cambridge on a boat called a punt. It was the best journey of my life!

We set off from one of the piers along the side of the River Cam and began our peaceful and relaxing journey down the river. We saw fantastic views and learnt interesting history from our boatman and guide. We saw the colleges of Cambridge University and learnt about the history of the buildings.

My favourite part was the Bridge of Sighs. It is a beautiful covered bridge that is named after the one in Venice. It is the main tourist attraction on the river.

Going down the River Cam was an amazing experience. No visit to Cambridge is complete without it.

Values

Ask Ss to explain the proverb in their mother tongue. Then initiate a class discussion about the meaning of the proverb and encourage all Ss to participate.

Suggested Answer

I think the proverb means that the only way to understand what a place is really like is to go there and see it for yourself.

Culture 3

Listening & Reading

1 Aim To introduce the topic, to skim a text

- Ask Ss to read the text quickly and find the names of five stations.
- Check Ss' answers.

Answer Key

Paddington, Farringdon, Chancery Lane, Mansion House, Bank

2 Aim To listen and read for specific information (sentence completion)

- Ask Ss to read the sentence stems and then play the recording. Ss listen and read the text and complete the sentences.
- Check Ss' answers and then elicit definitions for the words in bold from Ss around the class. Ss may use the Word List or their dictionaries to help them as necessary.

Answer Key

1 1863	4 Bank
2 Harry Beck	5 black
3 diamond	

Suggested Answer Key

line (n): a railway track
confusing (adj): difficult to understand
bold (adj): strong
curves (n): gradually bending lines
amusing (adj): funny
change (v): to get off one train and get on another
symbol (n): something that represents something else

- Give Ss time to look up the meanings of the words in the **Check these words** box in the Word List.
- Play the video for Ss and elicit their comments.

Speaking & Writing

3 Aim THINK To develop critical thinking skills; to discuss a design or symbol of one's country/capital city

- Ask Ss to talk in pairs and discuss what design or symbol reminds people of their country or capital city.
- Ask various Ss to tell the class.

Suggested Answer Key

A: I think one thing that reminds people of Italy is the Vespa motor scooter.

B: Yes, I agree. The streets of Rome are full of them and other towns and cities, too.

A: And they are used in films and TV advertisements set in Rome. I think they remind people of the 1960s.

B: That's true. The design has stayed the same since then and it is a typically Italian design that is easy to recognise.

4 **Aim** **ICT** **To develop research skills; to write about a design or symbol that represents a country or a capital city**

- Explain the task and give Ss time to research online and collect information about the design/symbol they discussed in Ex. 3. Ss make notes under the headings in their notebooks and then write a short text about it.
- Ask various Ss to read their text to the class.
- Alternatively, assign the task as HW and ask Ss to read out their texts in the next lesson.

Suggested Answer Key

Vespa

Who designed it: Piaggio

Where you can see it: on the streets of Rome and other Italian towns and cities

Why it reminds people of your country/capital city: seen every day and in films and TV advertisements set in Rome, 1960s look is a typically Italian design that is easy to recognise

The Vespa motor scooter designed by Piaggio is a symbol of Italy and especially of Rome. You can see them on the streets of Rome and in other Italian towns and cities. I think they remind people of Rome because they are seen every day and they are also seen in films and TV advertisements set in Rome. They have a 1960s look that is a typically Italian design and easy to recognise.

Review 3

Vocabulary

1 **Aim** **To consolidate vocabulary from the unit**

- Explain the task.
- Give Ss time to complete it.
- Check Ss' answers.

Answer Key

1 classic	5 uniforms
2 reed	6 sled
3 motor	7 zip-line
4 toboggan	

2 **Aim** **To consolidate vocabulary from the unit**

- Explain the task.
- Give Ss time to complete it.
- Check Ss' answers.

Answer Key

1 baggage	4 duty
2 passport	5 information
3 customs	

3 **Aim** **To practise prepositional phrases and phrasal verbs**

- Explain the task.
- Give Ss time to complete it.
- Check Ss' answers.

Answer Key

1 for	3 on	5 out of
2 over	4 in	6 on

Grammar

4 **Aim** **To practise the definite article (the)**

- Explain the task.
- Give Ss time to complete it.
- Check Ss' answers.

Answer Key

1 the	3 the	5 –	7 the
2 –	4 –	6 –	8 the

5 **Aim** **To practise the present perfect and the present perfect continuous**

- Explain the task.
- Give Ss time to complete it.
- Check Ss' answers.

Answer Key

1 has been raining	5 Have you been waiting
2 Has Jim ever stayed	6 has not/hasn't visited
3 have been driving	
4 has been	

6 **Aim** To practise the past perfect and the past perfect continuous

- Explain the task.
- Give Ss time to complete it.
- Check Ss' answers.

Answer Key

1 *left*   4 *came*
2 *Had you ever ridden*   5 *been cycling*
3 *been raining*

Everyday English

7 **Aim** To match exchanges

- Explain the task.
- Give Ss time to complete it.
- Check Ss' answers.

Answer Key

1 *d*   2 *a*   3 *e*   4 *c*   5 *b*

Competences

Ask Ss to assess their own performance in the unit by ticking the items according to how competent they feel for each of the listed activities.

Values: Philanthropy

1 **Aim** To identify the purpose of the text
- Ask Ss to guess the purpose of the text.
- Tell Ss to read the text quickly to find out.

Answer Key

The purpose of the text is to inform.

2 **Aim** To listen and read for comprehension
- Play the recording. Ss listen and read the text.
- Then give Ss time to write five comprehension questions based on the text.
- Have Ss swap papers with their partner and try to answer the questions.
- Ask various Ss around the class to read out the questions and answers.
- Then give Ss time to explain the meanings of the words in bold from the context or by looking up the meanings in their dictionaries if necessary.

Suggested Answer Key

1 *How did Carnegie become rich?*
He became rich from investing money in railways.
2 *How much money did Carnegie have left at his death?*
He had about 10% of his fortune left at his death.
3 *What did Carnegie think people should do for the first part of their lives?*
He thought they should educate themselves.
4 *How often did Carnegie go to Colonel Anderson's library?*
He went there every Saturday as a boy.
5 *Where was the first Carnegie Library set up?*
In Dunfermline, Scotland.

Suggested Answer Key

invest (v): *to put money into sth in order to make a profit*
fortune (n): *a large amount of money*
project (n): *a study of a subject done over time*
announce (v): *to tell people sth in an official way*
borrow (v): *to get sth from sb for a period of time before returning it*

- Play the video for Ss and elicit their comments.

3 **Aim** THINK To develop critical thinking skills
- Ask Ss to work in closed pairs and consider their answers to the questions.
- Ask Ss to discuss in pairs and then ask some pairs to share their answers with the class.

Suggested Answer Key

A: *I would donate my fortune to environmental organisations to fight climate change because I think we need to save our planet for future generations.*
B: *That's good. I would donate my fortune to charities that help poor people because I think there are too many people living in poverty. etc*

4 **Aim** ICT To talk about philanthropists
- Ask Ss to work in pairs or small groups and give them time to research online and collect information about other people who have donated their fortunes to charities.
- Then ask various Ss around the class to present them to the class.

Suggested Answer Key

Bill Gates is a famous philanthropist. He made his fortune as the cofounder of Microsoft. He has donated $27 billion in his life. Now, he runs the Bill and Melinda Gates Foundation which donates millions of dollars to organisations around the world that help libraries, agricultural development, emergency relief, poverty, health and education.
Warren Buffet is another famous philanthropist. He made his fortune through investing. He has donated $21.5 billion in his life and has promised to donate 99% of his wealth before he dies. He also encourages other billionaires to donate at least half of their fortunes. He supports many charitable foundations including Bill Gates'.

Public Speaking Skills

1 **Aim** **To present a public speaking task**

- Remind Ss of the purposes of presentations, i.e. They can entertain the audience, they can narrate events, they can inform the audience about something, or they can persuade the audience to do something.
- Ask Ss to read the task and elicit answers to the questions.

Answer Key

The purpose of the presentation is to inform and entertain. The situation is a tour. I am a tour guide. I will be talking about a statue and explaining its significance.

2 **Aim** **To analyse a model public speaking task**

- Read out the **Study Skills** box and tell Ss this tip will help them when writing a presentation of their own.
- Play the recording. Ss listen and read the model.
- Elicit answers to the questions.

Answer Key

He has included the story of how J. M. Barrie came up with the character of Peter Pan. It makes his presentation sound more interesting and entertaining.

3 **Aim** **ICT** **To prepare for and write a presentation**

- Give Ss time to research online about a statue of a fictional or mythical character and collect information under the headings.
- Then ask Ss to use their notes and the model to help them prepare a presentation on it.
- Ask various Ss to give their presentation to the class.
- Alternatively, assign the task as HW and have Ss give their presentations in the next lesson. If Ss have selected a statue in their area, you can arrange a visit to the place where the statue is with Ss and, pretending they are tour guides, they give their presentations.

Suggested Answer Key

name of the character: *The Little Mermaid*
where the statue is: *on a rock on Langelinie promenade by the waterside in Copenhagen*
why it is there: *in honour of Hans Christian Andersen who wrote the famous fairy tale with the same name and many others*
description of the statue: *a mermaid in human form sitting and looking sadly towards the land, bronze*
who made it: *it was commissioned by Carl Jacobsen, a Danish philanthropist, in 1909. It was sculpted by Edvard Eriksen.*
story: *Carl Jacobsen saw the ballet of 'The Little Mermaid' and came up with the idea of the statue. He wanted the ballerina Ellen Price to pose for the statue. The face of the statue is hers but the body is modelled on the body of the sculptor's wife.*
how well it shows the character: *captures the sad story of the mermaid*

Welcome to Langelinie promenade where we begin our tour of Copenhagen today. My name is Marcus Jensen, and I'm going to be your tour guide.
'She looked once more at the Prince, hurled herself into the sea, and felt her body dissolve into foam.' I'm too old for fairy tales now, but I've never forgotten my favourite fairy tale, 'The Little Mermaid'. And in Copenhagen I never have to because her statue is here. It's here to honour the Danish author Hans Christian Andersen who wrote the famous fairy tale and many others.
The bronze statue was commissioned by Carl Jacobsen a Danish philanthropist, in 1909 and it was sculpted by Edvard Eriksen. Carl Jacobsen saw the ballet of 'The Little Mermaid' and came up with the idea of the statue. He wanted the ballerina Ellen Price to pose for the statue. The face of the statue is hers but the body is modelled on the body of the sculptor's wife.
I think the statue really captures the sad story of the mermaid who has feelings for a prince and gives up everything for him only for him to fall in love with someone else. It shows a bronze mermaid in human form sitting on a rock and looking sadly towards the land. She looks like her heart is broken, don't you agree? I'm going to let you take a closer look at the statue now, but if you have any questions about it, please ask me.

Hard Times

4

Topic	
In this unit, Ss will explore the topics of stressful events and fears & physical reactions.	
4a Reading & Vocabulary	**30-31**
Lesson objectives: To learn vocabulary for stressful events, to read and listen for gist (multiple matching), to learn prepositional phrases, to practise words easily confused, to learn phrasal verbs with *take*, to write a short email about a stressful event, to give advice	
Vocabulary: Stressful events *(becoming unemployed, divorce/separation, serious injury/illness, moving house, starting a new job, taking exams, having financial problems, someone stealing your personal information)*; Nouns *(bill, day care, cause, promotion, CV)*; Verbs *(attract, quit, retire, afford, miss, volunteer, believe, think)*; Phrasal verbs *(pile up, give up, take after/off/over/up)*; Adjectives *(anxious, miserable, proud, active, useful)*; Phrases *(let sb go, fundraising event, positive attitude, professional networking site)*	
4b Grammar in Use	**32-33**
Lesson objectives: To learn/revise future tenses, to learn conditionals type 1, to learn time words	
4c Skills in Action	**34-35**
Lesson objectives: To learn vocabulary for fears & physical reactions, to listen for specific information (Yes/No statements), to act out a dialogue and practise everyday English for asking for/giving advice, to learn the pronunciation of /z/, /s/, to read for cohesion & coherence (word formation), to write an email giving advice	
Vocabulary: Fears & Physical reactions *(mouth goes dry, freeze, hands sweat, heart beats faster, hurt, run a mile, shake like a leaf, feel sick, hair stands on end, control fear, face fears, avoid – fear of bugs, fear of public speaking, fear of storms, fear of flying, fear of closed spaces, fear of heights)*	
Culture 4	**36**
Lesson objectives: To listen and read for gist, to read for specific information (comprehension questions), to talk about an annual festival, to write about a festival	
Vocabulary: Nouns *(bug, creepy-crawly, highlight, sample)*; Verbs *(host, wonder, forget)*; Adjectives *(rare, giant, brave, local, exciting)*; Adverb *(up close)*	
Review 4	**37**
Lesson objectives: To test/consolidate vocabulary and grammar learnt throughout the unit, to practise everyday English	

Go through the objectives box and tell Ss that these are the topics, skills and activities this unit will cover.

4a

Vocabulary

1 **Aim** **To present vocabulary related to stressful events**

- Ask Ss to look at the pictures and read out the words/phrases.
- Give Ss time to consider their answers and then ask various Ss to tell the class which three events they think are the most stressful and why.

Suggested Answer Key

I think divorce or separation is the most stressful because it can mean breaking up a family. I think having financial problems is very stressful too because if you can't pay your bills, you may lose your home. Finally, I think becoming unemployed is very stressful because it can lead to financial problems and family problems.

Reading & Listening

2 **a)** **Aim** **To present problems and introduce the topic of a text**

Ask Ss to look at the pictures 1-3 in the text and then read the problems a-c and match them.

b) **Aim** **To listen and read for gist (multiple matching)**

- Play the recording and have Ss follow the text in their books.
- Check Ss' answers around the class.

Answer Key

1 c	2 b	3 a

3 **Aim** **To listen and read for comprehension; to compare ideas and to consolidate new vocabulary**

- Explain the task. Play the recording. Ss match the people with the problems.
- Check Ss' answers around the class.

Answer Key

1 C	2 A	3 B

- Ask Ss to discuss in pairs if they agree with the advice Maggie gave to each person.
- Ask various Ss to share their thoughts with the class.
- Then give Ss time to explain the words in bold using their dictionaries to help them as necessary.

39

Suggested Answer Key

We would give the same advice as Maggie for No_ Luck_Lucy and for Hands_Full. For Brian, we thought he should take up a useful hobby like gardening or mending furniture. Maggie said he could work for a charity.

attract (v): *to bring in*
let sb go (phr): *to take away sb's job*
miserable (adj): *very unhappy*
quit (v): *to stop doing sth*
proud (adj): *satisfied*
active (adj): *always moving or busy*
useful (adj): *being helpful*
positive attitude (phr): *a way of thinking and acting in which you expect good results and success*
give up (phr v): *to stop trying*
miss (v): *to lose the chance*
fundraising events (phr): *events designed to collect money for a reason (usually a charity)*

- Give Ss time to look up the meanings of the words in the Check these words box in the Word List.
- Play the video for Ss and elicit their comments.

4 **Aim** To consolidate new vocabulary

- Ask Ss to read the words in the list and then give them time to complete the phrases with them.
- Check Ss' answers. Then give Ss time to write sentences using the phrases and elicit Ss' answers around the class.

Answer Key

1	tour	3	free	5	easy
2	day	4	positive	6	fundraising

Suggested Answer Key

*My cousin Tony works as a **tour guide** in the local museum.*
*Many parents leave their children in **day care** when they go to work.*
*I play football in my **free time**.*
*It is important to have a **positive attitude** when looking for a job.*
*When you are a working mother, there is no **easy answer** for how to combine work and family life.*
*Charities often hold **fundraising events**.*

NOTE: Ask Ss to add these phrases to the Collocations section in their notebook and revise them regularly.

5 **Aim** To consolidate prepositional phrases from a text

- Give Ss time to read the gapped phrases and fill the gaps with the correct prepositions.

- Then check Ss' answers by eliciting sentences using the completed phrases from Ss around the class.

Answer Key

1	for	5	of	9	in
2	from	6	at	10	about
3	about	7	in		
4	of	8	out of		

Suggested Answer Key

*I haven't applied **for** the post yet.*
*When I send my friend an email, I usually hear back **from** them quite quickly.*
*I am anxious **about** my exam results.*
*It isn't easy to work and take care **of** your children.*
*Paul is proud **of** his children.*
*I enjoy staying **at** home at weekends.*
*I am interested **in** science.*
*When you are unemployed, you are **out of** work.*
*You can call or text me if you want to get **in** contact with me.*
*I am excited **about** going on holiday next summer.*

NOTE: Ask Ss to add the phrases to the Prepositions section in their notebook.

6 **Aim** To understand words easily confused

- Explain the task and give Ss time to use their dictionaries (digital or printed) to help them complete it.
- Check Ss' answers.

Answer Key

1	reason	3	believe
2	cause	4	think

7 **Aim** To learn phrasal verbs with *take*

- Ask Ss to read the phrasal verbs box and make sure that Ss understand the definitions.
- Then give Ss time to complete the task and check their answers.
- Tell Ss to add the phrasal verbs to the Phrasal Verbs section at the back of their notebooks and write down any and all phrasal verbs that they come across in the units in exercises and in texts.

Answer Key

1	over	3	up	5	up
2	after	4	off	6	off

Speaking & Writing

8 **Aim** To write a short email asking for advice

- Explain the task and give Ss time to write a short email to Maggie asking for advice.

40

- Ask various Ss around the class to read out their emails.

Suggested Answer Key

Dear Maggie,
I am having financial problems and I am so stressed. I can't sleep. I can't concentrate and I don't know what to do. Please can you help me?
Helen_1986

9 Aim THINK **To practise giving advice**

- Ask Ss to swap their emails with their partner and then practise giving advice for the problem they have.
- Monitor the activity around the class and then ask some Ss to share their answers with the class. Ss can do the task orally or in writing.

Suggested Answer Key

Helen_1986: *You aren't alone. A lot of people these days have financial problems. You should make a list of all your bills. Work out which ones are the most important and then speak to the companies and try to arrange to pay them off in small amounts. You could also try to increase your income by taking a second job or selling some things to make some money. How about talking to your bank manager about a loan? Hope my advice helps!*

4b Grammar in Use

1 Aim To present/revise future tenses

- Ask Ss to read the dialogue and identify all the tenses used. Read out the list of uses and have Ss say which tense matches which use.
- Refer Ss to the Grammar Reference section for detailed information.

Answer Key

present simple: *the library closes*
present continuous: *I'm meeting*
future simple: *it'll be, I'll text, I'll be*
be going to: *I'm going to study, it's going to rain*

on-the-spot decisions: *future simple (will) – I'll text*
fixed arrangements in the near future: *present continuous – I'm meeting*
future plans & intentions: *be going to – I'm going to study*
timetables/programmes: *present simple – it closes*
predictions based on what we think or imagine: *future simple – it'll be, I'll be*
predictions based on what we can see or know: *be going to – it's going to rain*

2 Aim To listen for specific information; to practise *will/won't*

- Explain the task. Play the recording twice if necessary. Ss listen and complete the task.
- Check Ss' answers.

Answer Key

1 ✓   2 ✓   3 ✗   4 ✓   5 ✗   6 ✓

Suggested Answer Key

Jenny thinks she'll find a good job.
She hopes she'll share a flat.
Jenny expects she won't find a place with a garden.
She thinks she'll enjoy living there.
She expects she won't get bored there.
She thinks she'll miss her family.

3 a) Aim To listen for specific information; to practise *be going to*

- Explain the situation and ask Ss to make notes about Stan's holiday activities while they listen.
- Play the recording twice if necessary. Ss listen and complete the task.
- Check Ss' answers.

Answer Key

Stan is going to stay in a five-star hotel. He is going to stay on a Caribbean island. He's going to go for a swim every morning and he's going to sunbathe on the beach every afternoon. He's going to eat at lovely restaurants in the evenings and he's going to stay out late at night.

b) Aim To practise future plans and intentions

- Explain the task and give Ss time to complete it.
- Check Ss' answers.

Suggested Answer Key

... visit the Kasbah of the Udayas and the Hassan Tower as well as the Mausoleum of Mohammed V. I'm going to swim in the sea and sunbathe on the beach. I'm going to eat at local traditional restaurants and I'm going to buy lots of souvenirs.

4 Aim To practise *will* and *be going to*

- Explain the task and give Ss time to complete it.
- Then check Ss' answers. Ask Ss to justify their answers.

Answer Key

1 *will (on-the-spot decision)*
2 *am going to (future plan)*
3 *are going to (prediction based on what we see)*
4 *will (prediction based on what we think/imagine)*
5 *is going to (prediction based on what we know)*

5 **Aim** To practise the present simple and the present continuous (future meanings)

- Explain the task and read out the example.
- Give Ss time to complete the task and then elicit answers from Ss around the class.

Answer Key

2 is performing, finishes
3 are acting, ends
4 are visiting, opens
5 is giving, begins

6 **Aim** To practise future tenses

Explain the task and give Ss time to complete it and then check their answers.

Answer Key

1 Are you going to visit (future plan/intention)
2 am travelling (fixed arrangement)
3 is going to be (prediction based on what we know)
4 will have (prediction based on what we think/imagine)
5 leaves (timetable)
6 will be able to (prediction based on what we think/imagine)
7 will stop (on-the-spot decision)

7 **Aim** To present/revise conditionals type 1

- Present conditionals type 1. Say then write on the board: *If you ask me, I will help you.* Ask Ss to identify the **if**-clause *(If you ask me)* and which tense we use *(the present simple)*. Ask Ss to identify the **main clause** *(I will help you)* and the tense used *(the future simple)*. Explain that this is a type 1 conditional and we use them to talk about a real or likely situation in the present or future.
- Ask Ss to read the theory box. Focus on the first two examples and explain that we use a comma to separate the **if**-clause from the main clause if the **if**-clause precedes the main clause. Elicit that we use no comma to separate the two clauses when the main clause precedes the **if**-clause. Study the examples and then elicit an example from the dialogue on p. 32.
- Refer Ss to the **Grammar Reference** section for more information.

Answer Key

Example: *If there's a change of plan, I'll text you.*

8 **Aim** To practise conditionals type 1

- Explain the task and give Ss time to complete it.
- Check Ss' answers around the class.

Answer Key

1 e   2 a   3 b   4 c   5 f   6 d

1 The dog won't bite you unless you bother it.
2 I can take part in the match if you need me.
3 I'll pass the test unless I get stressed in the exam hall.
4 I'll be really nervous if there are many people in the audience.
5 I'll buy a new laptop if I can afford it.
6 We may go on a picnic unless it rains.

9 **Aim** To practise conditionals type 1

- Explain the task and ask Ss to read the thought bubbles and then continue the thoughts using conditionals type 1.
- Elicit answers from Ss around the class.
- You can divide the class into two teams. One team makes a sentence, the other team continues. Alternatively, Ss can do the task in closed or open pairs.

Suggested Answer Key

a) *... be late for work. If I am late for work, my boss will get angry. If my boss gets angry, he will shout at me. If he shouts at me, I will get upset. etc*
b) *... I won't get into university. If I don't get into university, I won't get a good job. If I don't get a good job, I won't earn much money. etc*

10 **Aim** To present time clauses

- Go through the theory box with Ss and then elicit examples from the dialogue on p. 32.
- Refer Ss to the **Grammar Reference** section for more information.

Answer Key

Examples: *when, after, if*

11 **Aim** To practise time clauses

Ask Ss to read the sentences and cross out the incorrect time words. Elicit answers from Ss around the class.

Answer Key

1 ✓   3 ✓   5 1st will
2 will   4 1st will 6 will

12 **Aim** To practise time clauses

Give Ss one minute to complete the sentences and then elicit answers from Ss around the class.

Suggested Answer Key

1 ... a good film comes out.
2 ... I will have dinner.
3 ... I will go to the gym today.
4 ... go home.

Background Information

Spain is a country in southwestern Europe. 45 million people live there and the capital city is Madrid. The official language is Spanish.

4c Skills in Action

Vocabulary

1 a) **Aim** **To present vocabulary for physical reactions**

- Ask Ss to read the sentences and, in closed pairs, choose the words in bold which best fit the sentences. Have Ss check their answers in the Word List.
- Check Ss' answers around the class.

Answer Key

1 goes dry, freeze	*4 shake, feel*
2 sweat, beats	*5 stood, control*
3 hurt, mile	*6 face, avoid*

b) **Aim** **To present vocabulary for fears**

- Ask Ss to read the fears A-F and then give them time to match them to the sentences from Ex. 1a.
- Elicit answers from Ss around the class.

Answer Key

1 C   2 B   3 A   4 D   5 F   6 E

Listening

2 **Aim** **To listen for specific information (Yes/No statements)**

- Read out the **Study Skills** box and tell Ss this tip will help them to complete the task successfully.
- Ask Ss to read statements 1-6 and underline the key words.
- Play the recording twice. Ss listen and mark the statements.
- Check Ss' answers. You can play the recording with pauses if you like for Ss to check their answers.

Answer Key

1 No	*3 Yes*	*5 No*
2 No	*4 No*	*6 Yes*

Everyday English

3 a) **Aim** **To introduce the topic and read for gist; to give advice**

Ask Ss to read the first exchange in the dialogue. Elicit what Alan's problem is and then ask various Ss around the class to give their advice.

Suggested Answer Key

I would advise Alan to prepare well so that he would be less nervous about forgetting what to say. I would also advise him to do some deep breathing before he went on stage and try to relax as much as possible.

b) **Aim** **To listen and read for specific information**

Play the recording. Tell Ss to follow the dialogue in their books and then elicit if any of their ideas from Ex. 3a were mentioned.

Suggested Answer Key

Being prepared was mentioned.

4 **Aim** **To role-play a dialogue asking for/giving advice**

- Explain the task and ask Ss to act out similar dialogues to the one in Ex. 3 in closed pairs using the prompts and the phrases in the box to help them.
- Write this diagram on the board for Ss to follow.

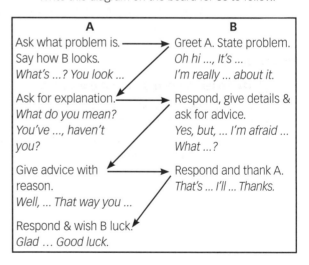

A	B
Ask what problem is. Say how B looks. *What's ...? You look ...*	Greet A. State problem. *Oh hi ..., It's ... I'm really ... about it.*
Ask for explanation. *What do you mean? You've ..., haven't you?*	Respond, give details & ask for advice. *Yes, but, ... I'm afraid ... What ...?*
Give advice with reason. *Well, ... That way you ...*	Respond and thank A. *That's ... I'll ... Thanks.*
Respond & wish B luck. *Glad ... Good luck.*	

- Monitor the activity around the class and offer assistance as necessary.
- Then ask some pairs to act out their dialogues in front of the class.

Suggested Answer Key

A: What's up James? You look a bit worried.
B: Oh, hi, Steve. It's this appointment I've got at the dentist's this afternoon. I'm really worried about it.
A: What do you mean? You've been to the dentist's before, haven't you?
B: Yes, but only for a check-up. I'm afraid I will need more work because one tooth is hurting. I'm terrified. What should I do?
A: Well, why don't you discuss the problem with the dentist? You could ask for some music to help you relax. That way, you won't feel so scared.
B: That's not a bad idea. I'll give it a try. Thanks Steve.
A: Glad to help. Good luck.

B

A: What's up Jenny? You look a bit worried.
B: Oh, hi, Amira. It's learning to drive. I'm really nervous about it.
A: What do you mean? You've been talking about getting driving lessons for ages, haven't you?
B: Yes, but I'm afraid I will freeze up when I am in the driving seat of a car. What's your advice?
A: Well, you should play some driving simulation games to get a general idea of what it's like. You'd better find a good instructor that you can trust too. That way you won't feel so anxious.
B: That's a very good idea. I'll give it a try. Thanks Amira.
A: Glad to help. Good luck.

Pronunciation

5 **Aim** To learn the pronunciations of /z/, /s/

- Read out the theory box.
- Model the sounds /z/ and /s/.
- Then play the recording. Ss listen and tick the pairs with different pronunciation.
- Check Ss' answers.
- Then elicit sentences from Ss around the class using the words in their own sentences.

NOTE: Point out that in American English, the spelling of both the noun and the verb 'practice' is with 'c' (no 's').

Answer Key

pairs to be ticked: *1,4*

Suggested Answer Key

I **advise** you to get fit.
Thanks for the **advice**.
An athlete **practises** hard every day.
Tony is having football **practice** this afternoon.
A pilot has to be **licensed** to fly a plane.

You need a valid driving **licence** to do this job.
We need to **devise** a plan.
A smartphone is a communication **device**.

Reading & Writing

6 a) **Aim** To read for cohesion and coherence (word formation)

- Read out the theory box and tell Ss that this information will help them to complete the task successfully.
- Read out the rubric and give Ss time to read the email and complete the task by forming a verb from the verb in brackets by adding a prefix to fill the gaps.
- Check Ss' answers.

Answer Key

1	disagree	4	rethink
2	dislikes	5	reconsider
3	disappear	6	misunderstand

b) **Aim** To identify the style of a piece of writing

Elicit the style of the email and ask Ss to give reasons for their answer.

Answer Key

The email is informal because the writer uses short forms (shouldn't, don't, they're), informal language (deal with it, how you get on) and omits pronouns (Sorry).

7 **Aim** To identify advice and expected results

Read out the **Writing Tip** box and then elicit what advice Conrad gives in the email and the expected results he mentions from Ss around the class.

Answer Key

Conrad advises Billy to imagine himself having a good time at the barbecue. The expected result is that he will have a better chance of enjoying himself.
He also advises Billy to think about how other people are feeling. The expected result is that if he focuses on other people, he will forget his own anxiety.

8 **Aim** To practise phrases for giving advice

Elicit the phrases Conrad uses to give advice and the expected results in the email from Ss around the class and then elicit alternative phrases from the box.

Suggested Answer Key

Give advice

why don't you – it would be a good idea to
you should – I advise you to

Expected results

This way, – This would mean that
By (focusing on other people) … – Then,

Writing

9 **Aim** **To prepare for a writing task**

Ask Ss to read the task and then elicit answers to the questions from Ss around the class.

Answer Key

I am going to write an email giving advice.
I am going to write to my English friend Max.

10 **a)** **Aim** **To prepare for a writing task**

- Ask Ss to read the gapped table.
- Then play the recording twice and have Ss listen and fill in the gaps.
- Check Ss' answers around the class.

Answer Key

1	reason	3	better	5	safe
2	fear	4	read	6	anxious

b) **Aim** **To write an email giving advice**

- Ask Ss to read the rubric in Ex. 9 again and then give them time to write their emails using their answers in Ex. 10a and following the plan.
- Ask various Ss to share their answers with the class.
- Alternatively, assign the task as HW and check Ss' answers in the next lesson.

Suggested Answer Key

Hi Max,

I'm sorry to hear about your fear of sailing, but I have some advice that I think will help. If you can overcome your fear, I think you will end up having a great time on your sailing trip.

First of all, why don't you try to identify why you are afraid? By understanding your fear, you can deal with it better.

Also, you should read about safety equipment online. This way you'll learn how to stay safe at sea and you'll feel less anxious.

I hope my advice helps. I'm sure you'll enjoy your sailing trip. Write and let me know how you get on.

Write soon,

Ali

Values

Ask Ss to think about the quotation. Then initiate a class discussion about the meaning of the quotation and encourage Ss to participate. You can ask Ss to research for similar quotations and present them in the next lesson.

Suggested Answer

A: *I think the quotation means that real bravery comes from not being afraid of things that we have nothing to actually fear, such as irrational fears and phobias.*

B: *I don't really agree with the quote. To me, courage is knowing that something is dangerous but doing it or facing it anyway, because the situation asks for it.*

Culture 4

Reading & Listening

1 **Aim** **To introduce the topic and listen and read for specific information**

- Ask Ss to read the words/phrases. Explain/Elicit their meanings and then play the recording.
- Elicit how they are related to Bug Fest.

Suggested Answer Key

Creepy-crawlies *are insects which Bug Fest is all about. You can **see** them **up close** there. There is an Xtreme Bugs exhibition which has **huge robot insects**. A local **sweet maker** makes sweets from insects you can eat and there is also a **cockroach race** at Bug Fest called the Roach Races Grand Prix.*

2 **Aim** **To read for specific information (comprehension questions)**

- Ask Ss to read the questions and then read the text and answer them.
- Check Ss' answers.

Answer Key

1 *It is a fear of insects.*
2 *the Academy of Natural Sciences*
3 *They can see huge robot insects.*
4 *a local sweet maker*

- Give Ss time to look up the meanings of the words in the **Check these words** box in the Word List.
- Play the video for Ss and elicit their comments.

3 **Aim** **To consolidate new vocabulary from a text**

- Direct Ss' attention to the words in bold in the text and ask them to read the list of words and match them as opposites.

- Tell Ss they can use their dictionaries to help them if necessary.
- Ask various Ss to share their answers with the rest of the class.

Answer Key

rare ≠ common
giant ≠ tiny
forget ≠ remember
brave ≠ afraid
local ≠ foreign
exciting ≠ boring

Speaking & Writing

4 **Aim** **THINK** **To discuss a similar festival**

Have Ss talk in pairs or small groups and think of a festival that celebrates something that people are commonly afraid of. Then ask various Ss to tell the class.

Suggested Answer Key

There is an annual festival in Mexico called the Day of the Dead. The festivities involve visiting cemeteries and include skeletons and skulls. Many people are afraid of these things. I think people should go to this festival to show that death is a part of life and there is nothing to be afraid of.

5 **Aim** **ICT** **To write a short text about a festival**

- Explain the task and give Ss time to research online and collect information about the festival in Ex. 4 and then write a short text about it.
- Ask various Ss to read their text to the class.
- Alternatively, assign the task as HW and ask Ss to read out their texts in the next lesson.

Suggested Answer Key

Name: *The Day of the Dead*
Place: *Mexico*
Date: *2nd November*
Reason: *To remember family members who are no longer alive*
Activities: *People visit cemeteries, light candles and decorate the graves of family members with gifts, flowers and cardboard skeletons. They make their favourite dishes and special sweets such as sugar skulls.*

The Day of the Dead is a festival that takes place in Mexico on 2nd November. People celebrate it to remember family members who are no longer alive. They visit cemeteries, light candles and decorate the graves of family members with gifts, flowers and cardboard skeletons. They make their favourite dishes and special sweets such as sugar skulls. It is a private

family event but if you are in Mexico at that time, you can enjoy displays in the streets.

Background Information

Philadelphia is the biggest city in the state of Pennsylvania in the USA. About 1.5 million people live there. It is very important in American history and was the capital city for a while before Washington, D.C. Today it is known for its arts, culture, education and historic landmarks.

Review 4

Vocabulary

1 **Aim** **To consolidate vocabulary from the unit**

- Explain the task.
- Give Ss time to complete it.
- Check Ss' answers.

Answer Key

1 *fundraising*	4 *injury*
2 *unemployed*	5 *financial*
3 *retirement*	6 *positive*

2 **Aim** **To consolidate vocabulary from the unit**

- Explain the task.
- Give Ss time to complete it.
- Check Ss' answers.

Answer Key

1 *taking*	3 *afford*	5 *believe*
2 *face*	4 *beating*	6 *hurt*

3 **Aim** **To practise phrasal verbs/prepositional phrases from the unit**

- Explain the task.
- Give Ss time to complete it.
- Check Ss' answers.

Answer Key

1 *in*	3 *about*	5 *up*
2 *off*	4 *of*	

Grammar

4 **Aim** **To practise future tenses**

- Explain the task.
- Give Ss time to complete it.
- Check Ss' answers.

Answer Key

1 will	4 are going to
2 is going to	5 will
3 will	

5 **Aim** To practise future tenses

- Explain the task.
- Give Ss time to complete it.
- Check Ss' answers.

Answer Key

1 leaves	4 'll be
2 's going to attack	5 's flying
3 's going to talk	

6 **Aim** To practise conditionals type 1

- Explain the task.
- Give Ss time to complete it.
- Check Ss' answers.

Answer Key

1 will scream	3 will quit	5 gets
2 arrive	4 will help	

Everyday English

7 **Aim** To match exchanges

- Explain the task.
- Give Ss time to complete it.
- Check Ss' answers.

Answer Key

1 e	2 d	3 b	4 a	5 c

Competences

Ask Ss to assess their own performance in the unit by ticking the items according to how competent they feel for each of the listed activities.

5 Citizen 2100

<table>
<tr><td colspan="2">Topic</td></tr>
<tr><td colspan="2">In this unit, Ss will explore the topics of cities of the future and future predictions.</td></tr>
<tr><td>5a   Reading & Vocabulary</td><td>38-39</td></tr>
<tr><td colspan="2">Lesson objectives: To learn vocabulary for cities of the future, to read for gist, (matching headings to paragraphs), to learn prepositional phrases, to practise words easily confused, to learn phrasal verbs with come, to design and present a city of the future

Vocabulary: Cities of the future (vertical farms, self-driving buses, 3D-printed houses, solar windows, drone deliveries, vacuum tube trains, floating buildings, charging stations for electric cars); Noun (traffic jam); Verbs (improve, construct, produce, increase, reduce, create, provide, deliver, transport); Phrasal verbs (come); Adjectives (crowded, perfect, lonely, alone); Phrase (take up space)</td></tr>
<tr><td>5b   Grammar in Use</td><td>40-41</td></tr>
<tr><td colspan="2">Lesson objectives: To learn/revise the future continuous and the future perfect, to listen for specific information (T/F statements)</td></tr>
<tr><td>5c   Skills in Action</td><td>42-43</td></tr>
<tr><td colspan="2">Lesson objectives: To learn vocabulary for future predictions, to listen for specific information (R/W/DS statements), to act out a dialogue and practise everyday English for discussing future plans, to learn the pronunciation of /uː/, /ʊ/, to read for order and structure, to practise word formation, to write an essay making predictions

Vocabulary: Future predictions (pollution levels in cities decrease, crime increases, people live in cities under the sea, people live longer, people go on holiday to other planets, there is more poverty)</td></tr>
<tr><td>Culture 5</td><td>44</td></tr>
<tr><td colspan="2">Lesson objectives: To listen and read for gist, to read for specific information (sentence completion), to make a plot outline, to write about a film or TV show about the future and the predictions it made

Vocabulary: Nouns (virtual assistant, task, weapon, nuclear bomb, automatic doors, satellite); Verbs (tap, attack, access, predict); Adjectives (voice-activated, latest, clear); Phrases (alien invasion, military vehicle)</td></tr>
<tr><td>Review 5</td><td>45</td></tr>
<tr><td colspan="2">Lesson objectives: To test/consolidate vocabulary and grammar learnt throughout the unit, to practise everyday English</td></tr>
</table>

Go through the objectives box and tell Ss that these are the topics, skills and activities this unit will cover.

5a

Vocabulary

1 **Aim** **To present vocabulary related to cities of the future**

- Go through the list of features with Ss and ask Ss to identify them in the picture.
- Give Ss time to decide which of the features they think will exist in 2100.
- Elicit answers from Ss around the class.

Suggested Answer Key

Features not in the picture: *self-driving buses, floating buildings*

I think in 2100 we will have self-driving buses, solar windows, drone deliveries and vacuum tube trains as well as charging stations for electric cars. I don't think we will have vertical farms, 3D-printed houses, or floating buildings.

Reading & Listening

2 **Aim** **To read for gist**

Ask Ss to read through the text quickly and then elicit how future cities will improve people's lives from Ss around the class.

Suggested Answer Key

Cities of the future will improve people's lives because they will have good public transport and fewer cars on the roads. Cars will be electric so there will be less pollution. Modern buildings will be 3D-printed and blocks of flats will float on rivers or off the coast so there will be more space. Buildings will have solar windows to generate solar power. All cities will have vertical farms to produce crops and a lot of green areas. Cities won't have that many shops because people will order everything online and drones will deliver their shopping to their home.

3 **Aim** **To read for gist (matching headings to paragraphs)**

- Ask Ss to read headings A-E and then give Ss time to read the text again and match the headings to the paragraphs. Ask Ss to look for words similar in meaning or thematically related to the words in the headings.
- Play the recording for Ss to listen and check their answers.

• Then give Ss time to look up the meanings of the words in bold in the Word List or in their dictionaries and ask various Ss around the class to share them with the rest of the class.

Answer Key

1 B (2100, hopeful, perfect places)
2 A (public transport, roads, cars, traffic jams)
3 D (build, houses, blocks of flats, buildings)
4 E (produce food close, vertical farms, food to people living nearby)
5 C (green areas, parks, green roofs, relaxing, exercising, order online)

Suggested Answer Key

increase (v): to become more
crowded (adj): full of people
perfect (adj): the best
reduce (v): to make less
create (v): to make something new
provide (v): to give
deliver (v): to take sth to sb

• Give Ss time to look up the meanings of the words in the **Check these words** box in the Word List.
• Play the video for Ss and elicit their comments.

4 a) **Aim** To consolidate new vocabulary

• Ask Ss to read the words in the lists and then give them time to match them.
• Check Ss' answers.

Answer Key

1 e   2 f   3 d   4 b   5 c   6 a

b) **Aim** To practise new vocabulary

Give Ss time to write sentences using the phrases and elicit Ss' answers around the class.

Suggested Answer Key

Modern technology is a big part of our lives these days.
We should all eat **healthy food** instead of burgers and pizzas.
My dad hates getting stuck in **traffic jams** so he goes to work by bus.
I hope **public transport** improves in the future as lots of people use it to commute daily.
A lot of houses in hot countries use **solar power** to produce energy.
I don't go shopping as online shops deliver the parcels to my **front door**.

5 **Aim** To consolidate prepositional phrases from a text

• Give Ss time to read the sentences and choose the correct prepositions.
• Then check Ss' answers.

Answer Key

1 with   3 off   5 In
2 within   4 about

Background Information

UAE (the United Arab Emirates) is a country in western Asia. It consists of seven emirates – Abu Dhabi, Ajman, Dubai, Fujairah, Ras al-Khaimah, Sharjah and Umm al-Quwain.

6 **Aim** To expand on vocabulary; to understand words easily confused

• Explain the task and give Ss time to use their dictionaries to help them complete it.
• Check Ss' answers.

Answer Key

1 lonely   3 transports
2 alone   4 delivers

7 **Aim** To learn phrasal verbs with *come*

• Ask Ss to read the phrasal verbs box and make sure that Ss understand the definitions.
• Then give Ss time to complete the task and check their answers.
• Then give Ss time to use the phrasal verbs in the box to make up a short story.
• Ask various Ss to share their stories with the class.
• Tell Ss to add the phrasal verbs to the Phrasal Verbs list in their notebooks and include the definitions and example sentences.
• Remind Ss to revise this list from time to time and to add to it every time they come across a new phrasal verb.

Answer Key

1 across   3 back
2 into   4 round/over

Suggested Answer Key

When James was helping his mum clear out some old papers, he **came across** a letter that said she **had come into** some money. The letter hadn't been opened. She was very surprised and glad that James **had come over** and told him to **come back** anytime.

Speaking & Writing

8 **Aim** To develop critical thinking skills; to design and present a city of the future

- Ask Ss to work in small groups and design a city of the future, thinking about where it will be and what it will have.
- You can brainstorm some ideas with Ss before they work in groups.
- Then ask various groups of Ss to present their city to the rest of the class.

Suggested Answer Key

Good morning. Our city of the future will be under the sea. All the buildings will either be under the sea floor or they will be on the bottom of the sea and they will have dome roofs to let in light and for people to see the sea life. People will get food from the sea and grow plants on the sea floor. People will get around in vacuum tube trains and they will travel to other cities in small underwater vehicles like submarines that can travel in the water or on the land. There will be no pollution and life will be simple.
That's our city of the future.
Does anyone have any questions? ... . Thank you for listening.

5b Grammar in Use

1 **Aim** To learn the future continuous

- Write on the board. *This time next week **I'll be flying** to Oman.* Ask Ss to look at the verb form in bold. Explain that this tense is the future continuous. Elicit use (action in progress at a certain time in the future).
- Elicit/Explain that we form the future continuous tense with *will/won't be* + main verb + *-ing*.
- Go through the theory box with Ss.
- Refer Ss to the **Grammar Reference** section for detailed information.
- Ask Ss to read the forum and elicit examples.

Answer Key

Examples: *will be receiving (result of an arrangement), we'll be using (result of an arrangement), we'll be seeing (result of a routine), I'll be taking (action in progress at definite future time)*

2 **Aim** To practise the future continuous

- Explain the task. Ss complete the task.
- Check Ss' answers.

Answer Key

1 will/'ll be visiting	5 will be giving
2 will not/won't be using	6 will be arriving
3 will/'ll be installing	7 will be learning
4 Will you be working	8 will/'ll be moving

3 **Aim** To practise the future continuous

- Explain the task and read out the example.
- Give Ss time to read the notes and complete the task.
- Check Ss' answers.

Answer Key

2 A: Will Kate be shopping at the supermarket at two o'clock next Tuesday?
   B: No, she won't. She will be shopping at the supermarket at three o'clock next Tuesday.
3 A: Will Kate be visiting a robot exhibition at ten o'clock next Friday?
   B: No, she won't. She will be visiting a robot exhibition at nine o'clock next Thursday.
4 A: Will Kate be flying to Barcelona at two o'clock next Friday?
   B: Yes, she will.

Background Information

Barcelona is a city in Spain. It is the second most populous city in Spain after its capital city, Madrid.

Speaking

4 **Aim** THINK To practise the future continuous and predict the future

- Explain the task and ask a pair to read out the example.
- Ask Ss to work in pairs and use the future continuous to make positive and negative predictions about the future. You can brainstorm for ideas with Ss before they do the task in closed pairs.
- Monitor the activity around the class and then ask various Ss to share their answers with the class.

Suggested Answer Key

A: In 30 years, people will be eating food from vertical farms.
B: In 30 years, people will be paying a lot of money for food.
A: In 30 years, people will be using VR headsets for entertainment.

B: *In 30 years, people won't be spending time with real people.*

A: *In 30 years, students will be using more technology in classrooms.*

B: *In 30 years, robots will be teaching in classrooms.*

A: *In 30 years, people will be driving electric cars.*

B: *In 30 years, only wealthy people will be driving cars.*

5 **Aim** **To learn the future perfect**

- Write on the board: *I **will have finished** my homework by 6 o'clock this afternoon.* Ask Ss to look at the verb form in bold and elicit/explain use (completed action in the future that will have happened before a stated time in the future). Explain that this tense is the future perfect.
- Explain/Elicit that we form the future perfect tense with *will have* + the past participle of the main verb.
- Go through the theory table with Ss.
- Refer Ss to the **Grammar Reference** section for more information.
- Then elicit two examples from the forum on p. 40.

Answer Key

Examples: *we will definitely have changed, I'll have sat*

6 **Aim** **To practise the future perfect**

- Explain the task and give Ss time to complete it.
- Then check Ss' answers around the class on the board.

Answer Key

1 will have moved
2 Will you have finished
3 will have discovered
4 won't have left
5 won't have finished
6 will have found

7 **Aim** **To practise the future perfect**

- Explain the task and ask two Ss to read out the example.
- Give Ss time to complete the task in closed pairs using the schedule, alternating roles so both Ss get to practise the future perfect.
- Monitor the activity around the class and then ask some pairs to ask and answer in front of the rest of the class.

Suggested Answer Key

A: *Will Max have finished his meeting with the sales department by 13:20?*

B: *No, he won't. Will Max have met Jerry by 18:45?*

A: *Yes, he will. Will Max have picked up Lisa by 20:30?*

B: *No, he won't.*

8 **Aim** **To practise the future continuous and the future perfect**

- Explain the task and give Ss time to complete it.
- Check Ss' answers.

Answer Key

1 will be travelling
2 Will underwater cities have been created
3 will have started
4 will be visiting
5 won't have finished
6 won't be seeing

Listening

9 **Aim** **To listen for specific information (T/F statements)**

- Explain the task and ask Ss to read statements 1-5.
- Play the recording twice. Ss listen and mark the statements,
- Check Ss' answers. You can play the recording with pauses for Ss to check their answers.

Answer Key

1 T   2 F   3 T   4 T   5 F

Speaking

10 **Aim** **To talk about the future, to practise the future continuous and the future perfect with personal examples**

Explain the task and give Ss time to consider their answers and then ask various Ss around the class to share their answers with the rest of the class following the example.

Suggested Answer Key

In five years' time, I'll have finished university and I'll be looking for a job. In ten years' time, I'll have bought a house and I'll be having my own family. In twenty years' time, I'll have got a promotion at work and I'll be earning a lot of money.

5c Skills in Action

Vocabulary

1 a) **Aim** **To present vocabulary for future predictions**

- Ask Ss to read the list of future predictions (1-6) and the list of reasons (a-f) and give them time to match them.
- Check Ss' answers and then elicit which predictions are positive and which are negative from Ss around the class.

Answer Key

1 b   2 f   3 c   4 d   5 e   6 a

Positive: *1, 4, 5*
Negative: *2, 3, 6*

b)  **Aim** To consolidate and expand new vocabulary

- Ask Ss to read the example and then use the linkers to expand the ideas in Ex. 1a using the future continuous or the future perfect.
- Elicit answers from Ss around the class.

Suggested Answer Key

By the year 2080, crime will have increased as criminals will be using advanced technology.

By the year 2080, people will be living in cities under the sea because regular cities will have become too crowded.

By the year 2080, people will be living longer because scientists will have found cures for serious diseases.

By the year 2080, people will be going on holiday to other planets because space travel will have become affordable.

By the year 2080, there will be more poverty since life will have become more expensive.

Listening

2 **Aim** To listen for specific information (R/W/DS statements)

- Ask Ss to read statements 1-6 and underline the key words.
- Play the recording twice. Ss listen and mark the statements according to what they hear.
- Play the recording with pauses for Ss to check their answers.

Answer Key

1 W   2 R   3 W   4 R   5 DS   6 R

Everyday English

3 **Aim** To listen and read for cohesion & coherence (missing words)

- Ask Ss to read the dialogue and complete the gaps with the missing words.
- Then play the recording for Ss to check their answers.

Answer Key

1 time	*3 then*	*5 like*
2 long	*4 to*	

4 **Aim** To role-play a dialogue discussing future plans

- Explain the task and ask Ss to act out a similar dialogue to the one in Ex. 3 in pairs using the advert and the language in the box to help them.
- Write this diagram on the board for Ss to follow.

A	B
Ask B about their summer plans. *Do you have any plans for …?*	Respond with details. *Haven't I told you? This time …*
Express surprise and ask how B found the job. *Really? How did you …?*	Respond. *There was …*
Ask what B's duties will be. *And what will you be …?*	Give details of responsibilities. *Mostly, I'll be …*
Show enthusiasm and ask about length of employment. *Wow! How long …?*	Give details, say what you'll use the money for & ask about A's plans. *Until … By then I'll have earned enough money to buy … What about …?*
Tell B your summer plans. *I'll be …*	Comment. *That sounds …*

- Monitor the activity around the class and offer assistance as necessary.
- Then ask some pairs to act out their dialogues in front of the class.

Suggested Answer Key

A: *Do you have any plans for the summer?*
B: *Haven't I told you? This time next week, I'll be working at a vertical farm.*
A: *Really? How did you find that job?*
B: *There was an advert online.*
A: *And what will you be doing there?*
B: *Mostly I'll be watering plants, changing soil and checking temperatures.*
A: *Wow! How long will you work there?*
B: *Until the end of August. By then I'll have earned enough money to pay part of my college fees! What about you?*
A: *I'll be working in my parents' shop.*
B: *Sounds like fun!*

Pronunciation

5 **Aim** To learn/practise the pronunciations of /uː/, /ʊ/

- Play the recording. Ss listen and tick the sounds they hear.
- Check Ss' answers.
- Play the recording again with pauses for Ss to repeat chorally and/or individually.

Answer Key

	/uː/	/ʊ/		/uː/	/ʊ/
pool	✓		fool	✓	
pull		✓	shoot	✓	
full		✓	should		✓

Reading & Writing

6 **Aim** To read for coherence (order paragraphs)

- Give Ss time to read the essay and put the paragraphs into the correct order.
- Check Ss' answers and then elicit in which paragraph the writer gives their opinion.

Answer Key

A 3   B 1   C 4   D 2

The writer gives their opinion in paragraphs 1 and 4.

7 **Aim** To present introductory techniques for an essay

- Read out the **Writing Tip**.
- Ask Ss to identify the technique the writer has used to start their essay and then give Ss time to write another introduction using the other technique mentioned in the **Writing Tip**.
- Ask various Ss to read out their introduction to the class.

Answer Key

The writer has made a statement.

Suggested Answer Key

Do you think people in the future will live to be 150 years old? In my opinion, this will soon be possible. In the future, we will improve healthcare so that people can live longer and healthier lives.

8 **Aim** To practise word formation

- Read out the box and explain the task. Then give Ss time to complete the task following the instructions.
- Check Ss' answers around the class.

Answer Key

1 lengthen   3 lessen
2 specialises   4 advertise

Writing

9 **Aim** To prepare for a writing task

- Ask Ss to look at the spidergram and identify which of the predictions are positive/negative.
- Then ask Ss to add their own ideas.
- Check Ss' answers around the class.

Suggested Answer Key:

Positive: longer lives, better paid jobs
Negative: meal pills, fewer wild animals, robot teachers, fewer friends, underground houses

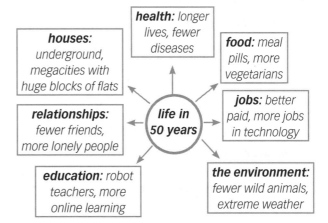

10 **Aim** To write an essay

- Ask Ss to read the rubric and then give them time to write their essay using their answers in Ex. 9 and following the plan.
- Ask various Ss to share their answers with the class.
- Alternatively, assign the task as HW and check Ss' answers in the next lesson.

Suggested Answer key

Do you think life in 50 years will be better or worse than today? In my opinion, we will improve many things and life will be better.

There are many positive predictions about the future. We will have robot teachers and more online learning so people everywhere can have access to education. People will live longer because of new medicines. Also, people will have better paid jobs.

On the other hand, there are also negative predictions for the future. We may have fewer friends because we will be always online. Also, the future food will be meal pills because real food will be very expensive.

Overall, I believe that we should be positive about the future. If we work towards a brighter future together, I think it will happen.

Values

Ask Ss to explain the quotation in their mother tongue. Then initiate a class discussion about the meaning of the quotation and encourage all Ss to participate. You can ask Ss to look for more quotes about determination and present them to the class.

Suggested Answer

I think the quotation means that we should not wait to see what happens in the future. We should try to make changes now that will make the future better for everyone.

Culture 5

Listening & Reading

1 Aim To introduce the topic, to listen and read for gist

*   Read out the questions in the rubric and elicit Ss' guesses in answer to them.
*   Then play the recording and have Ss listen and follow the text in their books to find out.

Answer Key

H G Wells wrote science-fiction books. He predicted a lot of things about the future in his books such as wireless communication, virtual assistants and weapons.

2 Aim To read for specific information (sentences completion)

*   Give Ss time to read the text again and complete the sentences.
*   Check Ss' answers.
*   Ss explain the words in bold.

Answer Key

1   20th centuries
2   email
3   information (about new products)
4   nuclear bombs
5   time machines

Suggested Answer Key

access (v): to have the opportunity to see/use sth
predict (v): to foretell
tasks (n): duties; assignments
latest (adj): the most recent
clear (adj): obvious

*   Give Ss time to look up the meanings of the words in the **Check these words** box in the Word List.
*   Play the video for Ss and elicit their comments.

Speaking & Writing

3 Aim THINK To develop critical thinking skills; to make a short plot outline for a novel set in the future

*   Explain the task and give Ss time to consider their answers and make a short plot outline for a novel set in 2100.
*   Then ask various Ss to share their answers with the class.

Suggested Answer Key

My novel will be set undersea on a planet in another galaxy in 2100. People will live in domes and will use special cars for transport. They can't go on land because it will be too dangerous as aliens have invaded the planet. They will use advanced technology to cure diseases, have vertical farms to grow their own food and use advanced robots. A special robot will lead them to attack the aliens and get their planet back.

4 Aim ICT To develop research skills; to write a short paragraph about a film/TV series set in the future and the predictions it contains

*   Give Ss time to research the topic online and give Ss some ideas to help them get started, e.g. *Star Trek* (space travel, alien races, medical advancements), *Blade Runner* (androids with emotions) or *Altered Carbon* (wear a body like clothes and change it when it breaks).
*   Give Ss time to write a short paragraph about the film or TV series and its predictions and then ask various Ss to share their answers with the rest of the class.
*   Alternatively, assign the task as HW and ask Ss to read out their texts in the next lesson.

Suggested Answer Key

In 'Star Trek', space travel is common and many people live in space on space stations or travel through space for their job as part of Space Fleet. Humans are exploring space and meeting alien races. Medical science is very advanced and surgeries happen without blood or cuts to the body. Scanners can tell what is wrong with someone straight away and machines cure them. There are also machines that transport people from one place to another within seconds.

*   As an extension, ask Ss which of the predictions from the film/TV series they think will come true.

Suggested Answer Key

I think space travel will become common in the future. There is already talk of a colony on Mars and tourists to the Moon, but I think it will be a few hundred years

from now. I think medical science will have machines like in 'Star Trek' in the near future. We already have MRI machines which scan the body. I don't think we will have the transport that they have in 'Star Trek' though, at least not for a very long time.

Review 5

Vocabulary

1 **Aim** To consolidate vocabulary from the unit

- Explain the task.
- Give Ss time to complete it.
- Check Ss' answers.

Answer Key

1 serious	4 crowded
2 floating	5 affordable
3 traffic	

2 **Aim** To consolidate vocabulary from the unit

- Explain the task.
- Give Ss time to complete it.
- Check Ss' answers.

Answer Key

1 delivers	3 Solar	5 stations
2 lonely	4 Vacuum	

3 **Aim** To practise prepositional phrases and phrasal verbs

- Explain the task.
- Give Ss time to complete it.
- Check Ss' answers.

Answer Key

1 with	3 into	5 within
2 across	4 about	

Grammar

4 **Aim** To practise the future continuous and the future perfect

- Explain the task.
- Give Ss time to complete it.
- Check Ss' answers.

Answer Key

1 will be living	4 will be starting
2 won't have fallen	5 will have run
3 won't be joining	

5 **Aim** To practise the future continuous and the future perfect

- Explain the task.
- Give Ss time to complete it.
- Check Ss' answers.

Answer Key

1 will have learnt	4 Will you be working
2 will be giving	5 will have increased
3 Will you have finished	

Everyday English

6 **Aim** To match exchanges

- Explain the task.
- Give Ss time to complete it.
- Check Ss' answers.

Answer Key

1 a	2 d	3 b	4 e	5 c

Competences

Ask Ss to assess their own performance in the unit by ticking the items according to how competent they feel for each of the listed activities.

6 The Big Screen

Go through the objectives box and tell Ss that these are the topics, skills and activities this unit will cover.

6a

Reading & Listening

1 **Aim** **To introduce the topic**

Ask Ss to look at the pictures and elicit if anyone recognises the characters. Then ask various Ss to say some typical film heroes and heroines and what they do.

Suggested Answer Key

The characters are C-3PO, Poe Dameron, Rey and Finn from 'Star Wars: The Force Awakens'.
Some typical film heroes are Iron Man, Robin Hood, Daisy Ridley and Luke Skywalker. They fight for what they believe in and they try to help other people.

2 **Aim** **To listen and read for specific information (T/F/DS statements)**

- Ask Ss to read out statements 1-5.
- Then play the recording and have Ss follow the text in their books and mark the statements according to what they read.
- Check Ss' answers around the class.

Answer Key

1 F	2 T	3 DS	4 F	5 DS

Background Information

George Lucas is an American film-maker. He is most famous for the Star Wars films and the Indiana Jones films. His films are very successful and have made a lot of money.

Luke Skywalker is a character in the Star Wars films. He is a young farm boy who has special powers. He wants to join the fight and become a Jedi knight.

Leia Organa is a character in the Star Wars films. She is a princess from Alderaan. She is part of the rebel forces that fight for freedom in the galaxy.

Han Solo is a character in the Star Wars films. He is a pilot. His ship is called the Millennium Falcon. He works with Chewbacca.

Darth Vader is a character in the Star Wars films. He is a commander in the Imperial Army and a Sith Lord. He wants to destroy the rebel forces.

3 **Aim** To read for comprehension, to consolidate new vocabulary (sentence completion)

- Ask Ss to read the text again and complete the sentences.
- Then give Ss time to explain the words in bold using their dictionaries to help them as necessary.

Suggested Answer Key

1 George Lucas
2 'Return of the Jedi'
3 John Williams
4 4th May (every year)

Suggested Answer Key

film-maker (n): *a person who makes films*
adventure (n): *an exciting journey*
queue (n): *a line of people waiting for sth*
force (n): *strength or power*
demand (v): *to ask for*
series (n): *a number of films/TV programmes/books of a similar kind happening one after the other*
appear (v): *to start to exist*
special effects (n): *illusions created for films using computer graphics and other methods*
proudly (adv): *in a way that shows a high opinion of sth*

- Give Ss time to look up the meanings of the words in the **Check these words** box in the Word List.
- Play the video for Ss and elicit their comments.

Vocabulary

4 **a)** **Aim** To present vocabulary relating to types of films

- Ask Ss to look at the pictures and read the film titles and the types of films in the list.

NOTE: Explain to Ss that while we talk about film genres using just these words, we need to add the word 'film' to some of them when talking about films themselves. Compare: "My favourite kind of film is horror." (genre) with "I saw a really scary horror film last night." (specific film). The genres that take the word 'film' are: action & adventure film, animated film, sci-fi film, crime film, horror film. Otherwise, we don't need it, e.g. 'Mamma Mia' is a musical.

- Give Ss time to consider their answers and match the film titles to the types of films and then check Ss' answers.

Suggested Answer Key

1 crime
2 action-adventure
3 thriller
4 animation
5 horror
6 western
7 sci-fi

- As an extension ask Ss to play in teams. One team says the name of a well-known film, the other says what type it is.

b) **Aim** To consolidate new vocabulary; to express opinion

- Ask Ss to read the adjectives in the list and then give them time to use them in exchanges talking about the types of films following the example.
- Elicit answers from Ss around the class.

Suggested Answer Key

A: *Do you like action-adventure films?*
B: *I love them. I find them exciting.*

A: *Do you like comedies?*
B: *I love them. I find them funny.*

A: *Do you like horror films?*
B: *I'm not crazy about them. I find them scary. etc*

5 **Aim** To practise collocations from the unit

- Give Ss time to complete the phrases with the words in the list.
- Then ask Ss to make sentences with them.
- Elicit answers from Ss around the class.

Answer Key

1 blockbuster
2 live-action
3 big
4 special
5 bad
6 celebrity

Suggested Answer Key

*I haven't seen a big **blockbuster film** for a while.*
*I enjoy watching **live-action TV series**.*
*I like to watch films on **the big screen**.*
***Special effects** in sci-fi films are amazing.*
*The **bad guy** in the 'Star Wars' films is Darth Vader.*
*This chat show has lots of **celebrity guests**.*

6 **Aim** To consolidate prepositional phrases from a text

- Give Ss time to read the gapped sentences and fill in the gaps with the correct prepositions.
- Then check Ss' answers around the class.

Answer Key

1 in
2 about
3 to
4 at
5 on

Background Information

C-3PO is a character in the Star Wars films. He is a robotic android (droid). He usually works indoors. He belongs to Luke Skywalker.

R2-D2 is a character in the Star Wars films. He is a robotic android (droid). He usually works on a spaceship. He belongs to Luke Skywalker.

7 (Aim) To understand words easily confused

- Explain the task and give Ss time to use their dictionaries to help them complete it.
- Check Ss' answers.

Answer Key

1	Audiences	4	created
2	effects	5	play
3	outside		

Suggested Answer Key

- *There were lots of spectators at the match.*
- *That film always affects me and makes me cry.*
- *We decided to watch the film outdoors in the garden on our laptop.*
- *They did a lot of work to make the costumes look realistic.*
- *Marvin acted his part very well.*

Background Information

Kurt Russell is an American actor. He is famous for action roles and comedy roles. Some of his films include: *Elvis* (1979), *Escape from New York* (1981), *The Thing* (1982), *Big Trouble in Little China* (1986), *Overboard* (1987), *Tombstone* (1993), *Stargate* (1994), *Death Proof* (2007), *The Hateful Eight* (2015) and *Guardians of the Galaxy Vol. 2* (2017).

Sylvester Stallone is an American actor, director and screenwriter. He is famous for action roles. Some of his film include: the Rocky series of films (1976–2015), the Rambo series of films (1982–2008), and The Expendables series of films (2010–2014).

8 (Aim) To learn phrasal verbs with *give*

- Ask Ss to read the phrasal verbs box and make sure that Ss understand the definitions.
- Then give Ss time to complete the task and check their answers.
- Tell Ss to add these phrasal verbs to the Phrasal Verbs section at the back of their notebooks.

Answer Key

1	up	2	back	3	in	4	away

Speaking & Writing

9 (Aim) To develop research skills; to write a fact sheet about a film

- Explain the task and give Ss time to think about their favourite film and prepare a 'Did you know?' fact sheet with five facts about the film.
- Ask various Ss around the class to read out their facts sheets to the class.

Suggested Answer Key

Did you know?

- *'The Matrix' was going to be a comic book instead of a film.*
- *The film's opening scene took six months of training and four days to film.*
- *The lead actors trained every day for four months to be able to do the fight scenes.*
- *The special effects were created specially for the film and did not exist before.*
- *The city in the film which is never named is Sydney, Australia.*

As an alternative, you can ask Ss to say various sentences about their favourite film and Ss in teams decide if each sentence is true or false.

6b Grammar in Use

1 (Aim) To do a quiz

- Ask Ss to read the quiz and then give them time to complete it.
- Play the recording. Ss listen and check their answers.

Answer Key

1 A	2 B	3 C	4 A	5 C

Background Information

Steven Spielberg is an American film-maker. He is probably the most popular film director and producer of all time. He has won two Academy Awards. He has a long list of famous films to his name including *Jaws* (1975), *Close Encounters of the Third Kind* (1977), the Indiana Jones series, *E.T. the Extra-Terrestrial* (1982), the Jurassic Park series, *The Color Purple* (1985), *Empire of the Sun* (1987), *Schindler's List* (1993), *Saving Private Ryan* (1998), *Munich* (2005), *Lincoln* (2012), *Bridge of Spies* (2015), *The Post* (2017), and *Ready Player One* (2018) as a director and *Back to the Future*, *Men in Black*, and the Transformers series as a producer.

2 **Aim** To present/revise the passive

- Write on the board:
  Active: They shot the film in Iceland.
  Passive: The film **was shot** in Iceland.
- Explain/Elicit that we form the passive tense with **the verb 'to be' + the past participle of the main verb**.
- Explain/Elicit that to change an active sentence to a passive sentence the object of the active verb becomes the subject of the passive verb and the active form changes to a passive form while the subject becomes the agent.
- Explain that we use the passive to talk about an action when we don't know who performed it or when it is obvious who performed it from the context or when the action is more important than the person who performed it.
- Go through the theory box with Ss. Ask Ss to find passive forms in the quiz.
- Check Ss' answers.
- Refer Ss to the **Grammar Reference** section for more information.

Answer Key

Examples: *were ... awarded, was ... named, to be filmed, were won, wasn't directed*

3 **Aim** To consolidate the passive

- Ask Ss to read the sentences and identify the items.
- Check Ss' answers and then elicit answers to the questions from Ss around the class.
- Refer Ss to the **Grammar Reference** section for more information.

Answer Key

George Lucas (subject)
directed (verb)
'Star Wars Episode IV: A New Hope' (object)
1 *The object of the active verb has become the subject of the passive verb. The active form has changed to a passive form and the subject has become the agent.*
2 *We form the passive tense with the verb 'to be' + the past participle of the main verb.*
3 *B*
4 *A*

4 **Aim** To practise the passive

- Explain the task and give Ss time to complete it.
- Check Ss' answers.

Answer Key

1 shown	3 are being	5 has
2 be bought	4 will be	6 are

5 **Aim** To practise *with* and *by* with the passive

- Go through the theory box with Ss and then give Ss time to complete the sentences.
- Check Ss' answers.

Answer Key

1 with (material)	4 by (person)
2 by (person)	5 by (person)
3 with (ingredient)	

> ### Background Information
>
> **Celine Dion** is a Canadian singer. Some of her most popular songs are: *My heart will go on, It's all coming back to me now, Because you loved me*, etc.
>
> **Leonardo DiCaprio** is an American actor and film producer. He has starred in lots of films such as: *Romeo & Juliet, The Aviator, The Revenant* (he won Best Performance by an Actor in a Leading Role – Academy Awards, USA), *The Wolf of Wall Street*, etc.

6 a) **Aim** To present passive questions

- Ask Ss to read the two sentences and then elicit answers to the questions.
- Refer Ss to the **Grammar Reference** section for more information.
- Elicit answers from Ss around the class.

Answer Key

*We form passive questions with 'who' by using '**who' + the verb 'to be' + subject + past participle of main verb + by.***
We cannot omit 'by' in this type of passive question.

b) **Aim** To practise questions in the passive

- Explain the task and read out the example.
- Give Ss time to complete it and then check their answers.

Answer Key

2 *Who was the title song from the film 'Skyfall' sung by? It was sung by Adele.*
3 *Who were the Harry Potter books written by? They were written by J. K. Rowling.*
4 *Who was the music to 'Star Wars' composed by? It was composed by John Williams.*

6

5   Who was the character of Sherlock Holmes created by? It was created by Sir Arthur Conan Doyle.
6   Which film studio was 'Avengers: Infinity War' made by? It was made by Marvel Studios.

Background Information

Marvel Studios is an American film studio which is part of Walt Disney Studios. It makes films based on Marvel comic book characters such as *X-Men*, *Spider-Man*, *The Hulk*, *Iron Man* and *The Avengers*. These films have made over $17 billion at the box office around the world.

John Williams (b. 1932) is an American composer, conductor and pianist. He has composed some of the most popular and critically acclaimed film scores in the history of cinema including the Star Wars series, *Jaws*, *Close Encounters of the Third Kind*, *Superman*, *E.T. the Extra-Terrestrial*, the Indiana Jones series, the first two Jurassic Park films, *Schindler's List*, and the first three Harry Potter films.

Adele (Adele Adkins) (b. 1988) is a British singer and songwriter. She was born in London and she has released three albums (*19*, *21*, *25*). She has sold an estimated 100 million records worldwide. She has won many awards including an MBE, an Academy Award, four Brit Awards, ten Grammys and a Golden Globe. She has a son, Angelo, with her partner Simon Konecki.

J. K. Rowling (b. 1965) is a British author, screenwriter and film producer. She is most well known for writing the Harry Potter series of books which is the best selling book series ever. She has won many awards and prizes and she has given huge amounts of money to charity. She has three children and lives in Scotland.

Sir Arthur Conan Doyle (1859-1930) was a British writer who wrote fantasy and science-fiction short stories and the world-famous Sherlock Holmes detective novels.

7   **Aim** To practise the passive

Explain the task. Point out that Ss need to pay attention to time words/phrases as these will help them use the correct tense in the passive sentence. Also, point out that Ss may need to add more words of their own as newspaper headlines omit articles, prepositions, etc. Do the first item with Ss, then Ss complete the task. Go round the class and offer help if needed. Elicit answers from Ss around the class.

Suggested Answer Key

A film premiere was called off yesterday because of bad weather.
A new cinema will be opened by the mayor on Monday evening.
'Dunkirk' was awarded three Oscars last night.
A cinema was destroyed in a fire last Saturday.
The theatre thieves have still not been caught.

8   **Aim** To practise the passive through sentence transformations

• Explain the task and give Ss time to complete it.
• Check Ss' answers around the class.

Answer Key

1   was directed by
2   will be closed
3   was made to pay (point out to Ss that when 'make' is used in the passive it is followed by to-inf)
4   have been sent
5   were shown to our seats
6   can be booked

9   **Aim** To present/practise reflexive/emphatic pronouns

• Go through the theory box and the example with Ss. Refer Ss to the **Grammar Reference** section for more information.
• Give Ss time to complete the task.
• Elicit answers from Ss around the class.

Answer Key

2   themselves – emphatic
3   herself – reflexive
4   himself/herself – emphatic
5   yourself/ourselves – reflexive
6   himself/herself – emphatic
7   yourself/yourselves – reflexive
8   himself – reflexive

10   **Aim** THINK To prepare a quiz

• Explain the task and give Ss time to prepare a quiz like the one on p. 48 using the passive.
• Give Ss time to complete the task and then ask various Ss to read out their quiz to the class.

Suggested Answer Key

1   Which film has won the most Oscars ever?
    A   'Gone With the Wind'
    B   'Titanic'
    C   'La La Land'

2   What was the name of Han Solo's spaceship in 'Star Wars'?
  Ⓐ   The Millennium Falcon
  B   The Enterprise
  C   Babylon
3   Which Star Wars film episode was filmed in Thailand?
  A   Episode I
  B   Episode II
  Ⓒ   Episode III
4   Which film was directed by Steven Spielberg?
  A   'Washington'
  Ⓑ   'Lincoln'
  C   'Reagan'
5   How many Oscars were won by Marlon Brando?
  A   4
  B   1
  Ⓒ   2

6c Skills in Action

Vocabulary

1 **Aim** **To present vocabulary for types of TV programmes**

- Ask Ss to read the list of adjectives and explain/ elicit the meanings of any unknown words.
- Ask two Ss to read out the example exchange and then ask Ss to discuss the TV programmes in the TV guide in pairs using the adjectives and following the example.
- Monitor the activity around the class.

Suggested Answer Key

A: Do you watch soap operas?
B: I love soap operas.
A: Really? I find soap operas awful.

A: Do you watch sitcoms?
B: To be honest, I'm not a fan. I find them silly.
A: Really? I find sitcoms funny. etc

Listening

2 **Aim** **To listen for specific information (multiple choice)**

- Ask Ss to read the questions and look at the picture options.
- Play the recording twice. Ss listen and chose their answers.
- Check Ss' answers. You can play the recording again with pauses for Ss to check their answers.

Answer Key

1   C   2   B   3   B

Everyday English

3 **a)** **Aim** **To introduce the topic and read for cohesion & coherence**

Ask Ss to read the dialogue and the missing sentences and decide which sentence matches which gap.

b) **Aim** **To listen and read for cohesion & coherence**

Play the recording. Tell Ss to follow the dialogue in their books and then check their answers to Ex. 3a.

Answer Key

1   C   2   E   3   A   4   F

4 **Aim** **To role-play a dialogue making a recommendation**

- Explain the task and ask Ss to act out a similar dialogue to the one in Ex. 3 in pairs using the phrases in the box to help them.
- Write this diagram on the board for Ss to follow.

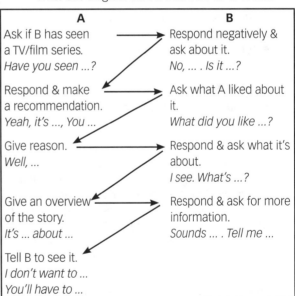

A	B
Ask if B has seen a TV/film series. *Have you seen ...?*	Respond negatively & ask about it. *No, ... Is it ...?*
Respond & make a recommendation. *Yeah, it's ..., You ...*	Ask what A liked about it. *What did you like ...?*
Give reason. *Well, ...*	Respond & ask what it's about. *I see. What's ...?*
Give an overview of the story. *It's ... about ...*	Respond & ask for more information. *Sounds ... . Tell me ...*
Tell B to see it. *I don't want to ... You'll have to ...*	

Suggested Answer Key

A: Have you seen 'The Guardians' yet?
B: No, I haven't. Is it any good?
A: Yeah, it's amazing. It's a must-see.
B: What did you like most about it?
A: Well, the acting is great.
B: I see. What's it about anyway?
A: It's a drama about life on a farm during World War I.
B: Sounds great. Tell me more.
A: I don't want to spoil it. You'll have to see it yourself.

6

Pronunciation

5 **Aim** **To learn the pronunciations of /ʌ/, /æ/**

- Get Ss to look at the words in the box.
- Model the sounds /ʌ/ and /æ/.
- Then play the recording. Ss listen and tick the correct sounds.
- Check Ss' answers.
- Then play the recording again with pauses for Ss to repeat chorally and/or individually.

Answer Key

	/ʌ/	/æ/		/ʌ/	/æ/
fan		✓	rang		✓
fun	✓		rung	✓	
sang		✓	stunned	✓	
sung	✓		stand		✓

Reading & Writing

6 **Aim** **To read for cohesion and coherence (word formation)**

- Read out the *Writing Tip*
- Read out the rubric and give Ss time to read the review and complete the task.
- Check Ss' answers and then elicit answers to the questions.

Answer Key

1	exciting	3	talented	5	realistic
2	powerful	4	amazing	6	wonderful

The writer has mostly used the present tense.
Paragraph A is about the title, type, director and cast of the film. Paragraph B is about the plot of the film. Paragraph C has comments about the cast, the special effects and other features of the film. Paragraph D is about the writer's recommendation.
The writer has not revealed the end of the film because this would spoil it for someone who has not seen it.

7 **Aim** **To practise topic-related vocabulary**

Explain the task and give Ss time to complete it and check their answers in their dictionaries.

Answer Key

1 *fast (could be used to describe plot)*
2 *slow (could be used to describe plot)*
3 *tired (audiences can be tired of sth)*
4 *slow (could be used to describe plot)*
5 *excited (audiences can be excited)*
6 *bored (audiences can be bored)*

8 a) **Aim** **To identify language used for recommending/criticising**

Go through the expressions one at a time and elicit whether each one recommends or criticises from Ss around the class.

Answer Key

Recommending: *Don't miss it. I highly recommend it., It's worth seeing., You should try to see it.*
Criticising: *It was disappointing. I wouldn't recommend it., Don't bother. It's a waste of time.*

b) **Aim** **To read for gist and practise recommending/criticising a film**

- Ask Ss to read the dialogue and elicit whether the speaker recommends the film or not.
- Then have Ss work in pairs and act out similar dialogues recommending/criticising a film using the expressions in Ex. 8a.
- Monitor the activity around the class.

Answer Key

The speaker recommends the film.

Suggested Answer Key

A: *Have you seen 'Venom'?*
B: *Yes, I have. You should definitely see it! The special effects are amazing.*

A: *Have you seen 'A Star is Born'?*
B: *Yes, I have. Don't bother. It's a waste of time. etc*

Writing

9 **Aim** **To prepare for a writing task**

- Ask Ss to read the task and find the key words. Then give Ss time to complete the spidergram in their notebooks.
- Check Ss' answers around the class.

Suggested Answer Key

Key words: *college English magazine, reviews about favourite films, 120-150 words*

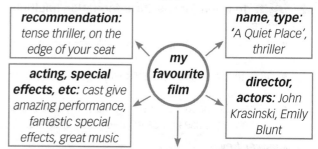

recommendation: *tense thriller, on the edge of your seat*

name, type: *'A Quiet Place', thriller*

my favourite film

acting, special effects, etc: *cast give amazing performance, fantastic special effects, great music*

director, actors: *John Krasinski, Emily Blunt*

summary of plot: *aliens on Earth, hunt people by noise, many people dead, one family tries to survive by being completely quiet*

10 **Aim** To write a film review

- Ask Ss to read the rubric in Ex. 9 again and then give them time to write their reviews using their answers in Ex. 9 and following the plan.
- Ask various Ss to share their answers with the class.
- Alternatively, assign the task as HW and check Ss' answers in the next lesson.

Suggested Answer key

If you're a fan of exciting thrillers, then 'A Quiet Place' is just the film for you. It is directed by John Krasinski who also stars in it along with Emily Blunt.

There are aliens on Earth that hunt people by noise. Many people are dead. One family tries to survive by being completely quiet. Will they make it?

All the actors, especially Emily Blunt and John Krasinski, give amazing performances. The special effects are fantastic and the music is great too – really scary!

'A Quiet Place' is a wonderful film for people who love watching tense thrillers and being on the edge of their seats. Don't miss it! I highly recommend it.

Values

Ask Ss to explain the quotation in their mother tongue. Then initiate a class discussion about the meaning of the quotation and encourage all Ss to participate.

Suggested Answer

I think the quotation means that people from all over the world and from all sorts of different backgrounds can appreciate a film regardless of what language it is in.

Culture 6

Reading & Listening

1 **Aim** To match extracts to types of music

- Elicit what type of music Ss like. Ask Ss to read the types of music in the list and then play the recording and have Ss match.
- Check Ss' answers.

Answer Key

1 d   2 a   3 c   4 f   5 b   6 e

2 **Aim** To read for specific information

Read out the rubric. Ask Ss to read the text and find out what type of music people can hear at the Festival of Film.

Answer Key

People can hear music from films at this festival.

3 **Aim** To read for cohesion and coherence (multiple choice cloze)

- Ask Ss to read the text again and fill in the gaps with one of the four options for each one. Ss need to pay attention to words before and after each gap as this will help them do the task.
- Check Ss' answers and then elicit explanations for the bold words from Ss around the class.

Answer Key

1 *A (passive voice)*
2 *B (collocation: live orchestra; alive = not dead; lively = happy)*
3 *C (collocation: takes place = happens; take over = get control of; take after= resemble; take off = remove clothes/(of planes) to leave the ground)*
4 *B (many of: used with countable nouns; 'lot' would need to be 'lots' or 'a lot' to be a correct answer; much + U noun; more = not appropriate in this context as it does not compare sth to sth else)*
5 *D (while: action happening at the same time; 'as' should be followed by subject + verb; then = 'afterwards' so irrelevant in this context)*

- Give Ss time to look up the meanings of the words in the **Check these words** box in the Word List.
- Elicit the meanings of the words in bold from Ss around the class. They may use their dictionaries if necessary.
- Play the video for Ss and elicit their comments.

Suggested Answer Key

theme (n): *a piece of music that accompanies a film*
showing (n): *performance*
composer (n): *a person who writes music*
realise (v): *to understand sth*
typical (adj): *common/usual*

Speaking & Writing

4 **Aim** **THINK** To develop critical thinking skills

Have Ss talk in pairs or small groups and think of films they would present at a film music festival and why. Then ask various Ss to tell the class.

Suggested Answer Key

I would present films where the title song or soundtrack has won an Oscar or I would feature the films where a particular composer has written the music and won an Oscar. For example, the title songs for films that won Oscars in recent years include: 'Let it Go' from 'Frozen', 'The Writing's on the Wall' from 'Spectre', 'City of Stars' from 'La La Land' and 'Remember Me' from 'Coco'. Also, composers who have won Oscars for soundtracks recently include: Alexandre Desplat for 'The Grand Budapest Hotel' and 'The Shape of Water'.

63

6

5 **Aim** **ICT** **To develop research skills; to make a poster about a music or film festival**

- Explain the task and give Ss time to research online and collect information about a music or film festival in their country and then make a poster for it.
- Ss can use the poster on p. 52 as a sample. Point out that the poster needs to contain information on place, type of event, time and a few catchy words to explain what it will be about. Ss can use photos and should present the information in an attractive way using bolded words, highlighted words and using different fonts and sizes.
- Alternatively, assign the task as HW.
- Put up the posters around the class.

Suggested Answer Key

> **BIFF**
> **The Bergen International Film Festival is back!**
>
>
>
> **Come to Bergen and take part in the largest film festival in Norway!**
> **Enjoy documentary films and short films from all over the world and see lots of interesting exhibitions, too!**
> **26th September – 4th October**

Review 6

Vocabulary

1 **Aim** **To consolidate vocabulary from the unit**

- Explain the task.
- Give Ss time to complete it.
- Check Ss' answers.

Answer Key

1 demanded	5 celebrities
2 sitcom	6 blockbuster
3 adventure	7 audience
4 episodes	8 queue

2 **Aim** **To consolidate vocabulary from the unit**

- Explain the task.
- Give Ss time to complete it.
- Check Ss' answers.

Answer Key

1 documentary	5 chat
2 effects	6 reality
3 soap	7 animated
4 role	8 series

3 **Aim** **To practise prepositional phrases and phrasal verbs**

- Explain the task.
- Give Ss time to complete it.
- Check Ss' answers.

Answer Key

1 in	3 away	5 to
2 to	4 in	

Grammar

4 **Aim** **To practise the passive**

- Explain the task.
- Give Ss time to complete it.
- Check Ss' answers.

Answer Key

1 is being shot, by
2 have already been covered, with
3 are not made, with
4 is loved, by
5 was reviewed, by
6 will be booked, by

5 **Aim** **To practise reflexive/emphatic pronouns**

- Explain the task.
- Give Ss time to complete it.
- Check Ss' answers.

Answer Key

1 ourselves	3 himself	5 yourself
2 themselves	4 herself	

Everyday English

6 **Aim** **To match exchanges**

- Explain the task.
- Give Ss time to complete it.
- Check Ss' answers.

Answer Key

1 b	2 d	3 a	4 c

Competences

Ask Ss to assess their own performance in the unit by ticking the items according to how competent they feel for each of the listed activities.

Values: Self-confidence

1 **Aim** To introduce the topic; to predict the content of the text; to listen and read for specific information

- Ask Ss to read the question and think of what advice might be given in the text. Elicit Ss' guesses.
- Play the recording. Ss listen and read to find out.

Suggested Answer Key

I think the advice will be about speaking clearly and confidently in front of people.

2 **Aim** To listen and read for specific information (T/F/DS)

- Ask Ss to read sentences 1-5 and then give them time to read the text. Ss mark the sentences according to what they read.
- Check their answers. Ss justify their answers.

Answer Key

1 T (*I've never done it before*)
2 DS
3 T (*Stand in front of ... it.*)
4 F (*Stand up ... the room.*)
5 F (*And don't rush*)

- Elicit explanations for the words in bold from Ss around the class. Alternatively, give Ss time to look up the meanings of the words in their dictionaries or in the Word List.

Suggested Answer Key

dry up (phr v): *to not be able to talk (informal)*
tip (n): *a piece of advice*
material (n): *task*
improve (v): *to get better*
deliver (v): *to give (a speech)*
lighten (v): *to make sth less serious*
raise your voice (phr): *to increase the volume of your voice*
rush (v): *to go faster than normal*

- Play the video for Ss and elicit their comments.

3 **Aim** **THINK** To develop critical thinking skills; to consolidate information in a text

Give Ss time to consider the questions and then elicit answers from Ss around the class.

Suggested Answer Key

Someone may feel unconfident about giving a presentation because they have not done it before. They may feel unconfident because they have a phobia of speaking in front of other people or they may not think the presentation they have prepared is very good. To change this, people can practise their presentation many times in front of a few friends to build up their confidence and overcome their phobia. They can also ask someone to look over the presentation and help them to improve it.

4 **Aim** **ICT** To research tips for public speaking

- Give Ss time to research online and find information about other tips for confident public speaking. Ss can work in close pairs or groups.
- Then ask various Ss to share their information with the class.

Suggested Answer Key

Visit the place where you will speak and get to know it. Practise walking onto the stage so you can feel more confident about it when the time comes.
Practise your speech in front of family and friends to feel more confident.
Practise positive body language using your hands and arms.

Public Speaking Skills

1 Aim To identify a type of speech

Ask Ss to read the task. Elicit the type of speech it asks for.

Answer Key

The type of speech is a ceremonial speech because it is for a festival opening.

2 Aim To analyse a model public speaking task; to introduce the use of cue cards

- Play the recording. Ss listen and read the model and number the cue cards in the correct order.
- Then ask Ss to complete gaps 1-3.
- Check Ss' answers.

Answer Key

A   3   B   1   C   2

1 Tye Sheridan
2 War of the Worlds
3 1946

3 Aim ICT To give a speech

- Ask Ss to think of a famous director and research online for information about them and then copy and complete the spidergram in their notebooks.
- Tell Ss to use their notes to prepare cue cards and number them.
- Ask various Ss to give their speech to the class.
- Alternatively, assign the task as HW and have Ss give their speeches in the next lesson.

Suggested Answer Key

| 'The Martian', sci-fi, 2015, set in the near future, mission to Mars goes wrong, Mark Watney (Matt Damon), Melissa Lewis (Jessica Chastain), gripping plot, great special effects, interesting characters |
| 'Alien', 'Blade Runner', 'Gladiator', 'The Martian' |
| worked for BBC, directed TV commercials, series and then films, first big success was 'Alien' (1979) |
| **Ridley Scott** |
| born County Durham, England, (1937), interest in sci-fi started as a child with H. G. Wells, attended Royal College of Art |

A
- *"I love different themes, different venues, different movies. I love to jump about and tackle different subjects."*
- *Ridley Scott*
- *'Alien', 'Blade Runner', 'Gladiator', 'The Martian'*

B
- *born County Durham, England*
- *interest in sci-fi started as a child with H. G. Wells*
- *worked for BBC, directed many TV commercials*
- *'Alien' (1979)*
- *sci-fi films*

C
- *'The Martian': sci-fi, 2015*
- *set in the near future, mission to Mars goes wrong*
- *Mark Watney (Matt Damon), Melissa Lewis (Jessica Chastain)*
- *gripping plot, great special effects, interesting characters*

Suggested Answer Key

Good evening, everyone, and welcome to our annual film festival. Every year, we celebrate a different director. "I love different themes, different venues, different movies. I love to jump about and tackle different subjects." These are the words of Ridley Scott, and show his creativity in film-making, which has made him one of the most important directors of our time. We'll be watching some of his classics this week, such as 'Alien', 'Blade Runner' and 'Gladiator' as well as some of his more recent films.

Scott was born in County Durham in England in 1937. He became interested in science-fiction as a child with H. G. Wells. He attended the Royal College of Art and after graduation he went to work for the BBC. He started to direct TV commercials, then TV series and later films. His first big success as a director came with 'Alien' in 1979 and he went on to make lots more successful films. He has made many types of films, but his great love has always been sci-fi, and we're going to see one of those today.

'The Martian' is a sci-fi film that was released in 2015. It is set in the near future, with the first manned mission to Mars. The main character Mark Watney, who is played by Matt Damon, accidentally gets left behind and must try to survive by himself. The rest of his crew led by Melissa Lewis, played by Jessica Chastain, must try to save him in a daring rescue. It's a film with a gripping plot, great special effects and interesting characters.

I'm sure you'll enjoy it just as much as I did. Now, I'm going to let the film speak for itself. Thank you for your time and let me present Ridley Scott's 'The Martian'.

Narrow Escapes

<table>
<tr><td>Topic</td></tr>
<tr><td>In this unit, Ss will explore the topics of disasters and emergency services.</td></tr>
</table>

<table>
<tr><td>7a   Reading & Vocabulary</td><td>56-57</td></tr>
</table>

Lesson objectives: To learn vocabulary for disasters, to listen and read for gist, to read for specific information (multiple choice questions), to learn prepositional phrases, to practise words easily confused, to learn phrasal verbs with *put*, to give a presentation on a cave rescue
Vocabulary: Disasters *(flood, explosion, earthquake, volcanic eruption, fire, thunderstorm, heavy snowfall, typhoon, avalanche)*; Nouns *(rescue, conditions, supplies, gear, efforts)*; Verbs *(trap, explore, discover, promise, tie, recover, hit, beat, strike, knock)*; Phrasal verbs *(put)*; Adjectives *(narrow, alive, unhurt, calm)*; Adverb *(meanwhile)*

<table>
<tr><td>7b   Grammar in Use</td><td>58-59</td></tr>
</table>

Lesson objectives: To learn/revise reported speech (statements, questions, orders, instructions, commands and reporting verbs)

<table>
<tr><td>7c   Skills in Action</td><td>60-61</td></tr>
</table>

Lesson objectives: To learn vocabulary for emergency services, to listen for specific information (multiple choice questions), to act out a dialogue and practise everyday English for calling the emergency services, to learn the pronunciation of /tʃ/, /dʒ/, to read for order of events, to read for cohesion & coherence (word formation), to write a news report
Vocabulary: Emergency services *(the police, the fire service, the coastguard, the mountain rescue service, the ambulance service, the cave rescue service)*

<table>
<tr><td>Culture 7</td><td>62</td></tr>
</table>

Lesson objectives: To listen and read for gist, to read for key information (matching headings to paragraphs), to retell a story, to write about a disaster
Vocabulary: Nouns *(trade, disaster, cure, guard, gunpowder, ruin)*; Verb *(spread)*; Phrasal verbs *(break out, put out, knock down, blow up)*; Adjective *(careless)*; Phrases *(royal court, high society)*

<table>
<tr><td>Review 7</td><td>63</td></tr>
</table>

Lesson objectives: To test/consolidate vocabulary and grammar learnt throughout the unit, to practise everyday English

Go through the objectives box and tell Ss that these are the topics, skills and activities this unit will cover.

7a

Vocabulary

1 **Aim** **To present vocabulary related to disasters**

- Ask Ss to look at the pictures and read the headlines.
- Give Ss time to choose the correct words and then ask Ss to check their answers in their dictionaries.

Answer Key

1 flood	4 earthquake
2 volcanic eruption	5 explosion
3 Fire	6 avalanche

2 **Aim** **To consolidate and expand new vocabulary**

- Ask Ss to read comments A-F and then give them time to match them to the disasters in Ex. 1.
- Check Ss' answers. Ask Ss which words helped them decide.

Answer Key

A   4 *(shaking)*
B   5 *(bang, ran outside)*
C   3 *(spread, wind)*
D   1 *(roof, rescue boats)*
E   6 *(warning signs, skiers)*
F   2 *(lava, mountainside)*

Listening & Reading

3 **Aim** **To introduce the topic of a text and listen and read for gist**

- Ask Ss to read the title and look at the map. Elicit Ss' guesses as to what the text is about.
- Play the recording. Ss listen to and read the text to find out if their guesses were correct.

Suggested Answer Key

The text is about the rescue of 12 boys and their football coach from a flooded cave in Thailand.

4 **a)** **Aim** **To read for specific information (multiple choice questions)**

- Ask Ss to read the questions and the possible answer choices and then give them time to read the text again and answer the questions.
- Check Ss' answers. Ask Ss to justify their answers.
- Play the video for Ss to watch and compare the information in it to the information in the text.

7 Narrow Escapes

Answer Key

1 D (para 1 – international news, rescue)
2 B (para 3 – a huge search)
3 C (para 3 – amazingly ... unhurt)
4 D (para 5 – hero)

b) Aim To consolidate new vocabulary

- Give Ss time to explain the words in bold using their dictionaries to help them as necessary.
- Check Ss' answers around the class.

Suggested Answer Key

trapped (adj): being unable to escape
explore (v): to look around a place
discover (v): to find
gear (n): equipment
recover (v): to get better
efforts (pl n): hard work
calm (adj): not upset or worried

- Give Ss time to look up the meanings of the words in the **Check these words** box in the Word List.
- Play the video for Ss and elicit their comments.

Background Information

Thailand is an Asian country in Southeast Asia. The capital city is Bangkok and the population is 66 million people. The language is Thai and the currency is the Baht. It is known for its natural beauty, its many historical sites and its cuisine.

Mae Sai is a town on the border between Thailand and Myanmar. It is next to the Mae Sai River. Around 200,000 people live in the area.

5 Aim To consolidate new vocabulary

- Ask Ss to read the words in the list and then give them time to complete the phrases in closed pairs.
- Check Ss' answers. Then give Ss time to write sentences using the phrases and elicit Ss' answers around the class.

Answer Key

1	international	5	clean
2	football	6	flooded
3	heavy	7	scuba
4	huge	8	real

Suggested Answer Key

The rescue made **international news**.
Twelve boys and their **football coach** got trapped in a cave.

Heavy rains flooded the cave.
A **huge search** began when their bikes were found.
The coach found **clean water** for the boys.
The boys had to swim through the **flooded tunnels** using **scuba gear**.
An old teammate said the coach was a **real hero**.

6 Aim To consolidate prepositional phrases from a text

- Give Ss time to read the gapped phrases and fill the gaps with the correct prepositions.
- Then check Ss' answers. Ask Ss to add these prepositional phrases to the Prepositions section in their notebook.

Answer Key

1	with	3	for	5	out
2	on	4	in	6	to

7 Aim To understand words easily confused

- Explain the task and give Ss time to use their dictionaries to help them complete it.
- Check Ss' answers.

Answer Key

1	hit	2	knocking	3	struck

8 Aim To learn phrasal verbs with put

- Tell Ss to write the phrasal verbs in the Phrasal Verbs list at the back of their notebooks and include the definitions. Tell Ss to revise this list from time to time and to add to it every time they come across a new phrasal verb.
- Ask Ss to read the phrasal verbs box and make sure that they understand the definitions.
- Then give Ss time to complete the task and check their answers.

Answer Key

1	on	2	off	3	up	4	out

Speaking & Writing

9 Aim ICT To develop research skills; to collaborate to collect information and exchange ideas; to develop public speaking skills; to show empathy; to give a presentation

- Give Ss time to look up more information online about this rescue and make notes. Ss work in groups.
- Ask Ss to use their notes and the text in Ex. 3 to prepare cue cards about the rescue. Then ask various Ss to present the rescue to the class from the perspective of one of the divers.

Suggested Answer Key

People: *12 boys aged 11-17 from the Wild Boars football team and their coach, Ekkapol Chantawong*

Key dates: *23rd June – boys got trapped in cave, 2nd July – divers found them, 10th July – everyone got out safely (18 days total)*

Rescue: *100,000 people involved, 100 divers, 1 diver died during rescue*

Conditions: *dark tunnels full of water, narrow and rocky, boys found 4 km into the cave*

Hello everyone. My name is Richard Stanton and I am a cave diver from the UK. I was one of the divers involved in the rescue of the people trapped in the Tham Luang cave in 2018.

Twelve boys aged 11-17 from the Wild Boars football team and their coach, Ekkapol Chantawong, went into the cave on the 23rd June and got trapped by flood waters. We found them on 2nd July after a long search. They were 4 kilometres into the cave.

Then the rescue operation started. It took eight days to get everyone out safely. There were 100,000 people involved in the rescue including 100 divers. It was a very difficult rescue and one diver died during this time. He was carrying oxygen to the trapped people but he didn't have enough for himself on his way out of the cave. The dark tunnels were full of water. They were narrow and rocky.

In the end, though, we managed to get everyone out by the 10th July. They were all taken to hospital where they recovered quickly.

Does anyone have any questions? … . Thank you for listening.

7b Grammar in Use

1 a) **Aim** To learn/revise reported speech

- Say then write on the board: *"I'm tired," Jane said.* Explain that direct speech is the exact words someone says and it is written in quotation marks. Say then write on the board: *Jane said (that) she was tired.* Explain that reported speech is the exact meaning of what someone says but not the exact words and we do not use quotation marks. Explain that we can use the word **that** to introduce reported speech or we can omit it.
- Refer Ss to the **Grammar Reference** section for detailed information.
- Ask Ss to study the examples. Then have Ss answer the questions. Refer Ss to the Grammar Reference section for more details.

Answer Key

1 The pronoun of the reported speech is changed to match the pronoun of the reporting verb.

2 The tenses change in reported speech as follows:
present simple → past simple
present continuous → past continuous
past simple → past simple or past perfect
present perfect → past perfect
past perfect → past perfect
present perfect continuous → past perfect continuous
past continuous → past continuous or past perfect continuous
will → would

3 There are no quotation marks in reported speech.

4 'Now' changes to 'immediately'.

b) **Aim** Ask Ss to read the newspaper clipping and find examples of direct/reported statements.

Answer Key

Direct speech: *"We've hit an iceberg. We need to go up on deck now."*

Reported speech: *Everyone said it was impossible for the ship to sink because it was so big. She said she had a bad feeling.*

Background Information

Titanic (RMS Titanic) sank on 15th April, 1912 in the early hours of the morning. It sank on the fourth day of its journey from Southampton in England to New York in America. It was the biggest passenger ship at the time and had 2,224 people on board. It hit an iceberg in the Atlantic Ocean on Sunday 14th April and sank 2 hours and 40 minutes later. There were not enough lifeboats on board for all the passengers and over 1,500 people died in the disaster.

2 **Aim** To review/practise using *say/tell* in reported speech

- Explain that when we report statements, we use **say** or **tell**. We use **say** in direct and reported speech without **to** when it is not followed by the person being spoken to (*e.g. Tina said, "I need help."/ Tina said [that] she needed help.*) and with **to** when it is followed by the person being spoken to (*e.g. Tina said to me, "I need help."/ Tina said to me [that] she needed help.*)
- Refer Ss to the **Grammar Reference** section for more information.

7 Narrow Escapes

- Explain the task. Ss complete the task in closed pairs.
- Check Ss' answers.

Answer Key

1 said	3 said	5 told	7 told
2 told	4 said	6 said	8 said

3 **Aim** To practise reported speech

- Explain the task and read out the example.
- Give Ss time to complete the task.
- Check Ss' answers.

Answer Key

2 The man said (that) he was phoning the ambulance then.

3 Craig told his wife (that) they wouldn't go out that night because of the storm.

4 The man said (that) they had just cleared the snow from the roads round there.

5 The man told the police (that) he had taken a photo of the accident that morning.

6 The reporter said (that) they had been fighting the fire all afternoon.

7 My friend told me (that) it had been raining there the day before/previous day.

4 **Aim** To present reported questions

- Go through the examples with Ss. Explain that we usually introduce reported questions with **asked** and we do not use a question mark. The verb is in the affirmative and the tenses, pronouns and time expressions change as in reported speech.
- Explain that when the direct question begins with a question word (e.g. who, where, what, why, when) then we use the same question word in the reported question, but when the direct question begins with an auxiliary verb (is, do, have, etc) then we use **if/whether** in the reported question.
- Refer Ss to the **Grammar Reference** section for more information.
- Elicit answers to the questions.
- Then elicit an example in the newspaper clipping.

Suggested Answer Key

1 asked

2 in questions that begin with an auxiliary verb

3 subject pronoun/noun + 'asked' + (object) + question word + subject + main verb in reported speech

Examples:

Reported speech: Eva asked her why she wasn't sleeping.

Direct speech: "Will you go and check what's happening?"

5 **Aim** To practise reported questions

- Explain the task and read out the example.
- Give Ss time to complete the task.
- Check Ss' answers.

Answer Key

2 She asked him where he was driving to in the snowstorm.

3 She asked him how long he was/had been trapped in his car.

4 She asked him when the emergency services had arrived.

5 She asked him if/whether he had ever had a similar experience.

6 She asked him if/whether he was planning to buy snow chains for his car.

6 **Aim** To present reported orders, instructions and commands

- Ask Ss to read the examples in the box. Explain that we usually use the verb **told + sb + (not) to-** **infinitive** in reported commands.
- Refer Ss to the **Grammar Reference** section for more information.
- Elicit examples from the newspaper clipping on p. 58.

Answer Key

Reported speech: The crew told people not to panic.
Direct speech: "Hold your mother's hand," he said to Eva.

7 **Aim** To practise reported orders, instructions and commands

Explain the task and give Ss time to complete it and then check their answers.

Answer Key

1 C	2 B	3 D	4 A

I told her not to let the children play near the pool.
I told her to keep hot irons away from the kids.
I told her to keep medicines out of reach of the children.
I told her not to leave the candle burning during the night.

8 **Aim** To present reporting verbs

- Read out the theory box and then the example.
- Give Ss time to complete the task by rewriting the sentences using the reporting verbs provided. Tell Ss to check in the **Grammar Reference** section for more details.
- Elicit answers from Ss around the class.

Suggested Answer Key

2   The teacher warned the children not to go too near the edge of the cliff.
3   She apologised for not checking/having checked the weather forecast.
4   He promised to return very soon with some help.
5   The guide offered to give us a tour of the volcano.
6   Tom agreed to bring his first aid kit along.

9   **Aim** To practise reported speech

- Explain the task and read out the example.
- Give Ss time to complete the task.
- Check Ss' answers around the class.

Answer Key

2   if/whether I had
3   not to forget
4   had been doing
5   the following/next

Speaking

10   **Aim** To practise reported speech

- Have Ss work in groups of three. Tell two Ss in the group to act out a short dialogue. Then have the third S report what they say to another group.
- Monitor the activity around the class and then have Ss swap roles so each S in the group has a chance to practise reported speech.

Suggested Answer Key

Ann: I watched a disaster film on DVD last night.
Bill: Really? Was it good?
Ann: Yes, it was.
Bill: What was it about?
Ann: It was about a huge skyscraper that came crashing down.

C: Ann said that she had watched a disaster film on DVD the night before. Bill asked her if it had been good. She said that it had been. Bill asked what it had been about. Ann replied that it had been about a huge skyscraper that had come crashing down.

7c Skills in Action

Vocabulary

1   **Aim** To present vocabulary for emergency services

Ask Ss to read the list of emergency services and then elicit which ones we contact for the situations in the list from Ss around the class.

Answer Key

a fire – the fire service
a crime – the police
a medical emergency – the ambulance service
a boating accident – the coastguard
a rock-climbing accident – the mountain rescue service
an emergency underground – the cave rescue service

2   **Aim** To consolidate and expand new vocabulary

- Ask Ss to read the comments (A-F) and then give them time to match them to the emergency services in Ex. 1.
- Check Ss' answers. Ss say which words helped them decide.

Answer Key

A   6 (trapped underground)
B   4 (summit)
C   2 (smoke)
D   1 (behaving suspiciously, bank)
E   5 (hospital, severe burns)
F   3 (boat, letting in water)

Listening

3   **Aim** To listen for specific information (multiple choice questions)

- Ask Ss to read questions 1-4 and the answer choices and underline the key words.
- Play the recording twice. Ss listen and choose their answers.
- Check Ss' answers. You can play the recording again with pauses for Ss to check their answers.

Answer Key

1   C   2   C   3   A   4   B

Everyday English

4   a)   **Aim** To introduce the topic; to read for gist and cohesion & coherence (missing sentences)

- Ask Ss to read sentences A-D and elicit what the problem is.
- Give Ss time to read the dialogue and complete the gaps with the missing sentences.

Answer Key

Someone's boat is sinking.

7 Narrow Escapes

b) Aim To listen and read for specific information

Play the recording. Tell Ss to follow the dialogue in their books and check their answers in Ex. 4a.

Answer Key

1 B   *2 A*   *3 D*   *4 C*

5 Aim To role-play a dialogue calling the emergency services

- Explain the task. Elicit which emergency service Ss need to contact (the fire service) and ask Ss to act out a similar dialogue to the one in Ex. 4 in groups of three using the prompts and the phrases in the box to help them.
- Write this diagram on the board for Ss to follow.

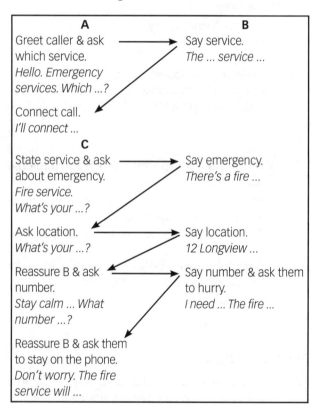

- Monitor the activity around the class and offer assistance as necessary.
- Then ask some pairs to act out their dialogues in front of the class.

Suggested Answer Key

A: Hello. Emergency services. Which service do you require?

B: The fire service.

A: I'll connect you now.

C: Fire service. What's your emergency?

B: Please help! There's a fire in my kitchen.

C: What's your address?

B: 15 Longview Road, Layton.

C: Please stay calm, sir. What number are you calling from?

B: It's 07746475588. I need help quickly. The fire is spreading!

C: Don't worry. The fire service will be there soon.

Pronunciation

6 Aim To learn/practise the pronunciation of /tʃ/, /dʒ/

- Read the words in the box.
- Model the sounds /tʃ/ and /dʒ/.
- Play the recording. Ss listen and tick the sounds they hear.
- Check Ss' answers.
- Play the recording again with pauses for Ss to repeat chorally and/or individually.

Answer Key

	/tʃ/	/dʒ/		/tʃ/	/dʒ/
damage		✓	*injury*		✓
chicken	✓		*coach*	✓	
reach	✓		*emergency*		✓

Reading & Writing

7 a) Aim To read for structure & content (order paragraphs)

- Give Ss time to read the news report and put the paragraphs into the correct order.
- Check Ss' answers and then elicit what each paragraph is about.

Answer Key

A 2   *B 3*   *C 1*

Paragraph A is about the damage caused by the disaster.
Paragraph B is about what the government will do and includes people's comments.
Paragraph C is about when and where the disaster happened and other facts.

b) Aim To read for cohesion & coherence (word formation)

- Go through the box with Ss .
- Ask Ss to read the news report again and fill the gaps using adjectives derived from the words in brackets.
- Check Ss' answers on the board.

Answer Key

1 suitable	4 hopeless
2 terrible/terrifying	5 environmental
3 natural	

8 (Aim) To identify features of news reports

Go through the **Writing Tip** box with Ss and then elicit examples of news report style in the text in Ex. 7 from Ss around the class.

Suggested Answer Key

facts: *12 noon, ten killed, 200 injured, a million homes without electricity, etc*

headline: *Typhoon Jebi hits Japan*

formal, impersonal style: *over one million ..., the government has said ..., in cities like ...*

full verb forms: *have been, has said, it will*

passive voice: *have been killed, have been destroyed*

direct speech: *"It was terrible.", "When you lose your home in a natural disaster like this, everything seems so hopeless!"*

9 (Aim) To practise impersonal style

- Ask Ss to read the extract and give them time to rewrite it in an impersonal style like in a news report including the elements mentioned in the **Writing Tip**.
- Ask various Ss around the class to read their answers to the class.

Suggested Answer Key

A gas explosion ripped through a chemical factory in Birmingham this morning. Many people were injured when the windows were blown out. "I'm very lucky I wasn't at work today," said one worker. Repairs are now being carried out and it is hoped that the factory will reopen next week.

Writing

10 a) (Aim) To prepare for a writing task

Ask Ss to look at the picture and the list of words and elicit what kind of news report they will hear.

Suggested Answer Key

*I think I will hear a news report about an earthquake in which some **people got injured** and some other people **lost their homes** and lots of **buildings** were **damaged**. I think there may be **electrical problems** afterwards and people may still be trapped in the **rubble**.*

b) (Aim) To prepare for a writing task

- Ask Ss to copy the spidergram into their notebooks. Then play the recording and have Ss listen and complete the spidergram.
- Check Ss' answers on the board.

Suggested Answer Key

comments and ongoing action: *"national emergency" (Mexican President); food, medicines, tents being sent*

place: *Mexico City*

action taken: *search for survivors; put out fires; treat injured*

disaster: earthquake

time: *1 pm local time today*

consequences: *damage to buildings, statues, national museum; fires; public transport stopped; fear of gas leaks*

what happened: *earthquake struck, 7.1 on Richter scale; 200 seriously injured; thousands homeless*

11 (Aim) To write a news report

- Ask Ss to read the rubric and then give them time to write their news report using their answers in Ex. 10 and following the plan.
- Ask various Ss to share their answers with the class.
- Alternatively, assign the task as HW and check Ss' answers in the next lesson.

Suggested Answer key

Earthquake hits Mexico City

A strong earthquake struck Mexico City today at 1 pm local time. The quake measured 7.1 on the Richter scale. At least 200 people have been seriously injured and thousands of people have lost their homes.

There has been lots of damage to property including famous buildings and statues as well as valuable objects in the national museum. Fires have started and the public transport system has stopped working. There is a fear of gas leaks and rescue workers and emergency services have been working around the clock searching for survivors in the ruins, putting out fires, and treating the injured.

"This is a national emergency," said the Mexican President. Other countries have been asked for their help, and food, medicines and tents are being sent to the area.

7 Narrow Escapes

Values

Ask Ss to explain the quotation in their mother tongue. Then initiate a class discussion about the meaning of the quotation and encourage all Ss to participate.

Suggested Answer

I think the quotation means that the only way to show that you really care about other people is to do something to help them – not just to say you feel sorry for them. I suppose it's another way to say 'actions speak louder than words'.

Culture 7

Listening & Reading

1 Aim To introduce the topic; to listen and read for gist; to consolidate and classify new vocabulary

- Ask Ss to look at the pictures. Elicit Ss' guesses as to how they are related to the Great Fire of London.
- Play the recording and have Ss listen and follow the text in their books to find out.
- Then give Ss time to look up the meanings of the words in bold in their dictionaries and elicit explanations for them from Ss around the class. Finally, elicit which of the words in bold are phrasal verbs.

Answer Key

The pictures show the Great Fire of London, the street where it started, the man who rebuilt London after the fire (Sir Christopher Wren) and a monument that was built to remind Londoners of the disaster.

Suggested Answer Key

disaster (n): *a tragic event*
break out (phr v): *to start to happen (of a fire, disease, etc)*
spread (v): *to move across a large area*
careless (adj): *not being careful*
put out (phr v): *to stop flames from burning*
knock down (phr v): *to demolish/pull down (a building)*
blow up (phr v): *to explode*
Phrasal verbs: *break out, put out, knock down, blow up*

- Give Ss time to look up the meanings of the words in the **Check these words** box in the Word List.
- Play the video for Ss and elicit their comments.

2 Aim To read for key information (matching headings to paragraphs)

- Ask Ss to read the headings and then give them time to read the text again and match the headings to the paragraphs.
- Check Ss' answers and elicit which words helped them decide on their answers.

Answer Key

1 D (*important times → trade, architecture, royal court, high society*)
2 F (*following the other → as if that wasn't enough*)
3 E (*began → it all started*)
4 A (*weather → long, hot, dry summer, strong wind*)
5 C (*cost → people dead, houses destroyed, without homes*)
6 B (*repairing → rebuild*)

3 Aim THINK To identify reference

- Direct Ss' attention to the highlighted words in the text and explain that these pronouns represent sth that has already been mentioned previously.
- Elicit what each one refers to from Ss around the class.

Answer Key

it = London
its = London
that = the Great Plague
His = Thomas Farynor
them = the houses near the bakery
they = buildings
this = knocking down the buildings
it = the fire
His = Sir Christopher Wren

Speaking & Writing

4 Aim THINK To develop critical thinking skills; to show empathy retelling a story from the point of view of an eyewitness

Ask various Ss around the class to retell the story of the Great Fire of London from the point of view of an eyewitness.

Suggested Answer Key

The Great Fire of London started early in the morning. I saw the smoke coming out of the baker's windows. I helped to try to put the fire out with buckets of water but it spread too quickly. We couldn't stop the fire. Soon, the other houses in the street were on fire, too. A strong wind started blowing and that made the fire even worse. The guards at the Tower of London blew up some buildings and that helped. Then three days after the fire started, it was finally under control. London looked terrible afterwards, though. Six people died and thousands of homes and buildings were destroyed. It was a tragedy.

Narrow Escapes

5 **Aim** **ICT** **To develop research skills; to write a short text about a disaster**

- Explain the task and give Ss time to research online and collect information about a disaster and then write a short text about it.
- Ask various Ss to read their text to the class.
- Alternatively, assign the task as HW and ask Ss to read out their texts in the next lesson.

Suggested Answer Key

The Great Lisbon Earthquake took place in Portugal in 1755. It happened on Saturday, 1st November in the morning at around 9:40 am. It measured between 8.5 and 9.0 on the Richter scale. After the earthquake, there were lots of fires and a tsunami. Lisbon was almost completely destroyed. Between 10,000 and 100,000 people died.

Background Information

Pudding Lane is a small street in London near London Bridge where the Great Fire of London started in 1666. It started in a bakery owned by Thomas Farynor, the King's baker.

London Bridge was originally a wooden bridge built by the Romans. It was rebuilt many times. In medieval times it became a stone bridge. This was rebuilt in the 19th century and today the bridge is made of concrete and steel. It has appeared in art, literature and songs and is most famous in the nursery rhyme 'London Bridge is Falling Down'.

Review 7

Vocabulary

1 **Aim** **To consolidate vocabulary from the unit**

- Explain the task.
- Give Ss time to complete it.
- Check Ss' answers.

Answer Key

1	flood	4 eruption
2	explosion	5 earthquake
3	avalanche	

2 **Aim** **To consolidate vocabulary from the unit**

- Explain the task.
- Give Ss time to complete it.
- Check Ss' answers.

Answer Key

1	ambulance	4 fire service
2	mountain rescue	5 police
3	coastguard	

3 **Aim** **To practise prepositional phrases and phrasal verbs**

- Explain the task.
- Give Ss time to complete it.
- Check Ss' answers.

Answer Key

1 out   2 off   3 for   4 out   5 up

Grammar

4 **Aim** **To practise reported speech**

- Explain the task.
- Give Ss time to complete it.
- Check Ss' answers.

Answer Key

1 said   2 told   3 said   4 said

5 **Aim** **To practise reported speech**

- Explain the task.
- Give Ss time to complete it.
- Check Ss' answers.

Answer Key

1 *Philip said (that) he was training to be a firefighter.*
2 *The forecaster said (that) the day after/the following day would be stormy.*
3 *He told us not to enter that cave.*
4 *He asked how long we had been waiting for help.*
5 *The guide said (that) they had had a horrible experience.*
6 *She asked me if/whether I had spoken to the police yet.*

6 **Aim** **To practise reporting verbs**

- Explain the task.
- Give Ss time to complete it.
- Check Ss' answers.

Answer Key

1 *Oliver offered to help the rescue team.*
2 *He advised us all to wear our helmets.*
3 *The guide apologised for not taking/having taken more care of the children.*
4 *Julia agreed that it was a very narrow escape.*

7 Narrow Escapes

Everyday English

7 **Aim** **To match exchanges**

- Explain the task.
- Give Ss time to complete it.
- Check Ss' answers.

Answer Key

1 c   2 d   3 a   4 b

Competences

Ask Ss to assess their own performance in the unit by ticking the items according to how competent they feel for each of the listed activities.

Topic

In this unit, Ss will explore the topics of work & jobs and work & education.

8a   Reading & Vocabulary   64-65

Lesson objectives: To learn vocabulary related to work and jobs, to listen and read for specific information, to read for specific information (multiple matching), to learn prepositional phrases, to practise words easily confused, to learn phrasal verbs with *carry*, to talk about a job, to interview sb about their job and write a short text about a job

Vocabulary: Work & Jobs *(work indoors/outdoors, work full-time/part-time, work shifts, work regular hours, wear a uniform at work)*, Nouns *(mountain guide, peak, life form, contract, possibility, overalls, pearl diver, oyster, surface, salary, wages)*; Verbs *(win, earn)*; Phrasal verb *(carry)*; Adjectives *(tricky, responsible, temporary, well-paid, pure, risky, poisonous)*; Phrases *(breathing equipment, watch out for)*

8b   Grammar in Use   66-67

Lesson objectives: To learn/revise conditionals types 2 & 3, to learn/revise wishes, to learn/revise question tags, to learn clauses of concession

8c   Skills in Action   68-69

Lesson objectives: To learn vocabulary related to work & education, to listen for specific information (multiple matching), to act out a dialogue and practise everyday English for talking about your job, to learn the pronunciation of /uː/, /juː/, to read for cohesion & coherence (choose linkers), to write a for-and-against article

Vocabulary: Jobs *(captain, travel agent, lawyer, lecturer, personal trainer, marine biologist, librarian, reporter, taxi driver, security guard, porter)*; Education *(certificate, marks, training, qualifications, advanced, course)*

Culture 8   70

Lesson objectives: To read for gist, to listen and read for cohesion and coherence (missing sentences), to talk about traditional jobs, to present a traditional job in one's country

Vocabulary: Nouns *(swan, prison, ceremony, occasion, rowing boat, riverbank, injury, disease)*; Verbs *(employ, lift, weigh, measure, affect, attack, preserve)*; Phrasal verb *(look after)*; Phrase *(keep track of)*

Review 8   71

Lesson objectives: To test/consolidate vocabulary and grammar learnt throughout the unit, to practise everyday English

---

Go through the objectives box and tell Ss that these are the topics, skills and activities this unit will cover.

8a

Vocabulary

1 **Aim** **To present vocabulary related to work and jobs; to expand on vocabulary**

- Read out the theory box and ask Ss to form nouns describing people's jobs from the words in the list.
- Give Ss time to complete the task and then ask Ss to check their answers in their dictionaries. Alternatively, check their answers on the board.

Answer Key

bank – banker, journal – journalist, photography – photographer, library – librarian, clean – cleaner, reception – receptionist, sail – sailor, engine – engineer, farm – farmer, sing – singer, publish – publisher

2 **Aim** **THINK** **To develop critical thinking skills; to consolidate and expand vocabulary relating to work & jobs**

- Ask Ss to read their answers in Ex. 1 again and decide which of these jobs involve the working conditions in the list.
- Give Ss time to consider their answers and then ask various Ss to tell the class.

Suggested Answer Key

Sailors and farmers work outdoors.
Bankers, librarians, cleaners, receptionists, singers and publishers work indoors.
Directors, journalists, photographers and engineers work indoors or outdoors.
Directors, bankers, journalists, sailors, engineers, farmers and publishers work full-time.
Photographers, librarians, cleaners, receptionists and singers work part-time or full-time.
Journalists and cleaners work shifts.
Bankers, librarians and receptionists work regular hours.
Cleaners wear a uniform at work.

Listening & Reading

3 **Aim** **To introduce the topic of a text and listen and read for gist**

- Ask Ss to quickly read the text and guess the people's jobs.
- Play the recording. Ss answer to the question.

Learning & Earning

8

Answer Key

A is a mountain guide.
B is a speleologist.
C is a pearl diver.

4 **Aim** To read for specific information (multiple matching)

- Ask Ss to read the questions and underline the key words. Give Ss time to read the text again and answer the questions. Ss in closed pairs discuss their answers.
- Check Ss' answers. Ss justify their answers.

Answer Key

1 B, C (in any order) – B: $90,000 a year, C: $1,200 a day
2 B (two-year contract)
3 C – In the old ... now.
4 C – Divers ... kill you!
5 A – you're responsible for people's safety
6 A – May to September

- Then give Ss time to explain the words in bold using their dictionaries to help them if necessary.
- Check Ss' answers around the class.

Suggested Answer Key

tricky (adj): difficult
responsible (adj): having the duty to take care of others or sth
peak (n): the top of a mountain
pure (adj): complete
possibility (n): chance
risky (adj): dangerous
watch out for (phr v): pay attention to sth; look out for sth
surface (n): the flat top part of sth

- Give Ss time to look up the meanings of the words in the **Check these words** box in the Word List.
- Play the video for Ss and elicit their comments.

Background Information

Nepal (the Federal Democratic Republic of Nepal) is a country in Central Asia in between China, India and Bangladesh. 26.4 million people live there and it is home to the world's ten tallest mountains including Mount Everest.

The Himalayas is a mountain range in Asia. It spreads across five countries: Nepal, Bhutan, India, China and Pakistan. It is home to Mount Everest and 52.7 million people live in the area.

Background Information

Mexico (the United Mexico States) is a federal republic in the southern part of North America. 124 million people live there. The capital is Mexico City and the people speak Spanish.

Australia is a large country in the Southern Hemisphere north of Antarctica and south of Indonesia. It has a population of 25 million people. The capital city is Canberra and the people speak English.

5 **Aim** To consolidate prepositional phrases from a text

- Give Ss time to read the gapped phrases and fill in the gaps with the correct prepositions.
- Then check Ss' answers.

Answer Key

1 for
2 in
3 on
4 out of
5 for
6 on
7 from
8 at

6 **Aim** To consolidate new vocabulary

- Ask Ss to read the words in the list and then give them time to complete the phrases with them.
- Check Ss' answers. Then give Ss time to write sentences using the phrases and elicit Ss' answers around the class.

Answer Key

1 mountain
2 temporary
3 snow
4 two-year
5 pearl
6 12-hour
7 breathing
8 poisonous

Suggested Answer Key

Mountain guides need to have suitable equipment when they climb mountains.
I want to find a **temporary job** this summer.
You need to wear **snow goggles** when you climb a mountain.
Mark has a **two-year contract** as a researcher with the university.
Pearl divers work underwater.
I don't think I could work a **12-hour shift**.
Pearl divers wear **breathing equipment** when they work underwater.
Pearl divers need to be careful because they may come across **poisonous fish** while working underwater.

7 **Aim** To understand words easily confused

- Explain the task and give Ss time to use their dictionaries to help them complete it.
- Check Ss' answers.

Answer Key

1	a salary	3	won
2	earn	4	wages

8 (Aim) To learn phrasal verbs with *carry*

- Ask Ss to read the phrasal verbs box and make sure that they understand the definitions.
- Then give Ss time to complete the task and check their answers.
- Tell Ss to write the phrasal verbs in the Phrasal Verbs list in their notebooks and include the definitions. Tell Ss to revise this list from time to time and to add to it every time they come across a new phrasal verb.

Answer Key

1 off	2 out	3 on

Speaking & Writing

9 (Aim) (THINK) To develop critical thinking skills, to talk about a job

- Ask Ss to work in pairs or small groups and give them time to consider their answers and then discuss which job they would choose [not] to do and why.
- Ask various Ss to share their answers with the class.

Suggested Answer Key

I would choose to be a speleologist because I think it would be very interesting to go below the ground and see caves and carry out research on tiny life forms. I think the job is well-paid and that's another reason I'd like to do it.

I would not choose to be a mountain guide in the Himalayas because I think it would be very dangerous. Also, I wouldn't like to do it because I'm not very comfortable with heights.

10 (Aim) To act out an interview about a job and write a short text about it

- Ask Ss to work in pairs and interview each other about a job covering all the points in the task. Elicit questions Ss can ask *(e.g. What do you do for a living?, What exactly do you do at work?, What are the working hours?, How much do you earn?, What do you like about your job?, Is there something you don't like about your job?)*
- Go round the class and monitor the task.
- Have Ss make notes of each other's answers and then use their notes to help them write a short text about their partner's job.
- Ask various Ss to read out their text to the class.
- Alternatively, assign the task as HW and ask Ss to share their answers in the next lesson.

Suggested Answer Key

what they do: *a pilot – flies planes*
the hours they work: *between 4 and 13 hours a day*
uniform: *airline uniform, a white shirt, a jacket and trousers, a tie and a cap*
salary/wages: *average salary £75,000 a year*
what they like/don't like about the job: *like – travel, free flights; don't like – long hours, being away from home*

John works as an airline pilot. He flies planes. He works between 4 and 13 hours a day. He wears a uniform at work. It's a white shirt, a jacket, trousers, a tie and a cap with the colours of the airline. He earns an average salary of £75,000 a year. He likes the travel and the free flights he gets. He doesn't like the long hours and being away from home.

8b Grammar in Use

1 (Aim) To learn/revise conditionals types 2 & 3

- Say then write on the board: *If I had a job, I would earn some money.* Ask Ss to identify the *if*-clause *(If I had a job)* and which tense we use *(the past simple)*. Ask Ss to identify the main clause *(I would earn some money)* and the verb form used *(would + infinitive without to)*. Explain that this is a type 2 conditional and elicit its use: we use it to talk about an unreal or unlikely situation in the present or future. Also, point out that we can use *were* instead of *was* in all persons.
- Say then write on the board: *If I had worked harder, I would have passed my exams.* Ask Ss to identify the *if*-clause *(If I had worked harder)* and which tense we use *(the past perfect)*. Ask Ss to identify the main clause *(I would have passed my exams)* and the verb form used *(would + have + past participle of the main verb)*. Explain/Elicit that we form a type 3 conditional with *if/when + past perfect + would have + past participle* and that we use it to talk about an unreal situation in the past.
- Go through the theory box with Ss and elicit examples from the forum.
- Refer Ss to the **Grammar Reference** section for more information.

Answer Key

We use type 2 conditionals to talk about an unreal or unlikely situation in the present or future. – if I were you, I would look for another job where you can use your waiting skills. If you did a short training course, you'd be able to apply for a job as a hotel receptionist or something like that.

We use type 3 conditionals to talk about an unreal situation in the past. – If I had given up, I wouldn't have made it this far.

Learning & Earning

2 **Aim** **To practise conditionals types 2 & 3**

- Explain the task and give Ss time to complete it.
- Check Ss' answers.

Answer Key

1 *had (type 2 conditional – could get)*
2 *have taken (type 3 conditional – would + have + pp)*
3 *had arrived (type 3 conditional – might have employed)*
4 *wouldn't have taken (type 3 conditional – wouldn't + have + past participle)*
5 *were (I'd apply – advice)*

3 **Aim** **To practise conditionals types 2 & 3**

- Explain the task and give Ss time to complete it and elicit the type of conditional. Ss can work in closed pairs.
- Check Ss' answers.

Answer Key

1 *had asked (type 3)*
2 *If the office canteen **served** better food, it might have more customers. (type 2)*
3 *If you **had written** down the date of the meeting, you wouldn't have forgotten it. (type 3)*
4 *If I were you, I **would hire** a professional painter for your house. (type 2)*
5 *If Karen were a bit more patient, she **would make** an ideal teacher. (type 2)*
6 *If the government **created** more jobs, fewer people would be unemployed. (type 2)*
7 *would move (type 2)*
8 *hadn't missed (type 3)*

4 **Aim** **THINK** **To develop critical thinking skills; to practise conditionals types 2 & 3 with personal examples**

- Explain the task and give Ss time to complete the sentences using personal examples.
- Elicit answers from Ss around the class.

Suggested Answer Key

1 *I would go on holiday*
2 *they worked less*
3 *I had not moved to London*
4 *we had robots to help*
5 *there would be less traffic*
6 *I might have become a farmer*
7 *I would move tomorrow*
8 *I finished my report before Friday noon*

5 **Aim** **To learn/revise wishes**

- Go through the theory box with Ss. Elicit that we introduce wishes with *If only/I wish*.
- Direct Ss' attention to the verb forms in each sentence. Ask: *What tense do we use to make a wish for the present?* (past simple) *What tense do we use to express regret about sth in the past?* (past perfect)
- Refer Ss to the **Grammar Reference** section for more information.
- Elicit examples from the forum.

Answer Key

Example: *I wish I had studied a bit harder.*

6 **Aim** **To practise wishes**

- Explain the task and give Ss time to complete it and then check their answers.
- Elicit reasons.

Answer Key

1 *hadn't forgotten (regret about past)*
2 *weren't/wasn't (wish to change – present)*
3 *had arrived (regret about the past)*
4 *worked (wish to change – present)*
5 *hadn't behaved (regret about past)*

7 **Aim** **To practise wishes and conditionals**

- Explain the task and read out the example.
- Give Ss time to complete the task and then check their answers.

Suggested Answer Key

2 *I hadn't missed the bus. If I hadn't missed the bus, I wouldn't have been late for work.*
3 *I didn't have a headache. If I didn't have a headache, I would be able to work faster.*
4 *I had been more careful. If I had been more careful, I wouldn't have deleted the files.*

8 **Aim** **To practise wishes using personal examples**

- Explain the task and read out the example.
- Give Ss time to complete the task in closed or open pairs using personal examples.
- Elicit answers from Ss around the class.

Suggested Answer Key

B: *I wish I were rich.*
A: *I wish I hadn't missed the bus this morning.*
B: *If only I had more free time.*
A: *If only my friends would call me more often.*
B: *I wish you hadn't told Tim my secret.*

9 (**Aim**) **To learn/revise question tags; to listen for rising/falling intonation**

- Write the first two examples in the theory box on the board. Explain/Elicit that question tags are short questions at the end of statements to confirm sth or to find out if sth is true. We form question tags with the auxiliary or modal verb of the main sentence with the correct subject pronoun.
- Explain/Elicit that when the verb of the sentence is in the present simple we form the question tag with *do/does* and the subject pronoun, and when the verb of the sentence is in the past simple we form the question tag with *did* and the subject pronoun.
- Explain/Elicit that when the sentence is positive the question tag is negative and vice versa. Explain/Elicit that when the question tag contains a word with a negative meaning (*never, hardly, seldom,* etc) then the question tag is positive.
- Go through the theory box with Ss.
- Refer Ss to the **Grammar Reference** section for more information.
- Give Ss time to fill in appropriate question tags and then check Ss' answers.
- Explain that when we aren't sure of the answer we use a rising intonation in the question tag and when we are sure of the answer we use a falling intonation in the question tag.
- Play the recording. Ss listen and tick the correct boxes for the items in Ex. 9.
- Play the recording again with pauses for Ss to repeat chorally and/or individually.

Answer Key

1 *isn't she*	4 *are you*	7 *didn't they*
2 *will you*	5 *aren't I*	8 *did they*
3 *isn't it*	6 *shall we*	

1 ↗	3 ↗	5 ↘	7 ↘
2 ↘	4 ↗	6 ↘	8 ↘

10 (**Aim**) **To present/practise clauses of concession**

- Write the examples in the theory box on the board. Explain/Elicit how clauses of concession are formed. Ask Ss to find an example in the forum. (*Although I work long hours, it pays very little.*)
- Refer Ss to the **Grammar Reference** section for more information.
- Give Ss time to do the task and then check Ss' answers.

Answer Key

1 *Even though he is hard-working, he didn't get a promotion.*
2 *Although she lives close to work, she drives there.*
3 *Despite working from home, he never feels lonely.*

4 *In spite of the fact that Ann knows a lot about computers, she doesn't have a degree.*

8c Skills in Action

Vocabulary

1 (**Aim**) **To present vocabulary related to work & education**

Ask Ss to look at the pictures and read the list of jobs. Elicit which ones are shown in the pictures. Then read out the places of study in the list and explain the meaning of any unknown words (*e.g. vocational school = a school that provides training in technical skills for a specific job*). Elicit which places of study match the jobs in the pictures.

Answer Key

A – lawyer	C – captain
B – lecturer	D – security guard

You can study to be a lawyer, a lecturer, a librarian, a marine biologist and a reporter at university.
You can study to be a captain at a vocational school.
A travel agent's job, a security guard's job, becoming a captain, a personal trainer, a taxi driver, a security guard and a porter does not require a degree.

2 (**Aim**) **To present and practise vocabulary related to education**

- Ask Ss to read gapped sentences 1-6 and then go through the words in the list. Have them look up the meanings of any unknown words in the Word List or in their dictionaries.
- Give Ss time to use the words to complete the sentences.
- Check Ss' answers around the class.

Answer Key

1 *marks*	4 *qualifications*
2 *certificate*	5 *advanced*
3 *course*	6 *training*

Listening

3 (**Aim**) **To listen for specific information (multiple matching)**

- Read out the **Study Skills** box and explain that this tip will help Ss to complete the task successfully.
- Ask Ss to read statements A-E and underline the key words.
- Play the recording twice. Ss listen and choose their answers.
- Check Ss answers and elicit guesses as to what each person's job is. You can play the recording with pauses for Ss to check their answers.

Learning & Earning

8

Answer Key

1 E	2 D	3 B	4 A

Suggested Answer Key

1 marine biologist
2 librarian
3 travel agent
4 personal trainer

Everyday English

4 **Aim** To read for specific information

- Read out the question.
- Then play the recording. Ss listen to and read the dialogue to find out.

Answer Key

Paul likes his job because it's very creative and it pays well.

5 **Aim** To role-play a dialogue talking about your job

- Explain the task and ask Ss to act out a similar dialogue to the one in Ex. 4 in pairs about a security guard job using the language in the box to help them.
- Write this diagram on the board for Ss to follow.

A	B
Congratulate B on their new job. *Hi, ... Congratulations on ... You work as a ... don't you?*	Thank A and say job. *Thanks. That's right. I'm a ...*
Comment and ask what they do. *What do you do ...?*	Say what your duties are. *I have to ...*
Ask what's the best part of the job. *What's the ...?*	Say the positives. *The ... is ... It's also ...*
Ask if B is happy in his job. *So, I guess you ..., don't you?*	Respond and say the negatives. *Yes, I do. Even though the ... and it's ...*
Ask about qualifications needed. *What qualifications did ...?*	Give details. *I had to have ... but I didn't need ...*

- Monitor the activity around the class and offer assistance as necessary.
- Then ask some pairs to act out their dialogues in front of the class.

Suggested Answer Key

A: *Hi, Steve. Congratulations on the new job! You work as a security guard now, don't you?*
B: *Thanks. That's right. I'm a security guard at the airport.*
A: *Wow. That's exciting! What do you do in your new job?*
B: *I have to search aircraft, passengers and luggage and patrol the airport.*
A: *What's the best part about the job?*
B: *The pay is pretty good! It's also great to work in a team.*
A: *So, I guess you like it, don't you?*
B: *Yes, I love it, even though the working hours are long and it's demanding and stressful at times.*
A: *I see. It sounds really interesting, though! What qualifications did you need?*
B: *I had to have a good general education and it's good to have experience, but it wasn't necessary to have any special qualifications.*
A: *Great!*

Pronunciation

6 **Aim** To learn the pronunciations of /uː/, /juː/

- Model the sounds /uː/ and /juː/.
- Then play the recording. Ss listen and repeat chorally and/or individually.

Reading & Writing

7 **Aim** To analyse a rubric

- Ask Ss to read the rubric and underline the key words.
- Then give them time to answers the questions and elicit answers from Ss around the class.

Answer Key

1 *I am going to write an article for a magazine.*
2 *I should write about the advantages and disadvantages of being a surgeon.*
3 *I should write 120-150 words.*

8 a) **Aim** To read for cohesion and coherence (linkers)

- Ask Ss to read the article and choose the correct linkers in bold.
- Check Ss' answers.

Answer Key

1	To begin with	6	Firstly
2	as a result	7	For example
3	Besides	8	In addition
4	For this reason	9	since
5	However	10	In conclusion

b) **Aim** **To identify features of formal style**

Read out the **Writing Tip** box and then elicit examples of formal style in the text in Ex. 8a from Ss around the class.

Answer Key

full verb forms: *that is, it is, it is, there is, there are, it is*

the passive: *is … admired, can be gained, is loved*

complex sentences: *Surgeons do an extremely difficult job and, as a result, their salaries are high, In conclusion … worth doing*

9 **Aim** **To learn about topic sentences**

* Read out the **Writing Tip**. Explain that topic sentences introduce the main idea of the paragraph. They are followed by supporting sentences that further develop the main idea providing points for/ against and justifications to support and elaborate on the main idea of the paragraph.
* Ask Ss to read the article again and identify the topic sentences, then choose suitable alternatives from the ones provided.
* Ask various Ss around the class to share their answers with the class.

Answer Key

Topic sentences: *A career as a surgeon has clear advantages.* → 2
However, being a surgeon has its disadvantages. → 1

Writing

10 a) **Aim** **To prepare for a writing task**

* Play the recording and have Ss listen and complete the table.
* Check Ss' answers.

Answer Key

1 *things*	4 *hours*
2 *meet*	5 *holidays*
3 *stressful*	

b) **Aim** **To write a for-and-against article**

* Explain the task and then give them time to write their article using their answers in Ex. 10a and following the plan.
* Ask various Ss to share their answers with the class.
* Alternatively, assign the task as HW and check Ss' answers in the next lesson.

Suggested Answer key

Being a journalist: the best and the worst

Working as a journalist may seem like a great job. What exactly are the advantages and disadvantages of this career choice, though?

The job clearly has some advantages. To start with, it improves one's knowledge. This is because journalists have to research every topic they write about. What is more, it can be exciting since they meet interesting people and interview celebrities and politicians.

However, being a journalist has its disadvantages. Firstly, it is very stressful since deadlines have to be met. Furthermore, journalists have to work long, unsociable hours. For example, they have to work at weekends and on public holidays.

In conclusion, although there are pros and cons to this job, I believe it is well worth doing. As Henry R. Luce said, "I became a journalist to come as close as possible to the heart of the world."

Values

Ask Ss to explain the saying in their mother tongue. Then initiate a class discussion about the meaning of the saying and encourage all Ss to participate.

Suggested Answer

A: *I think the saying means that a person who has done something badly will blame their equipment rather than admit their own lack of skill.*

B: *I agree. I think that it also means that skill is more important than equipment when it comes to doing a job.*

Culture 8

Reading & Listening

1 **Aim** **To introduce the topic and to read for gist**

* Ask Ss to look at the picture and read the introduction. Elicit Ss' guesses as to what sort of job the men do.
* Give Ss time to read the whole text to find out.

Suggested Answer Key

The men count and mark the swans on the River Thames and check on how the birds are doing.

2 **Aim** **To read for cohesion and coherence (missing sentences)**

* Ask Ss to read sentences A-F and then give them time to read the text again and match the sentences to gaps 1-4. Ask Ss to look for reference words within the sentences and the sentences before/ after each gap as this will help them do the task.

Learning & Earning

- Check Ss' answers and then give Ss time to explain the words in bold by using the Word List or their dictionaries to help them. Elicit explanations from Ss around the class.

Answer Key

1 E (count and mark the swans – kept a check on their numbers)
2 D (men, wear, uniforms – uppers, dressed, red and white, Swan Marker, red and gold jacket, feather in cap)
3 F (the swans up onto the riverbank – before sent back into the water)
4 B (come a long way – from protecting, it's now)

Suggested Answer Key

employ (v): to pay sb to do a job
look after (phr v): to take care of
occasion (n): a special event
riverbank (n): the land on the side of a river
affect (v): to have an effect on
attack (v): to try to hurt
preserve (v): to stop sth from being damaged or destroyed

- Give Ss time to look up the meanings of the words in the **Check these words** box in the Word List.
- Play the video for Ss and elicit their comments.

Speaking & Writing

3 **Aim** THINK **To develop critical thinking skills; to express an opinion**

Read out the question and give Ss time to consider their answers. Tell Ss to share their answers with their partner and then ask various Ss to share their answers with the class.

Suggested Answer Key

I think it is important to keep traditional jobs alive because it connects us with our past and keeps our culture alive. I also think that many traditional jobs still have a role to play in modern society such as the one in the text.

4 **Aim** ICT **To develop research skills; to write a short text about a traditional job in one's country**

- Explain the task and give Ss time to research online and collect information about a traditional job in their country (or elsewhere) and then write a short text about it.
- Ask various Ss to read their text to the class.
- Alternatively, assign the task as HW and ask Ss to read out their texts in the next lesson.

Suggested Answer Key

title of job: hermit (person who lives alone, far away from society)
origins: 1442
what the job involves: looking after the hermitage and St Martin's Chapel near Solothurn
why important today: preserve the buildings, currently the hermit's job is held by an ex-policeman from Germany, he lives there for free and gets a good wage

A hermit is a person who lives alone far away from society for various reasons. A hermit has taken care of the hermitage and St Martin's Chapel in the Verena Gorge near Solothurn in Switzerland since 1442. Someone needs to live there to preserve the buildings and take care of them. Currently the hermit's job is held by an ex-policeman from Germany. He lives there for free and gets a good wage, too! He is probably one of the last hermits in Europe.

Background Information

The River Thames is a 246-km long river that runs through London. The London Eye, Big Ben, the Houses of Parliament and the Tower of London are along its banks. You can cross the river by bridge or use a cable car.

Oxfordshire is a country in Southeast England. It lies between the River Thames, the areas known as the Chilterns, the Midlands and the Cotswolds. Oxford is the country town and Oxfordshire became a county in the early 10th century.

Review 8

Vocabulary

1 **Aim** **To consolidate vocabulary from the unit**
- Explain the task.
- Give Ss time to complete it.
- Check Ss' answers.

Answer Key

1 earns	4 temporary
2 shift	5 goggles
3 part-time	6 well-paid

2 **Aim** **To consolidate vocabulary from the unit**
- Explain the task.
- Give Ss time to complete it.
- Check Ss' answers.

Learning & Earning

Answer Key

1	degree	4	course
2	top	5	qualifications
3	training	6	certificate

3 **Aim** **To practise prepositional phrases and phrasal verbs**

- Explain the task.
- Give Ss time to complete it.
- Check Ss' answers.

Answer Key

1	for	3	for	5	out
2	on	4	from		

Grammar

4 **Aim** **To practise wishes/clauses of concession**

- Explain the task.
- Give Ss time to complete it.
- Check Ss' answers.

Answer Key

1	had	3	had applied
2	hadn't failed	4	Although

5 **Aim** **To practise conditionals**

- Explain the task.
- Give Ss time to complete it.
- Check Ss' answers.

Answer Key

1	had gone	4	would have got
2	would run	5	would use
3	hadn't been	6	had offered

6 **Aim** **To practise question tags**

- Explain the task.
- Give Ss time to complete it.
- Check Ss' answers.

Answer Key

1	don't they	4	don't you
2	aren't I	5	isn't it
3	will you	6	did they

Everyday English

7 **Aim** **To match exchanges**

- Explain the task.
- Give Ss time to complete it.
- Check Ss' answers.

Answer Key

1 c	2 e	3 d	4 a	5 b

Competences

Ask Ss to assess their own performance in the unit by ticking the items according to how competent they feel for each of the listed activities.

9 Want to play?

Topic
In this unit, Ss will explore the topics of sports & equipment, sports places, team sports and individual sports.

9a Reading & Vocabulary	72-73
Lesson objectives: To learn vocabulary for sports & equipment, to listen and read for specific information, to read for gist (matching headings to paragraphs), to learn prepositional phrases, to learn collocations, to practise words easily confused, to learn phrasal verbs with *turn*, to talk about extreme sports, to write a blog entry **Vocabulary:** Sports *(swimming, boxing, hockey, rugby, motor racing, climbing, squash, cricket)*; Equipment *(trainers, helmet, racket, swimsuit, rope, bat, boxing gloves, stick, ball)*; Nouns *(experience, situation, instructor, energy, element, risk, competition, prize, reply)*; Verbs *(face, experience, forget, whizz, attack, beat, win, earn, beat, gain)*; Phrasal verb *(hang)*; Adjective *(proper)*; Adverb *(fairly)*; Phrases *(to the limit, sales results, hidden away, deal with, ask for trouble)*	

9b Grammar in Use	74-75
Lesson objectives: To learn/revise the infinitive/-*ing* form, forms of the infinitive/-*ing* form and singular/plural nouns	

9c Skills in Action	76-77
Lesson objectives: To learn vocabulary for sports & places, to listen for specific information (gap fill), to act out a dialogue and practise everyday English for asking for information, to learn the pronunciation of /eɪ/, /aɪ/, to read for cohesion & coherence (word formation), to write a blog entry comparing ways to get fit **Vocabulary:** Sports *(badminton, baseball, basketball, cycling, diving, football, ice skating, jogging, golf, sailing, windsurfing, tennis, volleyball, water skiing)*; Places *(court, pitch, rink, track, field, course, sea, sports centre, swimming pool)*	

Culture 9	78
Lesson objectives: To listen and read for specific information, to read for detail (answer questions), to invent a sport, to write about a sport **Vocabulary:** Nouns *(record, shape)*; Verbs *(swing, score)*; Adjectives *(early, shaped)*; Conjunction *(except)*; Phrases *(in total, fast and furious)*	

Review 9	79
Lesson objectives: To test/consolidate vocabulary and grammar learnt throughout the unit, to practise everyday English	

Go through the objectives box and tell Ss that these are the topics, skills and activities this unit will cover.

9a

Vocabulary

1 a) **Aim** To present sports & categorise them

Ask Ss to look at the pictures and then elicit which ones are extreme sports, team sports, water sports or indoor sports from Ss around the class.

Answer Key

extreme sports: *motor racing, climbing*
team sports: *hockey, rugby, cricket*
water sports: *swimming*
indoor sports: *boxing, squash*

b) **Aim** To present vocabulary related to sports equipment

- Ask Ss to look at the equipment and then match the sports in Ex. 1a to the equipment.
- Elicit answers from Ss around the class. (Point out that we usually use the verbs *go/play/do* with sports but with some sports there are special verbs, e.g. *box*.)

Answer Key

You need a swimsuit to go swimming.
You need boxing gloves to box.
You need a stick to play hockey.
You need a ball to play rugby.
You need a helmet to go motor racing.
You need a rope to go climbing.
You need trainers and a racket to play squash.
You need a bat to play cricket.

Reading & Listening

2 **Aim** To introduce the topic of a text; to listen and read for specific information

- Go through the sentences with Ss and elicit answers. Alternatively, Ss in closed pairs do the task.
- Play the recording and have Ss listen to and read the article and check their answers.

Suggested Answer Key

2, 3, 4, 5, 6, 7

3 **Aim** To read for gist (matching headings to paragraphs)

- Read out the **Study Skills** box and tell Ss this tip will help them to complete the task successfully.
- Ask Ss to read the headings and underline the key words.

Want to play?

9

- Then give them time to read the text twice and complete the task following the tip in the **Study Skills** box.
- Check Ss' answers. Ss should justify their answers.

Answer Key

1 A (terrified ... thrilling / turn down ... fear?)
2 F (All of them ... a cliff!)
3 D (There's a love ... somewhere.)
4 B (But fear ... conditions.)
5 C (There is an element ... sports / extreme sports ... abilities)

- Then give Ss time to explain the words in bold using their dictionaries to help them as necessary.
- Check Ss' answers around the class.

Suggested Answer Key

experience (n): adventure
situation (n): condition at a certain time/place
turn down (phr v): to refuse to accept/agree to sth
experience (v): to face
forget (v): to not remember
hang off (phr): to be suspended from above with one part attached to sth, (e.g. hands holding on) and rest of body free
instructor (n): person who teaches a skill, e.g. skiing
hide away (phr v): to put something somewhere where no one can find it
fairly (adv): quite
attack (v): to try to injure or kill sb
energy (n): physical strength and power to be active
element (n): a part of sth
competition (n): a contest where people compete against each other
reply (n): sth said in response to sb

- Give Ss time to look up the meanings of the words in the **Check these words** box in the Word List.
- Play the video for Ss and elicit their comments.

4 **Aim** To consolidate prepositional phrases from a text

- Give Ss time to do the task referring back to the text as necessary.
- Then check Ss' answers. As an extension, you can ask Ss to use the prepositional phrases in sentences of their own.

Answer Key

1 to
2 about
3 at
4 of
5 in
6 with
7 under
8 for
9 in
10 with

Suggested Answer Key

1 She took sport to the limit when she did a bungee jump from the highest bridge in town.
2 Tom's mum is worried about him climbing up a glacier.
3 We skied down the slope at a speed of 60 miles per hour!
4 Trevor's love of danger made him decide to join a motor racing club.
5 In modern life, we are not very close to nature.
6 Swimming alone in the ocean helps me deal with my everyday problems.
7 It's difficult to keep a paraglider under control in windy conditions.
8 It's asking for trouble to ride a motorbike without a helmet.
9 I'm interested in all kinds of extreme water sports.
10 I don't really agree with Gill on this.

5 **Aim** To consolidate new vocabulary

- Explain the task and give Ss time to complete the phrases using the words in the list.
- Then check Ss' answers.

Answer Key

1 mind
2 call
3 chance
4 look

6 **Aim** To understand words easily confused

- Ask Ss to read the sentences and then complete them with the words in the list using their dictionaries if necessary.
- Check Ss' answers.

Answer Key

1 won
2 beat
3 gained
4 earn

7 **Aim** To learn phrasal verbs with *turn*

- Ask Ss to read the phrasal verbs box and make sure that Ss understand the definitions.
- Then give Ss time to complete the task and check their answers.

Answer Key

1 on, up
2 into
3 down
4 off, down

Want to play?

Speaking & Writing

8 **Aim** **THINK** **To develop critical thinking skills**

- Ask Ss to think of more extreme sports and why people do them. Give Ss time to consider their answers.
- Ask various Ss to tell the class.

Suggested Answer Key

Parascending, paragliding, hang-gliding, snowboarding, windsurfing, mountaineering, skydiving, bungee jumping, base jumping, etc

I think people do extreme sports for the excitement they feel when they are doing them. I think it makes them feel more alive and they forget about their worries and everyday lives.

9 **Aim** **To write a blog entry**

- Explain the task and give Ss time to write a blog entry including information for the points listed. Then ask various Ss to read their blog entry to the class.
- Alternatively, assign the task as HW and ask Ss to read out the blog entries in the next lesson.

Suggested Answer Key

Hi everybody!
There's an extreme sport called wing-walking. It isn't new because people started doing it not long after aeroplanes were invented. But it's not something that is available to everyone because you need a biplane to do it. Wing-walking involves being tied to the roof of the plane while it flies through the air and does lots of loops and turns. I think it sounds incredibly scary and exciting. I don't know about you, but I would like to try it one day because it seems very extreme! I think you would feel like you were really flying through the air.

9b Grammar in Use

1 **Aim** **To learn/revise the infinitive/-ing form**

- Ask Ss to read the advert and answer questions 1-7.
- Refer Ss to the ***Grammar Reference*** section for more information.
- Check Ss' answers.

Answer Key

2 -ing form	5 infinitive without to
3 to-infinitive	6 to-infinitive
4 infinitive without to	7 -ing form

2 **Aim** **To practise the infinitive/-ing form**

- Explain the task and give Ss time to complete it.
- Check Ss' answers.

Answer Key

1 playing	5 be, to try	9 to play
2 to join	6 meeting	10 leave
3 practise	7 running	
4 competing	8 getting	

3 **Aim** **To practise the infinitive/-ing form**

- Explain the task and give Ss time to complete it.
- Check Ss' answers.

Answer Key

1 taking part	4 to try	7 to find
2 to learn	5 being	8 practising
3 to play	6 exercising	9 become

4 **Aim** **To present the forms of the infinitive/-ing form**

- Go through the theory box and explain how the various forms of the infinitive/-ing form correspond to tenses.
- Refer Ss to the ***Grammar Reference*** section for more information.
- Give Ss time to complete the task and then check their answers.

Answer Key

1 practising	4 be climbing
2 catch	5 having been chosen
3 have been practising	6 have hurt

5 **Aim** **To practise the infinitive/-ing form**

- Remind Ss that some verbs, e.g. forget, stop, etc. can be followed by a *to*-infinitive or *-ing* form with a difference in meaning. Refer Ss to the ***Grammar Reference*** section for details. Explain the task and give Ss time to complete it.
- Check Ss' answers around the class.

Answer Key

1 going	4 to drop	7 to lift
2 changing	5 to tell	
3 driving	6 to book	

Speaking

6 **Aim** **To practise the infinitive/-ing form**

- Read out the first two sentences in the story and then ask various Ss around the class to continue the story using the verbs in the list in an infinitive or *-ing* form.

* Continue until all the Ss have had a turn using the verbs or using other verbs if necessary.

Suggested Answer Key

Sally and Jessie wanted to go surfing. They were looking forward to doing tricks on the waves. On their way to the beach, they **stopped** to buy some snacks. They **remembered** to buy some water, too. At the beach, they **tried** to do some surfing tricks, but the waves weren't big enough. They **should** have checked the weather forecast. So, instead, they **spent** the day lying on the beach and talking. Suddenly, it started raining, so they **needed** to go home. Sally **suggested** trying again next weekend.

7 **Aim** **To revise/learn singular/plural nouns**

* Read through the theory box and explain any points Ss are unsure of.
* Refer them to the **Grammar Reference** section for more information.
* Elicit examples in the advert on p. 74.

Answer Key

Examples: equipment, staff, advice

8 **Aim** **To practise singular/plural nouns**

* Explain the task and give Ss time to complete it.
* Check Ss' answers around the class.

Answer Key

1 is (distance)
2 Are (object consisting of two parts)
3 is (uncountable noun)
4 is (college subject)
5 is (sports)
6 is (noun that takes a singular verb form)
7 is (noun that takes a singular verb form)
8 are (object consisting of two parts)
9 is (disease)
10 are (object consisting of two parts)

9 **Aim** **To practise singular/plural nouns; to express a sentence in a different way**

Explain the task. Give Ss time to complete it and then check their answers.

Suggested Answer Key

1 my tracksuit trousers are
2 has (got) five members (in it)
3 is my favourite game/sport/hobby, etc
4 is needed (by someone)
5 is what I will get/will be given for the job

10 **Aim** **To practise the infinitive/-ing form; to express a sentence in a different way**

* Explain the task and give Ss time to complete it.
* Elicit answers from Ss around the class.

Answer Key

1 not warm enough to play
2 to be chosen
3 being told
4 is his favourite

9c Skills in Action

Vocabulary

1 **a)** **Aim** **To present vocabulary for sports**

* Ask Ss to read the list of sports.
* Then tell them to copy the Venn diagram into their notebooks and complete it using the sports in the list. Explain that the sports that go in both categories need to go in the middle section. Ss complete the task in closed pairs.
* Check Ss' answers on the board.

Answer Key

Team sports
baseball, basketball, football, volleyball

cycling diving sailing

Individual sports
badminton, ice skating, jogging, golf, windsurfing, tennis, water skiing

b) **Aim** **To present/practise vocabulary for sports places**

Explain the task. Ss do the task in closed pairs using their dictionaries if necessary. Check Ss' answers.

Suggested Answer Key

You can play badminton, basketball, tennis and volleyball on a court.
You can play football on a pitch.
You can go ice skating on a rink.
You can go cycling and jogging on a track.
You can play baseball on a field.
You can play golf on a course.
You can go sailing, go windsurfing and go water skiing in the sea.
You can play badminton and volleyball in a sports centre.
You can go diving in a swimming pool or in the sea.

9 Want to play?

2 **Aim** To practise new vocabulary

- Explain the task and give Ss time to complete it with the sports in Ex. 1a.
- Check Ss' answers around the class.

Answer Key

1 Jogging
2 basketball/volleyball
3 Sailing
4 Cycling
5 Ice skating

Listening

3 **Aim** To listen for specific information (gap fill)

- Ask Ss to read the gapped table and underline the key words.
- Play the recording twice. Ss listen and fill the gaps.
- Check Ss' answers. You can play the recording with pauses for Ss to check their answers.

Answer Key

1 fun
2 organise
3 success
4 lonely

Everyday English

4 **Aim** To listen and read for specific information

- Read out the questions in the rubric.
- Play the recording and ask Ss to listen and read the dialogue to find out the answers.

Answer Key

Bob is interested in TRX® classes.
The classes are on Tuesdays and Thursdays.
The classes cost £45 a month.

Background Information

The **TRX® System**, also known as **Total Resistance exercises**, is a specialised form of suspension training that uses equipment developed by former US Navy SEAL Randy Hetrick.

---

5 **Aim** To role-play a dialogue asking for information

- Explain the task and ask Ss to act out a similar dialogue to the one in Ex. 4 in pairs using the advert and the phrases from the language box.
- Write this diagram on the board for Ss to follow.

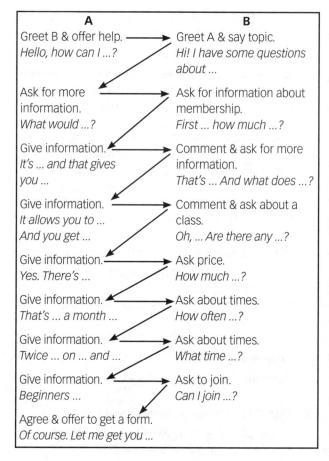

A	B
Greet B & offer help. *Hello, how can I ...?*	Greet A & say topic. *Hi! I have some questions about ...*
Ask for more information. *What would ...?*	Ask for information about membership. *First ... how much ...?*
Give information. *It's ... and that gives you ...*	Comment & ask for more information. *That's ... And what does ...?*
Give information. *It allows you to ... And you get ...*	Comment & ask about a class. *Oh, ... Are there any ...?*
Give information. *Yes. There's ...*	Ask price. *How much ...?*
Give information. *That's ... a month ...*	Ask about times. *How often ...?*
Give information. *Twice ... on ... and ...*	Ask about times. *What time ...?*
Give information. *Beginners ...*	Ask to join. *Can I join ...?*
Agree & offer to get a form. *Of course. Let me get you ...*	

- Monitor the activity around the class and offer assistance as necessary.
- Then ask some pairs to act out their dialogues in front of the class.

Suggested Answer Key

A: Hello, how can I help you?
B: Hi! I have some questions about the sports centre.
A: What would you like to know?
B: First of all, how much is the special offer for membership?
A: It's £180 and that gives you full annual membership.
B: That's great. And what does membership include?
A: It allows you to use the two swimming pools and the gym. And you get 20% off any exercise classes you take.
B: Oh, good. Are there any Zumba classes?
A: Yes. There's a beginners' and an advanced class.
B: How much do they cost?
A: That's ... £48 a month after your discount.
B: How often are they?
A: Twice a week, on Mondays and Wednesdays.
B: What time are they at?
A: Beginners from 7 to 8 pm, advanced from 8 to 9.
B: Can I join today?
A: Of course. Let me get you a form to fill in.

Want to play?

Pronunciation

6 **Aim** To learn the pronunciation of /ei/, /ai/

- Model the sounds /ei/, /ai/.
- Then play the recording. Ss listen and tick the sounds they hear.
- Play the recording again with pauses for Ss to repeat chorally and/or individually.

Answer Key

	/ei/	/ai/		/ei/	/ai/
skate	✓		mind		✓
weight	✓		sail	✓	
height		✓	fight		✓

Reading & Writing

7 **Aim** To read for cohesion & coherence

- Read through the Word formation box with Ss, explaining any unknown words.
- Give Ss time to read the text and complete the gaps with the correct words formed from the words in brackets.
- Then elicit answers from Ss around the class.

Answer Key

1 discussion
2 fitness
3 friendships
4 jogging
5 neighbourhood
6 achievement
7 difference
8 personality

8 **Aim** To learn about justifying arguments

- Go through the ***Writing Tip*** with Ss.
- Ask Ss to read the blog entry again and list the arguments, then find the reasons the writer gives. List Ss' answers on the board.

Suggested Answer Key

Team sports

Arguments	**Reasons**
sociable	→ lead to friendships
part of team ... continue	→ don't ... teammates

Individual sports

Arguments	**Reasons**
independent	→ flexible
responsible ... fit/proud	→ managed it alone

Writing

9 **Aim** To prepare for a writing task

- Ask Ss to read the rubric and then give them time to answer the questions.
- Check Ss' answers.

Answer Key

1 I am going to write a blog entry. It is for people interested in fitness.
2 I am going to write about the benefits of getting fit with a trainer and with an exercise class.
3 It should be 120-150 words long.

10 **Aim** To listen for ideas

Ask Ss to copy the table into their notebook and then play the recording twice. Ss listen and complete the table. Check Ss' answers.

Suggested Answer Key

1 different
2 encouragement
3 harder
4 friendship

11 **Aim** To write a blog entry about ways to get fit

- Explain the task and then give Ss time to write their blog entry using their answers in Ex. 10 and following the plan.
- Ask various Ss to share their answers with the class.
- Alternatively, assign the task as HW and check Ss' answers in the next lesson.

Suggested Answer key

Personal Trainer or Exercise Classes?

Today, I want to have a discussion about the benefits of both using a personal trainer and exercise classes to get fit.

Personal trainers

A personal trainer can give you personal attention. Everyone is different and you can work out a programme that suits you. Also, a personal trainer gives you encouragement. They are always next to you and they don't let you give up.

Exercise classes

Exercise classes involve a group of people so there is a great sense of team spirit. You encourage each other and this makes you try harder. Also, you can meet new people in an exercise class and develop friendships. This makes you want to attend the class more often because you will meet your friends.

So, whether you choose to get fit with a personal trainer or with exercise classes, both options have advantages. You should choose whichever suits you best.

Values

Initiate a class discussion about the meaning of the quotation and encourage Ss to participate.

9 Want to play?

Suggested Answer

A: I think the quotation means that we can win individual games in team sports if a few players are talented but to win more important competitions we need to work as a team.

B: Yes, I agree. I think it also means that there are a lot of people behind and around sportspeople who help them to progress and become champions.

C: This also applies to everyday life. Think of people at work. It definitely needs talent to achieve a goal, but when people work as a team, the results are often amazing.

Culture 9

Reading & Listening

1 **Aim** To introduce the topic; to listen and read for specific information

- Ask Ss to look at the picture, and elicit Ss' guesses in answer to the questions about hurling.

Suggested Answer Key

I think the sport is played on a field or pitch with a stick and a ball in a similar way to hockey. I think players try to score goals by putting the ball in the goal. I think it is a team sport.

- Play the recording. Ss listen to and read the text to find out.

2 **Aim** To read for detail (answer questions)

- Ask Ss to read the text again and then answer the questions.
- Check Ss' answers around the class.
- Then Ss explain the words in bold.

Answer Key

1 Over 3,000 years old
2 A stick made of ash wood that is flat with a wide end
3 70 minutes
4 3 points
5 150 km/h

Suggested Answer Key

earliest (adj): oldest or longest ago
shape (n): the physical form of sth
shaped (pp): having the shape/form of sth
score (v): to get a point or a goal in a sport or game
in total (phr): the amount you get when other amounts are added together

- Give Ss time to look up the meanings of the words in the **Check these words** box in the Word List.
- Play the video for Ss and elicit their comments.

Speaking & Writing

3 **Aim** To develop critical thinking skills

Explain the task and ask Ss to work in groups and consider their answers. Ask various Ss to share their answers with the class.

Suggested Answer Key

Name: tableball
Players: two teams of two players each
Equipment: table, football, net
Place: in a sports hall or large room
Rules: two players in each team use their feet or legs to hit a football over a net on a table. If the other team doesn't return the ball, the first team gets a point. The winning team is the one with the most points after 60 minutes.

Tableball is a sport with two teams of two players each. You need a table, a football and a net to play it. You play it in a sports hall or large room. The rules are that two players in each team use their feet or legs to hit a football over a net on a table. If the other team doesn't return the ball, the first team gets a point. The winning team is the one with the most points after 60 minutes.

4 **Aim** ICT To develop research skills; to write a short text about a sport

- Explain the task and give Ss time to research online and collect information about a sport that started in their country and is still played today. Ss make notes under the headings and then use their notes to write a short article about it.
- Ask various Ss to read their articles to the class.
- Alternatively, assign the task as HW and ask Ss to read out their articles in the next lesson.

Suggested Answer Key

name: lacrosse
players: 10 players in each team
equipment: ball, stick (crosse), helmet, gloves, shoulder pads
place: a lacrosse field (100 metres long and 55 metres wide)
rules: use a crosse to catch, carry, pass and shoot a solid rubber ball; score by shooting the ball into the opponent's goal

Lacrosse started in Canada hundreds of years ago. The Native Americans invented it around the 12th century. It is still played today and there are three different versions of it. In field lacrosse there are 10 players in each team. They play with a ball and a stick called a crosse which is triangular in shape and is strung with

loose netting. The players wear a helmet, gloves and shoulder pads because it is a full contact sport and they need to protect themselves from injury. They play on a lacrosse field which is 100 metres long and 55 metres wide. There are two goals. The players use a crosse to catch, carry, pass and shoot a solid rubber ball. They score by shooting the ball into the opponent's goal.

Background Information

Ireland (The Republic of Ireland) is a small island country on the western edge of Europe. The capital city is Dublin. It has a population of about 4.5 million.

Review 9

Vocabulary

1 (Aim) To consolidate vocabulary from the unit

- Explain the task.
- Give Ss time to complete it.
- Check Ss' answers.

Answer Key

1	boxing	4	ice skating
2	cricket	5	cycling
3	Motor racing	6	squash

2 (Aim) To consolidate vocabulary from the unit

- Explain the task.
- Give Ss time to complete it.
- Check Ss' answers.

Answer Key

1	win	5	court	9	beats
2	sailing	6	extreme	10	chance
3	element	7	pool		
4	face	8	team		

3 (Aim) To practise prepositional phrases and phrasal verbs

- Explain the task.
- Give Ss time to complete it.
- Check Ss' answers.

Answer Key

1	about	3	with	5	under
2	on	4	into		

Grammar

4 (Aim) To practise the infinitive/-ing form

- Explain the task.
- Give Ss time to complete it.
- Check Ss' answers.

Answer Key

1	going	3	to train	5	go
2	to record	4	working	6	to drink

5 (Aim) To practise forms of the infinitive/-ing form

- Explain the task.
- Give Ss time to complete it.
- Check Ss' answers.

Answer Key

1	to have been crying	3	to go
2	being hit	4	have stopped

6 (Aim) To practise singular/plural nouns

- Explain the task.
- Give Ss time to complete it.
- Check Ss' answers.

Answer Key

1 are	2 is	3 are	4 Is	5 is

Everyday English

7 (Aim) To match exchanges

- Explain the task.
- Give Ss time to complete it.
- Check Ss' answers.

Answer Key

1 c	2 b	3 e	4 a	5 d

Competences

Ask Ss to assess their own performance in the unit by ticking the items according to how competent they feel for each of the listed activities.

Values: Appreciation

1 **Aim** To introduce the topic; to predict the content of the text and to read for specific information

- Elicit what Ss do to show they are grateful to sb for sth. Elicit Ss' guesses as to whether this may be mentioned in the text.
- Ss read the text quickly to find out.

Suggested Answer Key

I say 'thank you', give a thank-you card, give flowers or buy the person a coffee, a gift or a meal depending what it was that they did for me.

The text mentions saying 'thank you', writing a thank-you note and buying a gift.

2 **Aim** To listen and read for specific information (matching headings to paragraphs)

- Ask Ss to read the headings A-F and then give them time to read the text and match them to the paragraphs.
- Play the recording for Ss to check their answers.
- Then Ss explain the words in bold.

Answer Key

1   D (can't you ... for a moment?)
2   F (It used ... the phrase!)
3   A (messages are ... more personal)
4   C (It doesn't have to ... with care; A pen ... write something.)

Suggested Answer Key

grateful (adj): *thankful*
appreciate (v): *to value*
facial expression (phr): *the look on sb's face*
frown (n): *an unhappy/angry expression*
personal (adj): *for a particular person*
old-fashioned (adj): *not modern*
in mind (idm): *in sb's thoughts*
pick up (phr v): *to lift sth using your hands*

- Play the video for Ss and elicit their comments.

3 **Aim** **THINK** To develop critical thinking skills; to identify the purpose of a text

Give Ss time to consider the questions and then elicit answers from Ss around the class.

Suggested Answer Key

The author's purpose is to entertain and inform the reader. She has been quite successful because it is interesting and entertaining to read.

4 **Aim** To consolidate information in a text and apply it to realistic situations

- Give Ss time to read the situations and consider their answers and then discuss their answers in closed pairs.
- Then ask various Ss to share their answers with the class.

Suggested Answer Key

If I spent my summer holidays at a friend's house, I would buy my friend and their parents a thoughtful gift and write a thank-you note to go with it to show my appreciation.
If my friend helped me with my homework, I would smile and say 'thank you' to show my appreciation.
If a person I worked with helped me move into my new flat, I would take him/her out for a meal or invite him/her to my flat and cook a meal for him/her to show my appreciation.

Public Speaking Skills

1 a) **Aim** To present a public speaking task

Ask Ss to read the task. Elicit what it asks for.

Answer Key

It is asking me to give a farewell speech for a colleague because it is his/her last day.

b) **Aim** To analyse a model public speaking task; to identify emotional language

- Play the recording. Ss listen and read the model and underline the emotional language.
- Check Ss' answers.

Suggested Answer Key

The speaker sounds sorry to see their colleague leave. Some phrases that communicate emotion are: the day has come for us to say goodbye, unfortunately for us, I can't imagine ... each day; we will miss you very much ... for the future, Jane, thank you ... good luck

2 **Aim** To identify content in a farewell speech

- Explain the task and give Ss time to do the task. Elicit Ss' answers.

Answer Key

To be ticked: *3 (become much better at building snowmen; I wish ... the cold; we will get some peace; get my hands on it first; to be honest ... eventually; which you can wear ... Celsius) 4 (positive attitude; Right from ... coffee; Jane has always made ... each day)*

3 **Aim** To give a farewell speech

- Explain the task and give Ss time to consider the situation and make notes under the headings in their notebooks.
- Tell Ss to then use their notes to prepare their farewell speech.
- Ask various Ss to give their farewell speech to the class.
- Alternatively, assign the task as HW and have Ss give their speeches in the next lesson.

Suggested Answer Key

It's time to say goodbye to our dear friend, Jack. Tomorrow, he sets off for a new life in Australia where he can learn to surf and become a barbecue expert. While we would like him to stay, we understand that avoiding poisonous insects and dangerous animals in Australia is what he wants to do in life, and so we wish him the very best. I asked if I could go with him, but it turns out his suitcase is already full!

I'll never forget the first day we met at college. I was so nervous when I arrived for my first lecture, but I was delighted to find someone who shared my love of video games and who had a silly sense of humour like me! Although, perhaps it would have been better to pay a bit more attention to that lecture!

During the five years that I've known Jack, he's shown himself to be generous, a great friend and only a little bit irritating.

Jack, we wish you lots of luck on your adventure in the land down under. You deserve the very best and you will definitely be missed by us all! Make sure you stay in touch ... or else!

10 Tech World

Topic	
In this unit, Ss will explore the topics of chores and digital communication.	
10a Reading & Vocabulary	**82-83**
Lesson objectives: To learn vocabulary related to chores, to listen and read for gist, to read for specific information & global understanding (multiple choice), to learn collocations, to learn prepositional phrases, to practise words easily confused, to learn phrasal verbs with *get*, to talk about the drawbacks of robot assistants, to write a comment to post on a blog **Vocabulary:** Chores (*do the laundry, feed the pet, mop the floor, do DIY, water the plants, make the bed, do the ironing, serve meals, lay the table, cook dinner, do the vacuuming*), Nouns (*trade show, technology, maid, device, designer, app*); Verbs (*serve, connect, share, take, bring*); Phrasal verb (*get*); Adjective (*high-definition*); Phrase (*household item*)	
10b Grammar in Use	**84-85**
Lesson objectives: To learn/revise modals & modals of deduction	
10c Skills in Action	**86-87**
Lesson objectives: To learn vocabulary relating to digital communication, to listen for specific information (multiple matching), to act out a dialogue and practise everyday English for giving instructions, to learn the pronunciation of /əʊ/, /ɔː/, to read for cohesion & coherence (word formation), to write an article giving an opinion **Vocabulary:** Digital communication (*chat using an instant messaging service, send a text message, write a post/comment on a social networking site, make a call using a mobile phone, send a tweet, write an email, create or comment on a vlog, write or comment on a blog entry, video chat, make a call using a landline*)	
Culture 10	**88**
Lesson objectives: To listen and read for gist, to read for cohesion and coherence (missing sentences), to talk about a museum, to write about a museum of technology **Vocabulary:** Nouns (*gramophone, decade, chance*); Verbs (*invent, display, handle*); Phrasal verb (*grow up*); Adjectives (*various, early*); Preposition (*throughout*)	
Review 10	**89**
Lesson objectives: To test/consolidate vocabulary and grammar learnt throughout the unit, to practise everyday English	

Go through the objectives box and tell Ss that these are the topics, skills and activities this unit will cover.

10a

Vocabulary

1 a) Aim To present vocabulary related to chores

- Ask Ss to read the chores in the list and look at the pictures, and say which ones they can see.
- Elicit answers from Ss around the class.

Answer Key

A do DIY	E feed the pet
B water the plants	F lay the table
C do the ironing	G cook dinner
D make the bed	

b) Aim To talk about household chores

Ask various Ss around the class to tell the rest of the class if and how often they do the chores in Ex. 1a.

Suggested Answer Key

I sometimes water the plants.
I usually feed the pet.
I often make the bed.
I never do the ironing.

Reading

2 Aim To introduce the topic of a text and listen and read for gist

- Ask Ss to tell the class how they think robots can help in our everyday life and elicit various suggestions from Ss around the class.
- Play the recording. Ss listen to and read the text to find out.

Suggested Answer Key

Robots can help in our everyday lives by doing the housework and chores.

3 Aim To read for specific information & global understanding (multiple choice)

- Ask Ss to read the questions and the answer choices and underline the key words. Explain that the first and the last question can be answered from the whole text.
- Then give them time to read the text again and answer the questions.
- Check Ss' answers. Ss justify their answers.

Answer Key

1   A (whole text)
2   C (Para 2 last sentence and Para 3)
3   D (Para 3 2nd sentence)
4   C (Para 4 1st sentence)
5   D (whole text)

- Then give Ss time to explain the words in bold using their dictionaries to help them as necessary.
- Check Ss' answers around the class.

Suggested Answer Key

technology (n): *the practical use of scientific discoveries*
maid (n): *a person who works as a servant in a home*
designer (n): *a person who thinks of sth new and draws plans for it*
serve (v): *to give food or drink to sb*
connect (v): *to join two things (physically, electronically or wirelessly)*
app (n): *a type of software that works on a smartphone*
share (sth with sb) (v): *to communicate; to pass on*
awesome (adj): *fantastic*

- Give Ss time to look up the meanings of the words in the **Check these words** box in the Word List.
- Play the video for Ss and elicit their comments.

4 Aim To consolidate new vocabulary

- Explain the task and give Ss time to complete the phrases using the words in the list.
- Then check Ss answers by having Ss use the phrases in sentences of their own.

Answer Key

1	trade	5	high-definition
2	robot	6	vacuum
3	household	7	smartphone
4	washing	8	family

Trade shows *are great places to learn about technology.*
It would be great to have a **robot maid** *to help with chores.*
Doing the ironing and the laundry are **household chores***.*
Most people have a **washing machine** *in their home these days to wash their clothes.*
My smartphone has a **high-definition camera** *so I can take amazing photos.*
We have a cordless **vacuum cleaner** *at home to vacuum the carpets.*
I can get directions on my phone through a **smartphone app***.*
All **family members** *in our home, mum, dad, my brother and I, help with the chores.*

5 Aim To consolidate prepositional phrases from a text

- Give Ss time to read the sentences and choose the correct prepositions.
- Then check Ss' answers. Ask Ss to add these prepositional phrases in the Prepositions section in their notebook.

Answer Key

1	with	3	to	5	between
2	on	4	on		

6 Aim To understand words easily confused

- Ask Ss to read the sentences and then complete them with either **take** or **bring** using their dictionaries if necessary.
- Check Ss' answers.

Answer Key

1	bring	2	take	3	take	4	bring

7 Aim To learn phrasal verbs with *get*

- Ask Ss to read the phrasal verbs box and make sure that Ss understand the definitions.
- Then give Ss time to complete the task and check their answers.
- Tell Ss to write the phrasal verbs in the Phrasal Verbs list at the back of their notebooks and include the definitions. Tell Ss to revise this list from time to time and to add to it every time they come across a new phrasal verb.

Answer Key

1	by	3	along/on	5	over
2	across	4	on		

Speaking & Writing

8 Aim THINK To develop critical thinking skills; to talk about the drawbacks of a robot assistant

- Ask Ss to work in closed pairs. Give them time to consider their answers and discuss what they think the drawbacks of having a robot assistant would be.
- Ask various Ss to share their answers with the class.

Suggested Answer Key

I think the main drawback would be that it would be expensive to buy a robot assistant and if it needed repairs that would be expensive too. I think another drawback would be that you would worry about it breaking down or going out of control, so you may feel you couldn't leave it to work by itself. You may have to stay home and watch it doing its work and this would be a waste of time.

10 Tech World

9 Aim To write a comment to post on a blog

- Give Ss time to consider their answers – both positive and negative – and present them to the class. Make notes on the board. Ss use the ideas to write a comment to post on the blog expressing their opinion on having robots as home assistants.
- Ask various Ss to read out their comments to the class.
- Alternatively, assign the task as HW and ask Ss to share their answers in the next lesson.

Suggested Answer Key

I think having a robot like this sounds great. It would save us from doing a lot of household chores. However, I also think that it would be expensive to buy and if it needed repairs that would be expensive too. I would also be concerned about leaving it to work by itself in my home in case it broke down or went out of control.

10b Grammar in Use

1 Aim To learn/revise modals

- Ask Ss to read the dialogue. Then elicit from Ss around the class what each of the modal verbs in bold are used to express from the list of uses. Ss can work in closed pairs to do the task. Check Ss' answers.

Answer Key

may – permission
have to – obligation
needn't – a lack of necessity
should – advice
mustn't – prohibition
shall – an offer
need to – necessity
might – possibility
would – a request
can – ability

2 Aim To practise modals

- Go through the theory box with Ss. You can ask Ss to provide their own examples if you like. Refer Ss to the **Grammar Reference** section for more information.
- Explain the task and give Ss time to complete it.
- Check Ss' answers.

Answer Key

1 *Shall (offer)*
2 *ought to (advice)*
3 *needn't (lack of necessity)*
4 *might (possibility)*
5 *Can (permission)*

6 *Would (request)*
7 *Could (request)*
8 *have to (obligation)*

3 Aim To practise modals

- Explain the task and give Ss time to complete it.
- Check Ss' answers.

Answer Key

1 *needn't*	4 *Shall*	7 *May*
2 *Would*	5 *can't*	8 *might*
3 *couldn't*	6 *should*	

4 Aim To practise modals

- Explain the task. Go through the rules and explain any unknown vocabulary. Point out that Ss need to pay attention to the beginning of each sentence as this will help them do the task. Read the example for the first sentence and explain that **it's not necessary** suggests that the modal to be used will be **needn't**. Give Ss time to complete the task using the list of rules and following the example.
- Elicit answers from Ss around the class.

Suggested Answer Key

You mustn't access social media on library computers.
You have to wear earphones when you use sound on a computer.
You should log out of your email account after using a computer.
You can use a computer for up to two hours.
Our IT department might check users' Internet activity.

5 Aim To practise modals

- Explain the task and give Ss time to complete it using the modals in the list. Point out that Ss need to pay attention to the beginning of each sentence as this will help them do the task.
- Check Ss' answers around the class.

Suggested Answer Key

1 *She wasn't able to find a Wi-Fi signal.*
2 *You mustn't download films without paying for them.*
3 *My older brother might give me his old tablet.*
4 *Would you help me create a presentation?*
5 *You can use the Internet to research for your project.*
6 *You need to have an email address to shop online.*

6 Aim To learn/revise modals of deduction

- Go through the examples in the theory box with Ss. Elicit that we use **must** when we are sure that sth is true, **can't/couldn't** when we are sure that sth is not

true and ***may/might/could*** to express possibility. Refer Ss to the **Grammar Reference** section for more information.

- Give Ss time to complete the sentences using the modals in the list.
- Check Ss' answers around the class.

Answer Key

1 can't/couldn't	4 may/might/could
2 can	5 must
3 may/might/could	

7 **Aim** To practise modals

- Explain the task and give Ss time to complete it. Point out that Ss need to use the correct form of the infinitive after **must**, **can't**, **may/might/could**.
- Check Ss' answers.

Answer Key

1 may be online	3 may not have found
2 can't have downloaded	4 must have sent
	5 can't be using

10c Skills in Action

Vocabulary

1 **Aim** To present vocabulary related to digital communication

- Ask Ss to look at the graph and read the list of communication habits.
- Draw Ss' attention to the language at the bottom and explain how we can refer to percentages.
- Read out the example and then ask various Ss to use the language to make similar sentences.

Suggested Answer Key

Three quarters of teens in the survey send text messages.
Most of the teens in the survey write posts/comments on social networking sites.
Half of the teens in the survey make calls using mobile phones.
A third of teens in the survey send tweets.
A quarter of teens in the survey write emails.
A few of the teens in the survey create or comment on vlogs, write or comment on blog entries and video chat.
Very few of the teens in the survey make calls using a landline.

2 **Aim** To personalise the topic

Ask various Ss around the class to tell the rest of the class about their communication habits.

Ss' own answers

Listening

3 **Aim** To listen for specific information (multiple matching)

- Ask Ss to read statements A-E and underline the key words.
- Play the recording twice. Ss listen and choose their answers.
- Check Ss' answers. You can play the recording again with pauses for Ss to check their answers.

Answer Key

1 E	2 B	3 C	4 D

Everyday English

4 **Aim** To listen and read for specific information

- Ask Ss to look at the steps in the pictures.
- Then play the recording. Ss listen to and read the dialogue and put the steps in the correct order.
- Check Ss' answers.

Answer Key

A 4	B 3	C 1	D 2

5 **Aim** To role-play a dialogue giving instructions; to sequence steps in instructions

- Explain the task and ask Ss to act out the dialogue in Ex. 4 in pairs.
- Write this diagram on the board for Ss to follow.

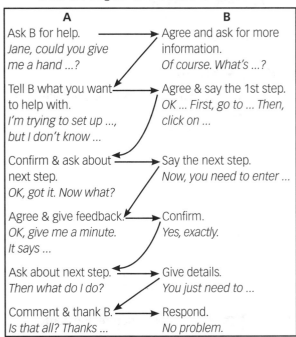

A	B
Ask B for help. *Jane, could you give me a hand ...?*	Agree and ask for more information. *Of course. What's ...?*
Tell B what you want to help with. *I'm trying to set up ..., but I don't know ...*	Agree & say the 1st step. *OK ... First, go to ... Then, click on ...*
Confirm & ask about next step. *OK, got it. Now what?*	Say the next step. *Now, you need to enter ...*
Agree & give feedback. *OK, give me a minute. It says ...*	Confirm. *Yes, exactly.*
Ask about next step. *Then what do I do?*	Give details. *You just need to ...*
Comment & thank B. *Is that all? Thanks ...*	Respond. *No problem.*

- Monitor the activity around the class and offer assistance as necessary.

10 Tech World

- Then ask some pairs to act out their dialogues in front of the class.

Suggested Answer Key

A: Jane, could you give me a hand with something?
B: Of course, Jack. What's the problem?
A: I'm trying to set up online banking but I don't know where to start.
B: OK, that's easy. First, go to the website of the bank. Then click on 'Register for online banking".
A: OK, got it. Now what?
B: Now, you need to enter the information it asks for and you'll get a customer number.
A: OK, give me a minute ... I've done that. Now it says they will send me the activation code.
B: Yes, exactly.
A: Then what do I do?
B: You just need to enter your customer number and code. After that, choose a PIN and password.
A: Is that all? Thanks for your help, Jane.
B: No problem.

Pronunciation

6 **Aim** To learn the pronunciations of /əʊ/, /ɔː/

- Play the recording. Ss listen and repeat chorally and/or individually.
- Elicit other words with these sounds from Ss around the class.

Suggested Answer Key

/əʊ/ blow, coat
/ɔː/ floor, taught

Reading & Writing

7 **Aim** To read for cohesion & coherence (word formation)

- Go through the theory box and explain any points Ss are unsure of.
- Then give Ss time to read the text and complete the gaps with the correct adverbs formed from the adjectives in brackets.
- Check answers on the board.

Answer Key

1 easily	4 quickly	7 strongly
2 definitely	5 directly	8 probably
3 extremely	6 specifically	

8 a) **Aim** To read for structure and content

- Ask Ss to read the article again and complete the table.
- Check Ss' answers on the board.

Answer Key

Viewpoints	Reasons/Examples
it is fast	you can read & reply quickly without connecting to the Internet
it is private	it goes directly from your phone to another phone

b) **Aim** To identify phrases used to express opinion

Read out the language box and then elicit examples of phrases used to express opinion in the article from Ss around the class.

Answer Key

To my mind ..., I strongly believe ...

9 **Aim** To identify starting/ending techniques in an article

- Read out the **Writing Tip** and answer any questions Ss may have about starting/ending techniques in an article.
- Then ask Ss to read the article again and identify the techniques the writer has used to start/end the article.
- Check Ss' answers.

Answer Key

start = general statement
end = addressing the reader directly

Writing

10 a) **Aim** To prepare for a writing task

- Ask Ss to read the rubric and underline the key words. Then give them time to match the viewpoints to the reasons/examples.
- Check Ss' answers.

Answer Key

Key words: English-language magazine, does social media improve communication? article, 120-150 words

1 b   2 a   3 c

b) **Aim** To write an article giving an opinion

- Explain the task and then give them time to write their article using their answers in Ex. 10a and following the plan.
- Ask various Ss to share their answers with the class.
- Alternatively, assign the task as HW and check Ss' answers in the next lesson.

Tech World 10

Suggested Answer Key

Many people these days use social media to communicate. But does it improve communication? To my mind, it does in a number of ways.

Firstly, social media is user-friendly. For example, it is simple to use and people can chat and post pictures and videos very easily.

Secondly, social media provides the opportunity to meet new people. You can join all sorts of different groups and make friends with people with similar interests to you.

All in all, I strongly believe social media improves communication because it is a great networking tool and it is easy to use. After all, don't most of us use it every day?

Values

Ask Ss to explain the quotation in their mother tongue. Then initiate a class discussion about the meaning of the quotation and encourage all Ss to participate.

Suggested Answer Key

A: *I think the quotation means that it doesn't matter if machines can or will be able to think, it matters if people can think.*

B: *Yes, I agree. It could also suggest that machines can only follow their programming and react to their environment in certain ways and people might be the same.*

A: *That's very interesting.*

Culture 10

Reading & Listening

1 **(Aim)** **To introduce the topic and to read for gist**
   - Ask Ss to look at the pictures and elicit what they show.
   - Then ask Ss to say how they are different to the modern versions we have of these devices.
   - Ss read the text to find out.

Suggested Answer Key

I can see old electronic devices. There's an old-fashioned telephone, a computer and a machine that looks like a metal box – it might be an old camera but I'm not sure.

Computers are much smaller nowadays and work faster. We also have laptops and tablets which we can take wherever we go.

Cameras these days are smaller and more advanced with high-definition photos.

Nowadays we use mobile phones and smartphones which are very light. They have built-in cameras that can connect to the Internet so we can do so many

more things with them than just calling as happened with old-fashioned telephones.

2 **(Aim)** **To read for cohesion and coherence (missing sentences)**
   - Ask Ss to read sentences A-E and then give them time to read the text again and match the sentences to gaps 1-4. Remind Ss there is one extra sentence. Ask Ss to look for words before/after each gap as this will help them do the task.
   - Check Ss' answers and then give Ss time to explain the words in bold by using the Word List or their dictionaries to help them. Elicit explanations from Ss around the class.

Answer Key

1   D (last 250 years – up until around 1760)
2   C (the Museum of Technology in Lincolnshire, England – This museum)
3   E (Most of the devices – handle lots of items – many still work)
4   B (younger people – A lot of children – older people)

Suggested Answer Key

invent (v): *to come up with the idea for a new object/ machine*
throughout (adv): *during a period of time*
various (adj): *different*
earliest (adj): *first, primitive, ancient*
chance (n): *opportunity*

   - Give Ss time to look up the meanings of the words in the **Check these words** box in the Word List.
   - Play the video for Ss and elicit their comments.

3 **(Aim)** **(THINK)** **To develop critical thinking skills; to express an opinion**
   - Read out the question and play the recording.
   - Ss listen to and read the text and then share their answers with their partner.
   - Ask various Ss to share their answers with the class.

Suggested Answer Key

I think a visit to this museum can be interesting to 10-year-old children because they will be able to see how fast technology has changed in recent history. They have grown up with smartphones, digital cameras and huge TVs and all the other modern devices we have today. They would see the difference between how these things are now and how they used to be and they would find it very exciting trying to imagine life then and compare it to their own.

10 Tech World

Speaking & Writing

4 **Aim** **ICT** **To write a short text about a museum of technology in one's country; to give a presentation**

- Explain the task and give Ss time to research online and collect information about a museum of technology in their country or another country and make notes under the headings. Ss use their notes to write a short article about it.
- Ask various Ss to present their articles to the class.
- Alternatively, assign the task as HW and ask Ss to present their articles in the next lesson.

Suggested Answer Key

Name: *Deutsches Teknikmuseum*
Location: *Berlin*
Opening times: *Tues – Fri 9 am to 5 pm, Sat – Sun 10 am – 6 pm, Mondays closed*
History: *founded in 1982, some of the collections date back 120 years*
Visitors can see: *old and new technology, wide range of exhibitions including film technology, photo technology, aerospace, telecommunications, transport, navigation and networks*

The Deutsches Teknikmuseum in Berlin is a fantastic technology museum that is very popular with both children and adults. Founded in 1982, some of the collections are 120 years old. Visitors can see old and new technology in a wide range of exhibitions including film technology, photo technology, aerospace, telecommunications, transport, navigation and networks. The Deutsches Teknikmuseum is open from Tuesday to Friday from 9 am to 5 pm and on Saturday and Sunday from 10 am to 6 pm. It is closed on Mondays. If you are ever in Berlin, be sure to pay a visit.

Background Information

Lincolnshire is a county in the East Midlands of England on the east coast. Major towns and cities include Lincoln, Grimsby, Scunthorpe, Boston, Cleethorpes and Skegness. It covers an area of about 7,000 km² and the population is just over 750,000 people. The city of Lincoln is the county town.

Review 10

Vocabulary

1 **Aim** **To consolidate vocabulary from the unit**

- Explain the task.
- Give Ss time to complete it.
- Check Ss' answers.

Answer Key

1 does	3 mopped	5 fed
2 take	4 do	

2 **Aim** **To consolidate vocabulary from the unit**

- Explain the task.
- Give Ss time to complete it.
- Check Ss' answers.

Answer Key

1 high-definition	6 text
2 instant	7 app
3 social	8 trade
4 blog	9 video
5 landline	

3 **Aim** **To practise prepositional phrases and phrasal verbs**

- Explain the task.
- Give Ss time to complete it.
- Check Ss' answers.

Answer Key

1 on	3 on	5 to
2 across	4 over	6 between

Grammar

4 **Aim** **To practise modals**

- Explain the task.
- Give Ss time to complete it.
- Check Ss' answers.

Answer Key

1 could	4 might
2 can	5 can't
3 wasn't able to	

5 **Aim** To practise modals

- Explain the task.
- Give Ss time to complete it.
- Check Ss' answers.

Answer Key

1 *couldn't open the file*
2 *don't have to download this program*
3 *may use my tablet*
4 *mustn't eat or drink in the computer lab*
5 *Would you help me print the document*

Everyday English

6 **Aim** To match exchanges

- Explain the task.
- Give Ss time to complete it.
- Check Ss' answers.

Answer Key

1 *d*   2 *c*   3 *e*   4 *b*   5 *a*

Competences

Ask Ss to assess their own performance in the unit by ticking the items according to how competent they feel for each of the listed activities.

11 Food for Thought

Topic
In this unit, Ss will explore the topics of food, ways of cooking, tastes and customer complaints.

11a Reading & Vocabulary	90-91

Lesson objectives: To learn vocabulary relating to ways of cooking and tastes, to listen and read for specific information, to read for specific information (T/F/DS), to learn prepositional phrases, to learn collocations, to practise words easily confused, to learn phrasal verbs with *keep*, to talk about street food, to research, write about and present street food in one's country
Vocabulary: Ways of cooking (*fried, roasted, grilled, baked, boiled*), Tastes (*spicy, sweet, salty, sour*), Nouns (*pitta, tzatziki, filling, gravy, topping, seconds, silkworm, vendor, toothpick, pastry, choice, dough, dessert, desert, course, plate, receipt, recipe, dish, meal*); Verbs (*ignore, trust*); Phrasal verb (*keep*); Adjectives (*nutritious, disgusted*); Phrase (*upright grill*)

11b Grammar in Use	92-93

Lesson objectives: To learn/revise comparisons, to learn/revise countable/uncountable nous, to learn/revise quantifiers & partitives, to learn/revise *some/any/no/every* & compounds

11c Skills in Action	94-95

Lesson objectives: To learn vocabulary for customer complaints, to listen for specific information (gap fill), to act out a dialogue and practise everyday English for making a complaint, to learn the pronunciation of /ð/, /z/, to read for cohesion & coherence (word formation), to write an online complaint form
Vocabulary: Customer complaints (*order, bill, manager, wrong change, sell-by date, credit card, full refund, receipt, note, change tables*)

Culture 11	96

Lesson objectives: To read for gist, to listen and read for cohesion and coherence (multiple choice cloze), to talk about organising a food festival, to present a food festival from one's country
Vocabulary: Nouns (*stall, tastes, grounds, food critic, workshop*), Verbs (*promote, sample, raise*); Adjectives (*delicious, annual, outdoor, fun*); Phrase (*sink your teeth into*)

Review 11	97

Lesson objectives: To test/consolidate vocabulary and grammar learnt throughout the unit, to practise everyday English

Go through the objectives box and tell Ss that these are the topics, skills and activities this unit will cover.

11a

Reading & Listening

1 **Aim** **To introduce the topic; to present cooking methods; to listen and read for specific information**

- Direct Ss' attention to the pictures and elicit which dishes are cooked in the ways listed. Explain/Elicit any unknown words in the cooking methods and then elicit what Ss think the dishes are made of.
- Play the recording. Ss listen to and read the article to find out.

Answer Key

Gyros is grilled. Poutine is fried. Beondegi is boiled. Empanadas are fried or baked.
Gyros is made from meat served in a pitta with onions, tomato, chips and a sauce called tzatziki.
Poutine is made from fried chips, soft cheese and gravy. Beondegi is made from boiled silkworms.
Empanada is made from pastry with chicken and onion or boiled eggs and olives.

2 a) **Aim** **To read for specific information (T/F/DS)**

- Ask Ss to read the statements and underline the key words.
- Then give them time to read the text again and mark the statements according to what they read.
- Check Ss' answers.

Answer Key

1 DS
2 T (The meat ... tzatziki)
3 T (This Canadian ... gravy.)
4 F (You can find this dish in fancy restaurants)
5 F (with a toothpick)
6 T (nutritious)
7 DS
8 F (Often, ... have.)

b) **Aim** **To consolidate new vocabulary**

- Give Ss time to explain the words in bold using their dictionaries to help them as necessary.
- Check Ss' answers around the class.

Suggested Answer Key

filling (adj): *making one feel full after eating sth*
ignore (v): *to pay no attention to sth*
trust (v): *to believe in sth*

Food for Thought

seconds (pl n): *a second serving*
disgusted (adj): *feeling strong dislike*
choice (n): *variety*

As an extension, ask Ss to read through the text and list words under the headings: meat – dairy products – vegetables – other.

Suggested Answer Key

meat: *meat, chicken*
dairy products: *yoghurt, cheese,*
vegetables: *onions, garlic, cucumber, tomato, olives*
other: *chips, sauce, tzatziki, gravy, silkworms, dough, boiled egg*

- Give Ss time to look up the meanings of the words in the **Check these words** box in the Word List.
- Play the video for Ss and elicit their comments.

Vocabulary

3 **Aim** To learn vocabulary related to tastes

- Go through the box with Ss making sure they understand the meanings. Ss use the words in bold to complete the sentences.
- Check Ss' answers.

Answer Key

1	salty	3	sour
2	spicy	4	sweet

4 **Aim** To consolidate prepositional phrases from a text

- Give Ss time to read the sentences and choose the correct prepositions.
- Then check Ss' answers.

Answer Key

1	At	3	with	5	of
2	For	4	with	6	for

5 **Aim** To consolidate new vocabulary

- Explain the task and give Ss time to complete the phrases using the words in the list, referring back to the text as necessary.
- Then check Ss' answers.
- Elicit Ss' own sentences using the phrases.

Answer Key

1	street	3	grilled	5	soft	7	paper
2	travel	4	fancy	6	food	8	boiled

Suggested Answer Key

Street food is usually cheaper than in restaurants.
Hank is a **travel writer** who publishes articles about all the places he visits.

Grilled meat is healthier than fried meat because you don't use oil.
Most **fancy restaurants** are too expensive for me!
The French are famous for **soft cheeses** like brie and camembert.
Snacks sold from **food trucks** are becoming very common in my city.
They serve home-made lemonade in **paper cups** at the street market.
I like my **boiled eggs** cooked for just two minutes before I take them out of the water.

6 **Aim** To understand words easily confused

- Ask Ss to read the sentences and then choose the correct words to complete them using their dictionaries as necessary.
- Check Ss' answers.

Answer Key

1	dessert	3	recipe
2	course	4	dish

- As an extension, ask Ss to make sentences using the other options.

Suggested Answer Key

1. The Sahara Desert is in Africa.
2. What's on your plate, Jeff?
3. Here's your change and receipt, sir.
4. Most people eat three meals a day.

7 **Aim** To learn phrasal verbs with *keep*

- Ask Ss to read the phrasal verbs box and make sure that Ss understand the definitions.
- Then give Ss time to complete the task and check their answers.
- Tell Ss to write the phrasal verbs in the Phrasal Verbs list at the back of their notebooks and include the definitions. Tell Ss to revise this list from time to time and to add to it every time they come across a new phrasal verb.

Answer Key

1	off	4	away from
2	out	5	on
3	up with		

Speaking & Writing

8 **Aim** **THINK** To develop critical thinking skills; to talk about street food

Give Ss time to consider their answers and then ask various Ss to share their answers with the class.

11 Food for Thought

Suggested Answer Key

I tried chimney cakes in Prague in the Czech Republic last year. It's a delicious pastry made with soft dough and covered in sugar and cinnamon. You can also add chocolate sauce. I really liked it because it was sweet and filling.

9 **Aim** ICT **To develop research skills; to write about and present street food in one's country**

- Give Ss time to research online and collect information about a popular street food in their country and make notes under the headings.
- Then give them time to use their notes to write a short paragraph about it.
- Ask various Ss to present their street food to the class.
- Alternatively, assign the task as HW and ask Ss to share their answers in the next lesson.

Suggested Answer Key

name of food: *pizza*
country: *Italy*
how it's made & ingredients: *type of bread dough topped with cheese and different toppings baked in the oven, cut into triangular slices*
how it's eaten: *with the hands*
why it's popular: *it's a tasty and filling snack*

In Italy, a popular street food is pizza. It is a type of bread dough topped with cheese and different toppings and baked in the oven. Then it is cut into triangular slices. You can buy it by the slice and eat it with your hands. It is popular because it's a tasty and filling snack.

Background Information

Greece is in southern Europe. The capital city is Athens and the population is around 11 million people.

Canada is a large country in northern North America. It is the world's second largest country. It has a population of about 34 million people. The capital is Ottawa.

South Korea is a country in East Asia. 51.4 million people live there and the capital city is Seoul.

Argentina is a large country in South America. The capital city is Buenos Aires and the people speak Spanish. The population is around 43 million people.

11b Grammar in Use

1 **Aim** To learn/revise comparatives

- Quickly revise formation of comparisons. Write on the board: *Paul's is cheaper than Pete's but Pete's is*

more crowded than Paul's. Steve's is the cheapest and the most crowded of the three restaurants. Paul's and Pete's are not as cheap and crowded as Steve's. Elicit comparative forms *(cheaper, more crowded)* and superlative forms *(cheapest, the most crowded)*, formation and use.

- Ask Ss to read the theory and explain the types of comparisons.
- Refer Ss to the **Grammar Reference** section for more information.
- Then ask Ss to read the advert and elicit examples of types of comparisons in it.

Answer Key

Examples: *more than a market, more luxurious, more relaxed, not as crowded as, much easier, the most exciting*

2 **Aim** To practise comparatives

- Explain the task and give Ss time to complete it.
- Check Ss' answers.

Answer Key

1 lot	3 much	5 than
2 least	4 as	

3 a) **Aim** To practise comparisons

- Explain the task and give Ss time to complete it.
- Check Ss' answers and elicit reasons.

Answer Key

1 the rudest *(superlative – compared to all shop assistants ever met)*
2 spicier *(expressing the degree of difference)*
3 the best *(superlative – compared to all cafés in a place)*
4 the sweetest *(superlative – compared to all the desserts on the menu)*
5 the most crowded *(superlative – compared to all the shopping streets in the world)*
6 saltier *(expressing the degree of difference)*

b) **Aim** To practise comparisons; to personalise the topic

- Explain the task and give Ss time to complete it. Ss can work in closed pairs if you like.
- Check Ss' answers.

Suggested Answer Key

Mario's restaurant is more elegant than BCB, but JFS is the most elegant of all.
Astor Pizza House isn't as large as Tony's Pizzeria.
JM Burger is a bit cheaper than Perfect Burger. etc

4 **Aim** **To learn/revise countable/uncountable nouns, quantifiers & partitives**

- Go through the theory box with Ss. Refer them to the **Grammar Reference** section for more information.
- Elicit examples in the advert.

Answer Key

Examples:

countable nouns: *visit, walk, market, herbs, spices, items, scarves, city, paths, lifts, levels, evening, nightspots, restaurants, cafés, experience, lifetime*
uncountable nouns: *jewellery*
quantifier: *plenty of*
partitive: *pieces of*

5 **Aim** **To practise countable/uncountable nouns**

- Explain the task and give Ss time to complete it. Refer Ss to the **Grammar Reference** for plural endings.
- Check Ss' answers around the class.

Suggested Answer Key

2	C steaks	10	U
3	U	11	U
4	C onions	12	U
5	U	13	U
6	C carrots	14	C cucumbers
7	U	15	U
8	U	16	C lemons
9	C cabbages		

6 **Aim** **To revise/practise partitives**

- Elicit as many food/drinks that match the partitives in the list as possible.

Suggested Answer Key

packet – pasta, biscuits, rice, cereals, nuts, crisps
loaf – bread
cup – tea, coffee
slice – bread, cake, pizza, cheesecake, pie, cheese, ham, bacon
bar – chocolate, soap
bunch – grapes, bananas, flowers
tin – soup, peas, sweetcorn, beans, tomatoes
can – cola, lemonade, soda, orangeade
bag – sugar, flour
carton – milk, (orange/fruit) juice

- Then explain the task and give Ss time to complete it.
- Check Ss' answers.

Answer Key

1	slice	5	can	9	tin
2	loaf	6	cup	10	carton
3	bar	7	bunch		
4	packet	8	bag		

7 **Aim** **To practise quantifiers**

Explain the task and give Ss time to complete it. Check their answers.

Answer Key

1 *any, several – bookshop*
2 *few – newsagent's*
3 *some, many – baker's*
4 *any, couple – clothes shop*

8 **Aim** **To practise quantifiers in situational dialogues**

- Explain the task and ask Ss to work in pairs and act out similar dialogues to the ones in Ex. 7 using the pictures and relevant quantifiers.
- Monitor the activity around the class and then ask some Ss to act out their dialogues in front of the rest of the class.

Suggested Answer Key

A: *Here's your coffee.*
B: *Thanks. Could I have some breadsticks as well, please?*

A: *Hi, have you got any roses?*
B: *Yes, we've got them in several colours.*

A: *I'd like a few croissants please.*
B: *Of course, how many do you want?*

9 **Aim** **To revise/practise** *some/any/no/every* **& compounds**

- Go through the table with Ss and refer them to the **Grammar Reference** section for more information.
- Then give Ss time to complete the exchanges and check their answers.

Suggested Answer Key

1 *anything, some*
2 *anywhere, Every*
3 *someone/somebody, anyone/anybody*
4 *everywhere, no one/nobody*
5 *nothing, everything*
6 *Everything, nowhere*

10 **Aim** **To practise grammar from the lesson**

- Explain the task and give Ss time to complete it.
- Check Ss' answers.

Answer Key

1 *a few people*
2 *cheaper than*
3 *cooks as well as/cooks better than*
4 *is nothing*
5 *want any*

11 Food for Thought

Background Information

Dubai is the biggest city and emirate in the United Arab Emirates (UAE). It is on the southeast coast of the Persian Gulf. 2.1 million people live there.

11c Skills in Action

Vocabulary

1 **Aim** To present vocabulary related to customer complaints

- Ask Ss to read out the list of words/phrases and then read the gapped sentences.
- Give Ss time to complete the gaps with the words/ phrases in the list and check their answers in their dictionaries.

Answer Key

1 credit card, manager
2 change, note
3 tables
4 order
5 bill
6 sell-by date, refund, receipt

2 **Aim** To practise language for making customer complaints

- Explain the task. Ss prepare their answers.
- Monitor the activity around the class and then ask some Ss to share their answers with the class.

Suggested Answer Key

I bought this carton of milk from your shop this morning, but it's past its sell-by date. So, I'd like another one, please. I have the receipt with me.

I'm sorry, but I've just checked the bill and there are some drinks on it that we didn't have. Could you check it, please?

Excuse me. This is not my order. I wanted the grilled chicken, not the steak.

Listening

3 **Aim** To listen for specific information (gap fill)

- Ask Ss to read the gapped complaint form and think about what part of speech each gap asks for.
- Play the recording twice. Ss listen and fill the gaps with the missing information.
- Check Ss' answers. You can play the recording again with pauses for Ss to check their answers.

Answer Key

1	Bolton	4 vegetables
2	30	5 free
3	(some) items	

Everyday English

4 **Aim** To listen and read for specific information

- Ask Ss to read the first two exchanges in the dialogue and elicit Ss' guesses about the customer's complaint and the action the manager will take. *(I think there is a complaint about something the customer bought from a shop yesterday. I think the manager will give the customer their money back.)*
- Play the recording for Ss to listen and read and find out.

Suggested Answer Key

The customer bought a carton of milk that was past its sell-by date. The manager gives the customer another carton of milk and a money-off coupon for next time.

5 **Aim** To role-play a dialogue making a complaint

- Explain the task and ask Ss to act out similar dialogues to the one in Ex. 4 in pairs using the prompts and the phrases from the language box.
- Write this diagram on the board for Ss to follow.

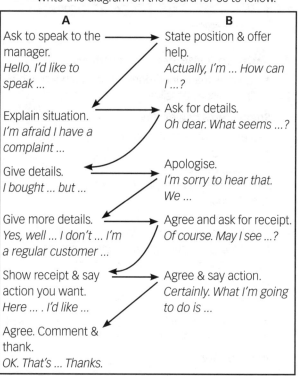

- Monitor the activity around the class and offer assistance as necessary.

- Then ask some pairs to act out their dialogues in front of the class.

Suggested Answer Key

A: Hello, I'd like to speak to the manager, please.

B: Actually, I'm the manager. How can I help you?

A: I'm afraid I have a complaint.

B: Oh dear. What seems to be the problem?

A: I bought a packet of butter yesterday, but when I got home I noticed it was past its sell-by date.

B: I'm sorry to hear that. We usually check them carefully.

A: Yes, well, I don't usually check the sell-by dates. I'm a regular customer and this has never happened before.

B: Of course not. May I see your receipt?

A: Here you are. I'd like a replacement or a refund.

B: Certainly. What I'm going to do is get you another packet of butter and here's a money-off coupon for your next visit.

A: OK. That's very kind of you. Thanks.

Pronunciation

6 **Aim** **To learn the pronunciation of /ð/, /z/**

- Model the sounds /ð/, /z/.
- Then play the recording. Ss listen and tick the sounds they hear.
- Play the recording again with pauses for Ss to repeat chorally and/or individually.

Answer Key

	/ð/	/z/		/ð/	/z/
clothe	✓		breathe	✓	
close		✓	with	✓	
breeze		✓	whizz		✓

Reading & Writing

7 **a)** **Aim** **To identify the type and context of a text**

Ask Ss to look at the heading and subheadings and elicit where you could see this form and what it is used for from Ss around the class.

Suggested Answer Key

I could see this form on a restaurant's website. It is used to deal with customer complaints and improve customer service.

b) **Aim** **To read for cohesion & coherence (word formation)**

- Give Ss time to read the text and complete the gaps with the correct words formed from the words in brackets.
- Then elicit answers from Ss around the class.

Answer Key

1 uncomfortable	4 apologise
2 constantly	5 rudely
3 service	6 disappointed

8 **Aim** **To learn about linkers**

Go through the **Writing Tip** with Ss. Ask Ss to read the form again and find and underline the linkers used for the functions given. Then elicit which paragraph states the action the writer expects to happen.

Answer Key

list complaints: *To begin with, What is more, Then, To make matters worse*

introduce the conclusion: *All in all*

Paragraph 3 states the actions the writer expects to be taken.

9 **Aim** **To practise language and phrases used to complain**

- Explain the task and give Ss time to complete it.
- Check Ss' answers around the class.

Answer Key

1 behaviour	4 waiter
2 new	5 order
3 apology	6 parking

Complaints: *1, 5, 6*
Actions expected to be taken: *2, 3, 4*

Writing

10 **a)** **Aim** **To prepare for a writing task; to listen for specific information**

- Ask Ss to read the gapped table and then play the recording and have them listen and fill in the gaps.
- Check Ss' answers.

Answer Key

1 food	4 chicken
2 meal	5 eat
3 quality	6 ten

Food for Thought

b) **Aim** To write a complaint

- Explain the task and then give Ss time to write their complaint using the information in Ex. 10a. Tell Ss to use the complaint form in Ex. 7 as a model.
- *Ask various Ss to share their answers with the class.*
- *Alternatively, assign the task as HW and check Ss' answers in the next lesson.*

Suggested Answer key

Customer's full name: *Harry Kemp*
Town/City of residence: *Dublin*
Email address: *h.kemp_69@mail.com*
Date of meal: *26/10/20...*

I am writing to complain about the catering you provided for our office dinner yesterday on 26th October.
To begin with, the food was not delivered on time. As a result, the meal was served one hour late. Secondly, the quality of the food was poor. For example, the chips were cold and the chicken was dry. What is more, there was not enough food for everyone to eat. We paid for food for thirty people but there was only enough food for around ten people.
All in all, I was very disappointed with your catering and I believe I am entitled to a full refund and a written apology. I look forward to your prompt reply.

Values

Ask Ss to explain the quotation. Then initiate a class discussion about the meaning of the quotation and encourage all Ss to participate.

Suggested Answer

A: *I think the quotation means that showing patience and being able to wait will serve you better than being passionate or angry.*
B: *Yes, I agree. I think it is also another way of saying that things will come to those who wait.*

Culture 11

Listening & Reading

1 **Aim** To introduce the topic and read for gist

- Ask Ss to read the title, the introduction and the headings and elicit Ss' guesses as to what is special about these events.
- Give Ss time to read the text to find out.

Suggested Answer Key

I think they are all popular food festivals in the UK.

2 **Aim** To read for cohesion and coherence (multiple choice cloze)

- Ask Ss to read the text again and choose the best word for each gap from the options provided.
- Play the recording for Ss to listen and check their answers.

Answer Key

| 1 C | 2 C | 3 B | 4 A | 5 B |

- Give Ss time to look up the meanings of the words in the **Check these words** box in the Word List.
- Play the video for Ss and elicit their comments.

3 **Aim** To consolidate new vocabulary

Give Ss time to match the words in bold to their synonyms in the list by using the Word List or their dictionaries to help them.

Answer Key

delicious: *tasty*   *outdoor: outside*
tastes: *flavours*   *raise: collect*
annual: *yearly*   *fun: enjoyable*
sample: *try*

Speaking & Writing

4 **Aim** **THINK** To develop critical thinking skills

- Explain the task and ask Ss to consider their answers and make notes under the headings.
- Ask various Ss to share their answers with the class.

Suggested Answer Key

name: *Street Food Fest*
where/when: *in the town square the first weekend in August every summer*
reason: *to celebrate street food and promote local businesses*
activities: *competitions, live music, rides for kids*
why it's special: *fun festival in summer for all the family*

My festival is called Street Food Fest. It would take place in the town square on the first weekend in August every year. It would celebrate street food and promote local businesses. There would be competitions, live music and rides for kids. It would be a fun summer festival for all the family.

5 **Aim** **ICT** To develop research skills; to write a short text about and present a food festival in one's country

- Explain the task and give Ss time to research online, collect information about a food festival in their country and make notes under the headings in Ex. 4. Then they use their notes to write a short article about it.

- Ask various Ss to present their food festival to the class.
- Alternatively, assign the task as HW and ask Ss to read out their articles in the next lesson.

Suggested Answer Key

name: *The Sagra del Risotto*
where/when: *Sessame, small town in the Piedmont region of Italy, first Sunday in May every year*
reason: *to celebrate the Italian dish risotto*
activities: *arts & culture events, large street market and lots of stalls serving risotto*
why it's special: *it is unique and dates back to the 13th century*

The Sagra del Risotto takes place in Sessame, a small town in the Piedmont region of Italy on the first Sunday of May each year. People celebrate risotto, an Italian rice dish, with a series of arts and culture events as well as a large street market where you can try lots of different types of Italian risotto. It is a unique festival that dates back to the 13th century.

Background Information

Shropshire is a county in the west Midlands of England. It borders Wales, Cheshire, Staffordshire, Worcestershire and Herefordshire. The county town is Shrewsbury and over 493,000 people live there.

Review 11

Vocabulary

1 (Aim) To consolidate vocabulary from the unit

- Explain the task.
- Give Ss time to complete it.
- Check Ss' answers.

Answer Key

1 refund	4 credit	7 change
2 street	5 vendor	8 course
3 fancy	6 dishes	

2 (Aim) To consolidate vocabulary from the unit

- Explain the task.
- Give Ss time to complete it.
- Check Ss' answers.

Answer Key

1 bill	3 order	5 refund
2 note	4 date	

3 (Aim) To practise prepositional phrases and phrasal verbs

- Explain the task.
- Give Ss time to complete it.
- Check Ss' answers.

Answer Key

1 For	3 off	5 with
2 of	4 away	

Grammar

4 (Aim) To practise quantifiers

- Explain the task.
- Give Ss time to complete it.
- Check Ss' answers.

Answer Key

1 any	3 lot	5 little
2 couple	4 plenty	

5 (Aim) To practise comparatives & superlatives

- Explain the task.
- Give Ss time to complete it.
- Check Ss' answers.

Answer Key

1 the worst	4 the best
2 faster	5 more slowly
3 the rudest	6 tastiest

6 (Aim) To practise *some/any/no/every* & compounds

- Explain the task and give Ss time to complete it.
- Check Ss' answers.

Answer Key

1 anyone	4 Every
2 somewhere	5 nothing
3 everyone	

Everyday English

7 (Aim) To match exchanges

- Explain the task.
- Give Ss time to complete it.
- Check Ss' answers.

Answer Key

1 c	2 d	3 e	4 b	5 a

Competences

Ask Ss to assess their own performance in the unit by ticking the items according to how competent they feel for each of the listed activities.

12 Earth, our Home

<table>
<tr><td colspan="2">Topic</td></tr>
<tr><td colspan="2">In this unit, Ss will explore the topics of the environment, environmental problems and eco-activities.</td></tr>
<tr><td>12a Reading & Vocabulary</td><td>98-99</td></tr>
<tr><td colspan="2">Lesson objectives: To learn vocabulary related to environmental problems, to listen and read for gist, to read for specific information (multiple choice), to learn collocations, to learn prepositional phrases, to practise words easily confused, to learn phrasal verbs with go, to talk about ideas for reusing plastic bottles, to make a poster
Vocabulary: Environmental problems (water pollution, rubbish, cutting down trees, air pollution, lack of rain, forest fires); Nouns (refugee camp, war, packaging, bucket, staff, wages, goat); Verbs (spoil, earn, receive, prove); Phrasal verb (go); Adjectives (clean, clear); Adverb (nearby); Determiner (little); Phrase (support myself)</td></tr>
<tr><td>12b Grammar in Use</td><td>100-101</td></tr>
<tr><td colspan="2">Lesson objectives: To learn/revise the causative, to learn/revise clauses of purpose, clauses of result and clauses of reason, to learn/revise determiners</td></tr>
<tr><td>12c Skills in Action</td><td>102-103</td></tr>
<tr><td colspan="2">Lesson objectives: To learn vocabulary for eco-activities, to listen for specific information (multiple choice), to act out a dialogue and practise everyday English for persuading, to learn the pronunciation of /d/, /dʒ/, to read for cohesion & coherence (word formation), to write an article providing solutions to a problem
Vocabulary: Eco-activities (Dos: take turns driving, take part in clean-up days, turn off the tap, send greetings using email, plant trees; Don'ts: buy fruit and vegetables that are out of season, use 'single-use' products, write on one side of paper, wrap food in plastic, leave computers, etc plugged in when not in use)</td></tr>
<tr><td>Culture 12</td><td>104</td></tr>
<tr><td colspan="2">Lesson objectives: To listen and read for gist, to read for cohesion & coherence (open cloze), to talk about plastic that gets washed ashore, to write a short article about an environmental organisation
Vocabulary: Nouns (mammal, sculpture, pile, jellyfish, octopus, puffin, exhibition); Verbs (increase, divide, remind); Phrasal verbs (set up, go on); Adjectives (giant, clean, curious); Adverb (ashore)</td></tr>
<tr><td>Review 12</td><td>105</td></tr>
<tr><td colspan="2">Lesson objectives: To test/consolidate vocabulary and grammar learnt throughout the unit, to practise everyday English</td></tr>
</table>

Go through the objectives box and tell Ss that these are the topics, skills and activities this unit will cover.

12a

Vocabulary

1 **Aim** **To introduce the topic of the environment**

Play the recording and ask Ss to listen to or read the poem and elicit what it is trying to tell us.

Answer Key

I think it is trying to tell us that we will only understand that we should protect the Earth when it is too late to undo the damage we have done.

2 **Aim** **To present vocabulary related to environmental problems**

- Ask Ss to read the problems in the list and look at the pictures and say which ones they can see.
- Elicit answers from Ss around the class.

Answer Key

A   forest fires
B   water pollution
C   air pollution
D   lack of rain
E   cutting down trees
F   rubbish

Listening & Reading

3 **Aim** **To introduce the topic of a text**

Ask Ss to read the introduction of the text and then elicit which of the environmental problems in Ex. 2 are mentioned.

Answer Key

rubbish and water pollution

4 **Aim** **To listen and read for gist**

- Ask Ss to look at the title of the text and the picture and think of a solution to the problem of plastic pollution which may be mentioned in the text.
- Elicit various guesses from Ss around the class.
- Play the recording. Tell Ss to listen to and read the text and find out.

Suggested Answer Key

I think the text might mention ways to collect plastic waste and either recycle it or use it to make something new.

5 **Aim** **To read for specific information (multiple choice)**

- Ask Ss to read the questions and the answer choices and underline the key words.
- Give Ss time to read the text again and answer the questions.
- Check Ss' answers. Ss justify their answers.

Answer Key

1   D (Paras 2, 3, 4)
2   C (escape from war)
3   B (wasn't a normal thing to do)
4   D (A camp ... plenty of work.)

- Then give Ss time to explain the words in bold using their dictionaries to help them as necessary.
- Check Ss' answers around the class.

Suggested Answer Key

spoil (v): *make unsuitable (to eat/drink)*
nearby (adv): *close to sth*
little (adj): *not much*
pick up (phr v): *to collect*
look after (phr v): *to take care of*
join in (phr v): *to take part in sth*
staff (n): *people who work at a place; workers*
receive (v): *to get*
wages (n): *the money sb gets paid for doing a job*
prove (v): *to show*

- Give Ss time to look up the meanings of the words in the **Check these words** box in the Word List.
- Play the video for Ss and elicit their comments.

6 **Aim** **To consolidate new vocabulary**

- Explain the task and give Ss time to complete the phrases using the words in the list referring back to the text as necessary.
- Then check Ss' answers.

Answer Key

1	plastic	4	eco-friendly
2	environmental	5	capital
3	drinking	6	recycling

7 **Aim** **To consolidate prepositional phrases from a text**

- Give Ss time to read the sentences and choose the correct prepositions.
- Then check Ss' answers.
- Tell Ss to add these prepositional phrases to the Prepositions list in their notebooks and include examples if they like. Tell Ss to revise this list from time to time and to add to it every time they come across a new prepositional phrase.

Answer Key

1   in   2   of   3   in   4   by

8 **Aim** **To understand words easily confused**

- Ask Ss to read the sentences and complete them with either *clean* or *clear*, using their dictionaries if necessary.
- Check Ss' answers.

Answer Key

1   clear   2   clear   3   clean   4   clean

9 **Aim** **To learn phrasal verbs with *go***

- Ask Ss to read the phrasal verbs box and make sure that Ss understand the definitions.
- Then give Ss time to complete the task and check their answers.
- Tell Ss to write the phrasal verbs in the Phrasal Verbs list at the back of their notebooks and include the definitions. Tell Ss to revise this list from time to time and to add to it every time they come across a new phrasal verb.

Answer Key

1   out   2   on   3   off   4   on   5   off

Speaking & Writing

10 **Aim** ICT **To develop critical thinking skills; to research the reuse of plastic bottles; to make and present a poster**

- Ask Ss to work in groups and give them time to research online and collect information on different ideas for reusing plastic bottles.
- Then give Ss time to use these ideas to make a poster and present it to the class.
- Alternatively, assign the task as HW and ask Ss to share their answers in the next lesson.

Suggested Answer Key

Plastic bottles can be reused in many ways such as:

planters

12 Earth, our Home

craft projects

lampshades

Plastic bottles can be reused for all kind of things. Our poster shows a few of them. We can reuse plastic bottles as planters to grow plants in. They can also be used in craft projects. We can paint them and make them into something pretty. We can also reuse plastic bottles or plastic cups to make lampshades.

Background Information

Kenya is a country in East Africa. Over 49 million people live there. It borders Ethiopia, Somalia, Tanzania, Uganda and South Sudan. Its capital city is Nairobi, the largest city in East Africa. The country gets its name from Mount Kenya. People there speak Swahili and English.

12b Grammar in Use

1 **Aim** To learn/revise the causative

- Write on the board. *I cut my hair.*
  I have my hair cut.
- Elicit which sentence suggests that the action is done for me by another person *(the second one)*. Explain/Elicit that we use the causative to talk about actions that we do not do ourselves but we have them done for us by somebody else. Elicit that we form the causative with **have** + **object** (person) + **past participle of the main verb**.
- Go through the theory box with Ss. Refer Ss to the **Grammar Reference** section for more information.
- Then ask Ss to read the dialogue and elicit an example of the causative from the dialogue.

Answer Key

Example: *I'll have it serviced regularly*

2 **Aim** To practise the causative

- Explain the task and give Ss time to complete it.
- Check Ss' answers.

Answer Key

1 had the leaky tap fixed
2 is having a greenhouse built
3 should have your air conditioner serviced
4 were having a herb garden planted
5 will have her groceries delivered

3 **Aim** To practise the causative

- Explain the task and read out the example.
- Give Ss time to complete the task.
- Check Ss' answers.

Answer Key

2 will have their car checked by a mechanic.
3 have had all my old light bulbs replaced with LED ones by the electrician.
4 are having solar panels installed on our roof by a local company.
5 was having the grass in her garden cut by a gardener at 10 am this morning.
6 should have the newspapers taken to the recycling centre.

4 **Aim** To learn/revise clauses of purpose

- Write on the board. *He uses buckets to collect rainwater.* Explain/Elicit that *to collect rainwater* expresses purpose, the reason why somebody does something.
- Ask Ss to read out the theory box and refer Ss to the **Grammar Reference** section for more information.
- Elicit how we introduce clauses of purpose and ask Ss to find examples in the dialogue.

Answer Key

We use to / so as [not] to / in order [not] to / so that / in case to introduce a clause of purpose.
Examples: *I'll have it serviced regularly so that it'll use less petrol. We should be eating more vegetables in order to reduce our carbon footprint.*

5 **Aim** To practise clauses of purpose

- Explain the task and give Ss time to complete it using the clauses in brackets.
- Check Ss' answers around the class.

Suggested Answer Key

1 Mark turned on the TV in order to watch a wildlife programme.
2 Please switch off the lights when you leave so as not to waste electricity.
3 They're going to close the factory so that it won't cause any more pollution.
4 Take gloves in case you plant some trees.
5 Jake went to the bottle bank to recycle some bottles.

6 (Aim) To learn clauses of result

- Go through the examples in the theory box with Ss.
- Elicit how we introduce clauses of result and ask them to find examples in the dialogue. Refer Ss to the **Grammar Reference** section for more information.

Answer Key

We use so / such [a/an] / such + adj / so + adj/adv to introduce a clause of result.
Examples: Our cities are so polluted by car fumes that ... So, from now on, I plan to have meat just once a week.

7 (Aim) To practise clauses of result

Explain the task, give Ss time to complete it and then check their answers.

Answer Key

1 so	3 such	5 so
2 such a	4 so	

8 (Aim) To learn clauses of reason

- Go through the examples in the theory box with Ss. Elicit that clauses of reason explain why sth happens. Elicit how we introduce clauses of result and ask Ss to find an example in the dialogue.
- Refer Ss to the **Grammar Reference** section for more information.

Answer Key

We use as / since / because / the/a reason for + noun/-ing form + is/was + noun/-ing form / the/a reason why + is/was + noun/-ing form/that clause to introduce a clause of reason.
Example: we should be eating less meat because producing it is bad for the environment.

9 (Aim) To practise clauses of reason

Explain the task, give Ss time to complete it and then check their answers.

Answer Key

1 The/A reason why I buy organic food is that it's better for the environment.
2 Don't swim in the river because it's polluted./ Because it's polluted, don't swim in the river.
3 Since she's free on Saturday, Jean will join the park clean-up./Jean will join the park clean-up since she's free on Saturday.
4 A reason for air pollution is cars.
5 As there weren't any buses to the city centre, we shared a taxi./We shared a taxi as there weren't any buses to the city centre.

10 (Aim) To present/revise determiners

- Go through the theory box with Ss and explain any points they are unsure of.
- Focus Ss' attention on the singular or plural form of the verb after nor/or.
- Refer Ss to the **Grammar Reference** section for more information.
- Then elicit examples from the dialogue.

Answer Key

Example: every person

11 (Aim) To practise determiners

Explain the task and give Ss time to complete it. Then check Ss' answers.

Answer Key

1 nor	4 Both	7 Every
2 whole	5 Each	8 All
3 either	6 None	

As an extension, ask Ss to make their own sentences using the determiners in the theory box.

12c Skills in Action

Vocabulary

1 a) (Aim) To present vocabulary related to eco-activities

- Ask Ss to look at the lists of dos and don'ts and read the words in the rubric.
- Give Ss time to complete the gaps with the words in the list.
- Play the recording for Ss to check their answers.

12 Earth, our Home

Answer Key

✓		✗	
1	take	1	buy
2	take	2	use
3	turn	3	print
4	send	4	wrap
5	plant	5	leave

b) Aim To personalise the topic

Ask various Ss around the class to tell the rest of the class which of the actions in Ex. 1a they do/ don't do.

Suggested Answer Key

I often take part in clean-up days and I always turn off the tap when brushing my teeth. I never wrap food in plastic to put in the fridge or take with me to work, and I always unplug my computer when I'm not using it.

Listening

2 Aim To listen for specific information (multiple choice)

- Ask Ss to read the questions and answer choices and underline the key words.
- Play the recording. Ss listen and choose their answers.
- Check Ss' answers. You can play the recording again with pauses for Ss to check their answers.

Answer Key

1 B   2 C   3 C   4 C

Everyday English

3 a) Aim To read for cohesion and coherence

Ask Ss to read the list of missing phrases and then read the dialogue and complete the gaps.

b) Aim To listen for cohesion and coherence

Play the recording. Ss listen to and read the dialogue and check their answers in Ex. 3a.

Answer Key

1	come along	4	pick you up
2	need more	5	See you
3	could manage		

4 Aim To role-play a dialogue trying to persuade sb to do sth

- Explain the task and ask Ss to act out similar dialogues to the one in Ex. 3 in pairs, using the prompts and the phrases from the language box.

- Write this diagram on the board for Ss to follow.

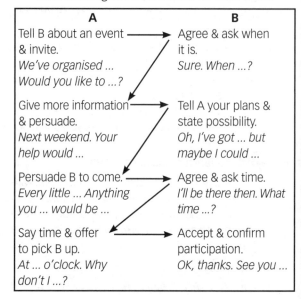

- Monitor the activity around the class and offer assistance as necessary.
- Then ask some pairs to act out their dialogues in front of the class.

Suggested Answer Key

A: We've organised a clean-up day at the local beach. Would you like to join us?
B: Sure. When is it?
A: Next weekend. Your help would mean a lot.
B: Oh, I've got to study for my exams next weekend, but maybe I could spare a couple of hours.
A: Every little helps! Anything you can manage would be great.
B: Well, I'll be there then, what time are you meeting?
A: At 11 o'clock on Saturday morning. Why don't I pick you up?
B: OK, thanks. See you on Saturday.

A: We've organised a recycling day. Would you like to join us?
B: Sure. When is it?
A: Next weekend. Your help would mean a lot.
B: Oh, I've got to study for my exams next weekend, but maybe I could spare a couple of hours.
A: Every little helps! Any help is welcome.
B: Well, I'll be there then. What time are you meeting?
A: At 11 o'clock on Saturday morning. I'd be glad to give you a lift there.
B: OK, thanks. See you on Saturday.

Earth, our Home

Pronunciation

5 **Aim** To learn/practise the pronunciation of /d/, /dʒ/

- Play the recording. Ss listen and tick the sounds they hear.
- Play the recording again with pauses for Ss to repeat chorally and/or individually.

Answer Key

	/d/	/dʒ/		/d/	/dʒ/
paid	✓		hard	✓	
page		✓	large		✓
jeep		✓	jog		✓
deep	✓		dog	✓	

Reading & Writing

6 a) **Aim** To read for cohesion & coherence (word formation)

- Give Ss time to read the text and complete the gaps with the correct words formed from the words in brackets. Ss should identify what part of speech each gap asks for, then think of appropriate derivatives.
- Then elicit answers from Ss around the class. Check accurate spelling on the board.

Answer Key

1 terrible/terrifying
2 global
3 easily
4 reuse
5 action
6 improvement

b) **Aim** To learn about linkers

- Read out the **Writing Tip** with Ss.
- Ask Ss to read the article again and look at the linking words/phrases in bold.
- Elicit which ones serve which purpose from Ss around the class.

Answer Key

give explanations/examples: *In other words, For instance*
make suggestions: *One useful suggestion is to, Another way around the problem is to*
present expected results: *That way, This means that*

7 **Aim** To read for structure

- Ask Ss to read the article again and copy the table into their notebooks and complete it.
- Check Ss' answers on the board.

Answer Key

Suggestions	Explanations/ Examples	Expected results
recycle	**1) take plastic, glass, paper and metal items to recycling bin**	**2) environment will be cleaner**
3) reuse	*keep things in empty jars, tins, bottles*	**4) they don't end up in rubbish bin**

Writing

8 **Aim** To analyse a task

- Ask Ss to read the task and then give them time to answer the questions.
- Check Ss' answers.

Answer Key

1 *I am going to write an article providing solutions to a problem for an environmental magazine.*
2 *I should write about how to reduce plastic in our everyday lives.*
3 *120-150 words*

9 a) **Aim** To listen for ideas

Ask Ss to copy the table into their notebooks and then play the recording. Ss listen and complete the table.

Answer Key

Suggestions	Explanations/ Examples	Expected results
1) use own shopping bag	*use it again & again – avoid plastic bags*	*cleaner environment*
Don't buy things sold in plastic	**2) plastic water bottles – use a glass one & refill it**	**3) don't need to do recycling**

b) **Aim** To write an article providing solutions to a problem

- Explain the task. Remind Ss to give their article a title – a short catchy one to attract readers' attention. Brainstorm titles with Ss and write them on the board.
- Give Ss time to write their article using their notes in Ex. 9a and following the plan.
- Ask various Ss to share their answers with the class.
- Alternatively, assign the task as HW and check Ss' answers in the next lesson.

Earth, our Home

Suggested Answer key

Goodbye Plastic!

Far too many things these days are made of plastic. This creates huge amounts of plastic waste and is a global problem. So, how can we reduce the plastic we use in our everyday lives?

One useful suggestion is to use our own shopping bag. This way, we can use it again and again and avoid plastic supermarket bags altogether. This will help to create a cleaner environment.

Another solution to the problem is to stop buying things sold in plastic. For example, plastic water bottles create a lot of waste. We can use a glass bottle and refill it. This way we can reduce the need to recycle.

In conclusion, by not using plastic bags or plastic water bottles we can greatly reduce plastic waste in our everyday lives. If everyone takes small steps like these to reduce plastic waste, we can make a difference. 'Small changes, big differences,' as the saying goes.

Values

Ask Ss to explain the quotation in their mother tongue. Then initiate a class discussion about the meaning of the quotation and encourage all Ss to participate.

Suggested Answer

A: *I think the quotation means that we should all only have a positive effect on the Earth by making it a better place than it was before we were born.*

B: *Yes, I agree. It also means that we shouldn't have a negative effect on the Earth by causing pollution.*

Culture 12

Reading & Listening

1 **Aim** To introduce the topic and to listen and read for gist

- Ask Ss to look at the picture and read the title, then elicit Ss' guesses as to what Washed Ashore is.
- Play the recording. Ss listen to and read the text to find out.

Suggested Answer Key

I think Washed Ashore is a project that takes plastic rubbish that washes up on our beaches and turns it into art.

2 **Aim** To read for cohesion and coherence (open cloze)

- Ask Ss to read the text again and then read the summary and think of an appropriate word for each gap.
- Check Ss' answers around the class.

Answer Key

1 rubbish	5 USA
2 animals	6 pollution/plastic
3 sculptures	7 exhibitions
4 washes	8 website

- Give Ss time to look up the meanings of the words in the **Check these words** box in the Word List.
- Play the video for Ss and elicit their comments.

3 **Aim** To ask and answer questions based on a text; to consolidate new vocabulary

- Do the first question and answer with Ss on the board as an example. E.g. *A: How long can plastic bottles take before they disappear? B: 450 years.*
- Ss then continue to ask and answer questions based on the text in closed or open pairs. If necessary, go around the class and monitor the activity. Set a time limit on the activity.
- Have a pair of Ss model their questions and answers in front of the class.

Suggested Answer Key

A: *How many animals and birds die from plastic pollution in the seas every year?*

B: *100,000 sea turtles and mammals and 1,000,000 sea birds.*

A: *How much plastic ends up in our oceans each year?*

B: *8 million metric tons. etc*

- Give Ss time to explain the words in bold by using the Word List or their dictionaries to help them. Elicit explanations from Ss around the class.

Suggested Answer Key

increase (v): *to get bigger/more*
giant (adj): *very big*
set up (phr v): *to create sth*
remind (v): *to call to mind*
clean (adj): *free of pollution*
go on (phr v): *to continue doing sth*
curious (adj): *wanting to know more about sth*

Speaking & Writing

4 **Aim** THINK To develop critical thinking skills

- Explain the task and ask Ss to consider their answers and make a list and then compare it with their partner.
- Ask various Ss to share their answers with the class.

Suggested Answer Key

plastic bottles and caps
fishing lines/nets
plastic cups
flip flops
plastic bags
plastic for wrapping food

5 **Aim** ICT To write a short text about an environmental organisation in one's country

- Give Ss time to research online and collect information about an environmental organisation in their country or another country and make notes under the headings. Ss then use their notes to write a short article about it.
- Details of organisation.
- Ask various Ss to read their articles to the class.
- Alternatively, assign the task as HW and ask Ss to read out their articles in the next lesson.

Suggested Answer Key

Name: *Greenpeace*
Details of organisation: *founded in 1971, now operates 27 branches in 55 countries*
What it does: *fights environmental problems including global warming, deforestation, overfishing and more; uses non-violent creative protests to get people's attention*
How to get involved: *become a member, donate, join a campaign, visit their website*

Greenpeace is an international environmental organisation. It was founded in 1971, and now operates 27 branches in 55 countries. It works to fight world issues such as global warming, deforestation, overfishing, and more. It uses non-violent, creative protests to get people's attention and make them think seriously about those problems. You can get involved by becoming a member, donating or joining a campaign. You can find out more information by visiting their website, www.greenpeace.org.

Background Information

Oregon is a state in the Pacific Northwest region of the United States. The capital city is Salem and the population is around 4 million people.

Angela Haseltine Pozzi was born in Portland, Oregon. She is an artist. She is the founder and artistic director of the non-profit organisation Washed Ashore Project. She started it in 2010 in Bandon, Oregon to combat the amount of plastic pollution she saw on the beaches.

Review 12

Vocabulary

1 **Aim** To consolidate vocabulary from the unit

- Explain the task.
- Give Ss time to complete it.
- Check Ss' answers.

Answer Key

| 1 d | 2 e | 3 a | 4 c | 5 b |

2 **Aim** To consolidate vocabulary from the unit

- Explain the task.
- Give Ss time to complete it.
- Check Ss' answers.

Answer Key

1 leaves	4 takes
2 buys	5 wraps
3 plants	

3 **Aim** To practise prepositional phrases and phrasal verbs

- Explain the task.
- Give Ss time to complete it.
- Check Ss' answers.

Answer Key

| 1 in | 2 off | 3 off | 4 in | 5 on |

Grammar

4 **Aim** To practise clauses and determiners

- Explain the task.
- Give Ss time to complete it.
- Check Ss' answers.

Answer Key

1 for	5 Because	9 Whole
2 in order to	6 None	10 Both
3 such	7 Each	
4 in	8 Neither	

5 **Aim** To practise the causative

- Explain the task.
- Give Ss time to complete it.
- Check Ss' answers.

Answer Key

1 *have our car serviced by a mechanic every six months*
2 *should have his water pipes fixed*
3 *will have our posters printed on recycled paper*

12 Earth, our Home

4   *has had her old clothes repaired by her mum*
5   *had their picture taken by Marta*

Everyday English

6 **Aim** **To match exchanges**

- Explain the task.
- Give Ss time to complete it.
- Check Ss' answers.

Answer Key

1 c   *2 d*   *3 b*   *4 a*

Competences

Ask Ss to assess their own performance in the unit by ticking the items according to how competent they feel for each of the listed activities.

Values: Caution

1 **Aim** **To introduce the topic; to predict the content of the text and to listen and read for specific information**

- Ask Ss to read the title and the introduction of the article and elicit what Ss think a virtual villain is.
- Ask Ss to look at the pictures and elicit Ss' guesses as to what they are going to read about.
- Then play the recording. Ss listen and read to find out.

Suggested Answer Key

I think a virtual villain is a person who we should be careful about meeting online. I think the text will talk about online bullies.

2 **Aim** **To read for specific information (multiple matching)**

- Ask Ss to read questions 1-5 and then give them time to read the text again and match them to the villains.
- Check their answers.

Answer Key

1 CB (electronic data ... future.)
2 CF (They post ... that isn't theirs)
3 T (They try ... trouble)
4 T (It is ... ignore them.)
5 CB (negative information ... future/report ... police.)

- Play the video for Ss and elicit their comments.

3 **Aim** **To consolidate new vocabulary**

Give Ss time to look up the meanings of the words in bold in their dictionaries or in the Word List and elicit explanations from Ss around the class.

Suggested Answer Key

nasty (adj): *very unpleasant*
mean (adj): *very unkind; rude*
embarrassed (adj): *feeling ashamed*
electronic data (phr): *digital information*
deal with (v): *to find a solution to a problem*
fake (adj): *false; not real*
upsetting (adj): *causing sb to feel unhappy or angry*
suspicious (adj): *having reason to doubt sb/sth is true*
bitter (adj): *angry and unhappy*
offensive (adj): *aggressive*

4 **Aim** **THINK** **To develop critical thinking skills; to discuss/personalise the topic**

Give Ss time to consider the questions and discuss them in pairs. Then elicit answers from Ss around the class.

Suggested Answer Key

I have experienced some cyberbullying by a person who posted a picture of me online without asking for permission.

5 **Aim** **ICT** **To develop research skills; to expand the topic and write a short text**

- Give Ss time to research online and collect information about hackers and use their information to write a short text like the ones in the article.
- Then ask various Ss to share their answers with the class.
- Alternatively, assign the task as HW and ask Ss to read out their texts in the next lesson.

Suggested Answer Key

The hacker

A hacker is a person who uses their computer knowledge to break into systems they are not allowed into or to get access to information they don't have a right to. Some hackers do this to show off their computer skills, but others do it for criminal reasons. For example, a hacker may use someone's personal information to commit identity theft. Watch out for any posts on social media supposedly made by you but you don't recognise them. If this happens, contact the police immediately.

D Public Speaking Skills

1 **Aim** To present a public speaking task

Ask Ss to read the task and then elicit answers to the questions from Ss around the class.

Answer Key

1 *I am going to speak to a class of students.*
2 *The talk is going to be about the right way to use smartphones.*
3 *The purpose of the talk is to inform and persuade.*

2 **Aim** To analyse a model; to identify persuasive approaches

- Read out the **Study Skills** box and tell Ss this tip will help them to complete the task successfully.
- Ask Ss to read the persuasive approaches (1-3) and the underlined parts of the talk.
- Play the recording. Ss listen to and read the model and match.
- Check Ss' answers.

Answer Key

1 *Well, ... others.*
2 *Imagine ... it wasn't!*
3 *I think ... too much.*

3 **Aim** To identify opening/closing techniques

Ask Ss to look at the introduction and the conclusion again and then elicit which techniques the speaker has used from Ss around the class.

Answer Key

The talk addresses the audience and makes a statement to open, and closes by addressing the audience.

4 **Aim** To brainstorm for ideas; to develop public speaking skills

- Explain the task and give Ss time to consider the situation and prepare their talk.
- Ask various Ss to give their talk to the class.
- Alternatively, assign the task as HW and have Ss give their talks in the next lesson.

Suggested Answer Key

Hello everyone. Today, I want to talk to you about the right way to use social media.

Who uses social media? Hands up! Around 68% of adults in the UK have a social media account, and why not? It's a useful and fun way to communicate. However, it's important to use social media correctly. So, ask yourself three questions.

Firstly, are you using social media in a healthy way? Some people use social media for many hours every day – even when they are in bed. I think you'll all agree that's too much. Staring at a screen before you go to

bed will stop you from being able to sleep properly, according to scientists. So, don't use social media for at least an hour before you go to bed to sleep well.

Second, are you using social media in a safe way? You should make sure that your personal information is private and don't share too much information such as your real name, your home address, the college you go to and your current location. This way, you can avoid being the victim of identity theft. How would you feel if a stranger got into your bank account?

Finally, are you using social media in a responsible way? Do you use social media at mealtimes, during lectures or in the cinema? There is a time and a place for using social media and these are not good examples. Also, make sure you use social media responsibly by not posting mean comments about others and treating people with respect.

There's no doubt that social media is a great way to stay connected with friends and family, to share ideas and to meet people with similar interests. However, we should keep it under control and follow some basic rules about privacy, suitable times and places for using it, and respect for others. After all, it's for our own good, right?

CLIL: Literature

Listening & Reading

1 **Aim** **To introduce the topic**

- Ask Ss if any of them are familiar with the story of 'The Old Man and The Sea'. Then ask the ones who aren't whether they can guess the story from the picture.
- Ask various Ss to tell the class.

Suggested Answer Key

I have read the story and I know that it is about an old Cuban fisherman who struggles with a huge marlin off the coast of Cuba.
I haven't read the story but I think from the picture that it is about an old man who goes fishing in a small boat and comes across a huge fish.

2 **Aim** **To listen and read for specific information (T/F); to consolidate new vocabulary**

- Ask Ss to read statements 1-5.
- Play the recording. Ss listen to and read the text and mark the statements according to what they read.
- Check Ss' answers. Ss justify their answers. Then elicit explanations for the words in bold.

Answer Key

1 T (the moon was below the hills)
2 T (He was rowing steadily ... was flat.)
3 F (Now, the man ... proper depths.)
4 T (He kept his lines ... they were.)
5 F (I may have ... lucky.)

- Give Ss time to look up the meanings of the words in the **Check these words** box in the Word List or in their dictionaries.

Suggested Answer Key

head for (phr v): *to make one's way towards a place*
fond of (phr): *keen on*
flat (adj): *level and smooth*
gently (adv): *in a soft and calm way*
wish (v): *to want*

3 **Aim** **To present/identify personification**

- Ask Ss to read the **Study Skills** box and explain anything Ss are unsure of.
- Then elicit examples of personification from the extract.

Answer Key

the boats were silent
flying fish ... were his friends
when luck comes

Speaking & Writing

4 **Aim** **THINK** **To develop critical thinking skills; to predict what happens in a story**

Give Ss time to consider what they think happens next in the story and ask various Ss to tell the class.

Suggested Answer Key

I think after a long struggle, he catches a big fish like the one in the picture.

5 **Aim** **ICT** **To develop research skills; to develop public speaking skills**

- Give Ss time to research online to collect information about Ernest Hemingway and his works.
- Then give Ss time to prepare a presentation.
- Ask various groups of Ss to give their presentations to the class.
- Alternatively, assign the task as HW and ask Ss to make their presentations in the next lesson.

Suggested Answer Key

Hello, everyone. "My aim is to put down on paper what I see and what I feel in the best and simplest way." said Ernest Hemingway, one of the greatest American authors and journalists. Ernest Hemingway was born in 1899 and died in 1961. He wrote novels and short stories. When he was 18, he drove an ambulance in World War I, and he was a reporter in World War II. Many of his novels are about these experiences. His works include: 'Indian Camp' (1924), 'The Sun Also Rises' (1926), 'A Farewell to Arms' (1929), 'For Whom the Bell Tolls' (1940) and 'The Old Man and the Sea' (1952) that got a Pulitzer Prize. He won the Nobel Prize for Literature in 1954.
Ernest Hemingway was a titan of 20th-century literature. Are there any questions? ... Thanks for listening.

B CLIL: Film Studies

Listening & Reading

1 **Aim** To listen and read gist

- Elicit Ss' guesses in answer to the questions.
- Play the recording. Ss listen and read to find out.

Suggested Answer Key

A 3D film has the added dimension of depth that a normal film doesn't have. We need 3D glasses to be able to watch a 3D film.

2 **Aim** To read for specific information (sentence completion)

- Ask Ss to read the gapped sentences (1-5) and then give them time to read the text again and complete them.
- Check Ss' answers and then elicit explanations for the words in bold.

Answer Key

1 flat	4 projector
2 depth	5 glasses
3 lenses	

Suggested Answer Key

float (v): *to move lightly in the air*
stand for (phr v): *to represent sth*
possible (adj): *able to be done/achieved*
mixture (n): *a combination of things*
slightly (adv): *to a small degree*
display (v): *to show to sb*

Speaking & Writing

3 **Aim** **THINK** To develop critical thinking skills; to talk about cinema in the future

- Ask Ss to consider the questions and discuss them with their partner.
- Ask various Ss around the class to share their answers with the rest of the class.

Suggested Answer Key

A: *I think in the future cinemas will add extra special effects to make the films more realistic and to make us feel that we are involved in the action. For example, the seats may move or a wind may blow in the cinema.*

B: *That's interesting. I just think that film technology will improve so that the films themselves are more realistic and lifelike. We already have high-definition films and 3D technology, but I think another type of new technology will improve the quality of the films we watch.*

4 **Aim** **ICT** To develop research skills; to write a review of a 4D film

- Give Ss time to research online and find information about a film that was made in 4D and write a short review of it. Ss should make notes under the headings: name – director – cast – plot – general comments – recommendation
- Ask various Ss to read their reviews to the class.
- Alternatively, assign the task as HW and ask Ss to read out their reviews in the next lesson.

Suggested Answer Key

name: *Jurassic World: Fallen Kingdom*
director: *J A Bayona*
cast: *Chris Pratt, Bryce Dallas Howard*
plot: *a dinosaur theme park manager and scientist try to rescue dinosaurs on a fictional island before it is destroyed by a volcano*
general comments: *a fast-paced film full of action, excellent acting, visually stunning special effects, spectacular 4D effects (moving seats, lightning, rain, wind)*
recommendation: *well worth seeing*

'Jurassic World: Fallen Kingdom' is a high-tech science fiction adventure about a dinosaur theme park manager and a scientist who try to rescue dinosaurs on a fictional island before the island is destroyed by a volcano. It is directed by J A Bayona and stars Chris Pratt and Bryce Dallas Howard.

This fast-paced film is full of action and the acting is excellent. The special effects are visually stunning and the 4D effects are really spectacular. In particular, you feel the rain and wind on your face and the cinema lights up with flashes of lightning. Your seat moves around so much you think you're on a rollercoaster ride!

I definitely recommend this film. You actually feel you are in it instead of just watching it. It's well worth seeing, but the 4D version is only available in certain cinemas.

Background Information

A **4D film** combines a 3D film with effects that occur in the theatre in synchronisation with the film. 4D films are shown in custom-built theatres. Some cinemas, though, can present 4D versions of 3D films.

Listening & Reading

1 **Aim** **To listen and read for specific information**

- Ask Ss how earthquakes happen.
- Play the recording. Ss listen and read the text to find out.
- Check the answers around the class.

Suggested Answer Key

Earthquakes happen when pressure that has built up from tectonic plates pushing against each other is released.

2 **Aim** **To read for specific information**

- Ask Ss to look at the diagram and label it using the highlighted words/phrases in the text.
- Check Ss' answers.

Answer Key

1 *epicentre*	4 *seismic waves*
2 *fault line*	5 *focus*
3 *tectonic plates*	

3 **Aim** **To read for specific information**

- Ask Ss to read statements 1-4 and then give them time to read the text again and mark them as true or false according to what they read.
- Check Ss' answers around the class. Ss justify their answers.
- Elicit explanations for the words in bold from Ss around the class. Alternatively, give Ss time to look up the meanings of the words in bold in the Word List or in their dictionaries

Answer Key

1 *T (at speeds of around two to five centimetres a year)*
2 *T (The places where two plates meet ... and make a mountain)*
3 *F (they often get stuck at the edges ... The plates keep trying to move in the same direction)*
4 *F (If a lot of energy is released ... and cause shaking in and around the epicentre)*

Suggested Answer Key

layer (n): *a level of material*
rise up (phr v): *to move upwards*
smooth (adj): *flat and even*
pressure (n): *the force sth produces when it presses against sth*
build up (phr v): *to increase gradually*
shaking (n): *the action of moving side to side or up and down repeatedly*

- Give Ss time to look up the meanings of the words in the **Check these words** box in the Word List.

Speaking & Writing

4 **Aim** **To consolidate information in a text**

Ask various Ss to explain how earthquakes happen using the diagram.

Suggested Answer Key

Tectonic plates are huge pieces of flat rock under the surface of the Earth. They move all the time and they meet at fault lines. They often get stuck and unstuck and when this happens, they move past each other very quickly and cause an earthquake. The place where they get unstuck below the surface is the focus of the earthquake and the epicentre is the place on the surface above it. The energy of the earthquake travels in seismic waves.

5 **Aim** **ICT** **To develop research skills; to prepare a presentation on safety measures in the event of an earthquake**

- Ask Ss to work in small groups and give them time to research online and find out information about earthquake safety measures and prepare a presentation.
- Ask various Ss to give their presentations to the class.
- Alternatively, assign the task as HW and have Ss tell the class in the next lesson.

Suggested Answer Key

Good morning everyone! Today I'm going to talk about earthquake safety measures. Of course, we can't know when an earthquake will happen but there are a number of things we can do if one happens to try to stay safe.
First of all, if an earthquake happens, you should stay calm. Panicking will only make matters worse. You shouldn't run. You should stay wherever you are until it is over. If you are indoors, move quickly towards a wall near the centre of the building, stand in a doorway or crawl under a heavy piece of furniture such as a desk or a table. Stay away from windows and outside doors. Do not use the lift, because you will get trapped in there.
If you are outside, stay in the open but keep away from buildings, telephone poles, power lines or anything that could fall on you.
If you are in the car, you should stop the car and wait inside it until the earthquake is over.
After the earthquake, check yourself and others for injuries and give first aid. Are there any questions?... Thank you for listening.

CLIL: Geography

Listening & Speaking

1 **Aim** **To listen and read for specific information**

- Elicit Ss' guesses as to how caves are formed.
- Play the recording. Ss listen and read the text to find out.

Suggested Answer Key

Caves are formed over long periods of time by nature. They are formed by erosion of soft rock by water in the form of rain, melted snow, waves from the sea or carbonic acid over many years.

2 **Aim** **To read for specific information**

- Ask Ss to read the gapped sentences (1-5) and then read the text again and complete them accordingly.
- Check Ss' answers and then elicit explanations for the words in bold from Ss around the class.

Answer Key

1	soft rock	4	Stalagmites
2	carbon dioxide	5	equipment
3	Karst caves		

Suggested Answer Key

break down (phr v): *to separate into smaller parts*
create (v): *to make sth start to exist*
tiny (adj): *very small*
drop (n): *a very small amount of a liquid*
explore (v): *to look around a place*
enter (v): *to go into a place*

- Give Ss time to look up the meanings of the words in the **Check these words** box in the Word List.

Speaking & Writing

3 **Aim** **ICT** **To develop research skills; to write a leaflet about a cave in one's country**

- Ask Ss to research online and collect information about a cave in their country, make notes under the headings and use them to write a leaflet advertising it to tourists, adding photos or drawings. Ss can work in closed pairs or groups.
- Ask various Ss to share their leaflets with the class, then display the leaflets around the class.
- Alternatively, assign the task as HW and have Ss share their leaflets in the next lesson.

Suggested Answer Key

name: *Eisriesenwelt (= world of the ice giants)*
where it is: *Werfen, Austria, in the Hochkogel Mountain in the Tennengebirge section of the Alps*
how big it is: *42 km long*
special features: *biggest ice cave in the world*
history: *it was formed by the erosion of the Salzach River, it was discovered in 1879 but it wasn't explored until 1912, today there is a cable car to the cave*

Amazing caves – Eisriesenwelt cave

Come and explore the unique Eisriesenwelt cave in Werfen, Austria, in the Hochkogel Mountain in the Tennengebirge section of the Alps. Its name means 'world of the ice giants' and, at 42 km long, it is the biggest ice cave in the world! It was formed by the erosion of the Salzach River. It was discovered in 1879, but it wasn't explored until 1912. Modern explorers can walk up the mountain or arrive in style on the cable car.

Student's Book Audioscripts

UNIT 1 – In Character

1c – Exercise 2 (p. 8)

Claudia: Hello, David. Sorry about last week. Opening a new clothes shop in London means I don't have any time free at the moment!

David: Don't worry. You're just in time to see my new summer collection.

Claudia: Great. I can't wait to see it. You know how much I love your clothes!

David: Well, this year, I have a completely new line to add to the collection. I feel like the older customers know me, so it's time to appeal to the younger crowd. Come over here and see my new sportswear line! There are brightly-coloured tracksuits with matching basketball trainers and sleeveless T-shirts with exciting patterns and designs on them. I think sporty and fashionable young people will love them!

Claudia: Yes, I'm sure they will. But this year, I'm thinking of selling something a little smarter. I'm looking for some stylish suits and some fairly expensive evening dresses. You know – the kind of thing you would wear to a special event at your company, or on a business trip. The sort of clothes people are happy to pay a high price for.

David: Hmm … I see. But don't you sell mostly casual clothes in your shops?

Claudia: Yes, in the ones south of the river. But now I have the new shop – the one in Halifax Street. It's just to the east of Knightsbridge, so wealthy customers come in there regularly – and even a celebrity from time to time!

David: Oh, I see. That's great! You might like this outfit, then. It's a long, red, silk skirt, with a matching red blouse and scarf. It goes with a long, black, velvet coat and looks fantastic!

Claudia: Yes, it's beautiful. Do you have it in different sizes?

David: Yes. We have it in small, medium and large.

Claudia: Good. Let me take five outfits in each size and see how they sell. Now, what about some trendy shirts, jackets and ties?

David: I don't have any new designs in shirts, I'm afraid. But, I do have a new range of formal ties, including some rather interesting bow ties. Bow ties are coming back into fashion this year – you have my word.

Claudia: Oh, I love this one, and that one's great, too! It's so hard to choose.

David: This is a new direction for me, so let me make you an offer. Put the whole collection in your shop window in Halifax Street and we can see how it goes.

Claudia: There's an offer I can't refuse!

UNIT 2 – Reading Time

2c – Exercise 2b (p. 16)

It was a sunny morning in early spring, and Harriet was walking in the mountains with her sister Patsy. They were in the trees, where there was still thick snow on the slope.

Harriet was feeling a little tired, falling behind Patsy. Suddenly, she heard a noise like thunder, and snow began to slide downwards. It was an avalanche!

Luckily, she was right next to a large tree. She managed to get behind it, so it protected her from the snow. Then she stretched her hand out to Patsy, who was just going past, and pulled her to safety. "Phew!" she said to her sister, as they looked down at the moving snow. "That was a close one!"

Once the avalanche stopped, they used Patsy's mobile phone to call for help. They were both amazed to be alive, but they never went walking in the mountains in early spring again. I mean, would you?

2c – Exercise 10a (p. 17)

Mark and Paul were walking along the beach carrying their surfboards. The sun was shining and the waves were crashing on the beach. It was a perfect day for surfing.

While Paul was cleaning his board, Mark went surfing. Paul was relaxing on the beach when he saw a dark shape in the water moving towards Mark. It was a shark!

Paul jumped up and shouted to Mark to get out of the water. Mark was riding a wave and at first, he didn't hear him. Paul started waving his hands and shouting louder. Mark saw him and paddled as fast as he could. Paul ran to meet him and pulled him out of the water just in time.

As they watched the shark swim away, they both felt relieved. "I was almost that shark's lunch!" said Mark.

UNIT 3 – All around the world

3a – Exercise 2b (p. 20)

It's an amazing world out there, travellers, and here at Transit Travel we find weird and wonderful experiences and put them in a package to satisfy every customer.

Take a reindeer sled ride over the snow in beautiful Finland. Try the famous toboggan ride down the slopes of Monte on the sunny Portuguese island of Madeira. Zip line through the warm, wet rainforests of Costa Rica. Wherever you choose, we can put you on track to the holiday of a lifetime. Do you want to ride on the bamboo train in tropical Cambodia? We can make it happen.

Student's Book Audioscripts

Everything from sailing on the reed boats of Peru's Lake Titicaca to riding through the streets of Cuba's capital, Havana, in a classic car, let us do the work. Visit our website today at transittravel.co.uk and save 50% on all holidays!

3c – Exercise 2 (p. 24)

Man: Next, please. ... Good afternoon. Where are you travelling to?
Woman: Hi there! I'm flying on flight number AG533 to New York. The flight takes off at 8:30 – or at least I hope so!
Man: I'm sure it will. All our flights have left on time so far today. Could I have your passport, please?
Woman: Of course – here you are.
Man: Thank you. Now, how many bags are you checking in?
Woman: Just one, but it's big!
Man: Did you pack it yourself?
Woman: Yes, I did.
Man: Would you like a window seat or ...
Woman: A window seat, please. I want to see New York as we arrive! I've never been before – it's going to be so interesting!
Man: I'm sure it will. So, here's your passport back, and your boarding pass. You're in seat 24A.
Woman: Thank you. And where does it say the gate?
Man: Right here. It's Gate 23.
Woman: Oh yes. Sorry about all the questions. It's just that it's my first foreign holiday, so I'm a bit nervous.
Man: That's quite alright. I'm sure everything will go very smoothly.
Woman: One last thing ... is this the boarding time here? 7:30?
Man: That's right. Have a pleasant flight!
Woman: I'm sure I will. Thank you!

UNIT 4 – Hard Times

4b – Exercise 2 (p. 32)

Nancy: Hi, Jenny. Ben just told me you're moving to London! Is it true?
Jenny: Yes, it is. I was just about to tell you.
Nancy: What made you decide to do that?
Jenny: Work, mainly. I think I'll find a good job there.
Nancy: OK, but where are you going to live?
Jenny: I'm still looking for places online. I hope I'll share a flat with somebody else – that way the rent will be a lot cheaper.
Nancy: That's a good idea. Are you going to take your dog with you?
Jenny: No, he's going to stay with my parents. I expect I won't find a place with a garden, so he'll be more comfortable in the countryside.
Nancy: That's probably for the best. But aren't you worried about moving to a big city on your own?

Jenny: Not really. I think I'll enjoy living there! There's so much to see and do in London! I expect I won't get bored there at all!
Nancy: And what about your family? Won't you miss them?
Jenny: Yeah, I suppose I'll miss them a little – but I can always visit at weekends.
Nancy: Well, I just hope you'll invite me to visit when you get settled!
Jenny: Of course I will, Nancy!

4b – Exercise 3a (p. 32)

Boss: Have you finished the report yet, Stan?
Stan: Not yet, Mr Thompson, but I promise I'll finish it soon.
Boss: OK, just make sure it's on my desk by the end of the day. You go on holiday tomorrow, don't you?
Stan: That's right, Mr Thompson. I can't wait! I'm going to stay in a five-star hotel on a Caribbean island. I'm going to go for a swim every morning, and then I'm going to sunbathe on the beach in the afternoons. Also, I'm going to eat at lovely restaurants in the evenings, and I'm going to stay out late at night. As well as that, I'm going to ...
Boss: Stan, stop daydreaming about your holiday! I need that report!
Stan: Oh, sorry, Mr Thompson.

4c – Exercise 2 (p. 34)

Man: You're listening to *Ask Vic* – England's number one phone-in radio show. The phone lines are open, so give me a call on 555-2567. If you've got a problem and need some advice, I'm here for the next two hours. Oh, I see we've got our first caller. Hello, you're on the air.
Woman: Hi, Victor. My name's Pam. Over the years, I've heard you give advice to lots of people with phobias, so I was wondering if you could help me, too.
Man: I'll certainly try. What phobia do you suffer from?
Woman: OK, don't laugh, but I've got globophobia – a fear of balloons. My parents say it started on my first birthday, when a balloon popped in my face. I can't remember it, of course, but I must have got a terrible shock. Now, I can't even enter a room where there's one! And if I come across one by accident, I have a shortness of breath and feel extremely weak.
Man: But what do you at parties?
Woman: I just avoid them. For example, last month it was my best friend's birthday, but I told her I was ill. Only family members know about my condition, you see.
Man: That's a shame. Well, basically, the treatment that works best for most phobias is exposure therapy. This involves facing the thing you're scared of little by little. So, in your case, on the first day, you might begin by looking at a picture of a balloon, then move on to a video of a balloon, then maybe a real balloon but from distance. Eventually, you might be comfortable enough to touch one. I don't want

you to go through this alone, though. You need to see a psychologist for the best results.

Woman: Oh, I feel ill just thinking about balloons! But I'll give it a try, Victor!

Man: OK, all the best, Pam!

4c – Exercise 10a (p. 35)

A: Hi, Kate. Is something wrong? You look as white as a ghost!

B: Oh, hi, Bill. I've just got off the phone with Laura. She's invited me to go on a sailing trip with her family next month.

A: So, why do you look so worried? That sounds like great fun!

B: Haven't I ever told you? I'm terribly scared of the sea! It's called thalassophobia and I've had it since I was a little kid.

A: Oh, I had no idea. But surely there are ways to get over your problem. My dad says the best way to treat a phobia is exposure therapy – that's when you expose yourself to the thing you're afraid of little by little.

B: Go on …

A: Well, I'm not an expert, but maybe it would be a good idea for you to try to identify the reason for your fear. Did something happen? If you can understand why you are afraid better, you can deal with it.

B: That's a good idea.

A: And you could also read about the safety equipment online. This way, you'll learn about how to stay safe at sea and you'll feel less anxious.

B: OK. That's not a bad idea, too. Thanks for the advice.

A: OK. I hope it helps.

UNIT 5 – Citizen 2100

5b – Exercise 9 (p. 41)

Presenter: Welcome back to the show. With us, we have the best-selling novelist, Robert Ellis. Robert, let's talk about the future. Do you see yourself writing novels in ten years' time?

Robert: Oh, yes, I'll definitely still be writing then. I can't imagine myself doing anything else.

Presenter: OK. And how many more novels will you have written by then? I mean, will you continue to write a novel a year, like you do now?

Robert: I doubt that. I want to slow down a little, so, let's say around four more by then.

Presenter: I see. And, continuing with this theme, do you think you'll still be living in New York in ten years' time?

Robert: Well, a lot of people move out of New York when they get older, but that doesn't interest me. I love it there.

Presenter: A lot of people have said your novels would

make great films. In ten years' time, do you see yourself working on film versions of your books?

Robert: Yes, why not? I've had lots of offers from producers, so one of these days, I'm going to say 'yes' – and I'd definitely like to be involved.

Presenter: Very interesting! And one more question. In the next 10 years, do you think you'll win the Nobel Prize?

Robert: If it happens, I'd be delighted - but, no, I seriously doubt it. There are lots of other novelists that deserve it more.

Presenter: A lot of your fans would disagree, Robert. Thanks for talking to us today.

Robert: My pleasure.

5c – Exercise 2 (p. 42)

Anna: Hi Jason. Have you finished your project about the world in 2080 yet?

Jason: Oh, hi Anna. No, I haven't got far with it. It's due on Monday, right?

Anna: Yes, you've still got the weekend. But what are you going to write about?

Jason: Well, I'm focusing on the environment. I think many well-known animals like tigers and elephants will have become extinct by then. So, I'll write about that.

Anna: Oh, you're so negative! Do you think there'll be lots of air pollution in the future, too?

Jason: No, because we'll all be driving electric cars then. There'll be lots of water pollution, though. A lot of sea animals will become extinct because the water isn't clean enough.

Anna: Well, I'm far more positive about the future. I'm mainly writing about food for my project and I believe there'll be lots of food for everyone in 2080.

Jason: No way! The world population could be double by then. How will there be enough food for everyone?

Anna: We'll be able to print food using 3D printers! It'll be easy.

Jason: Hmm, I'm not so sure. But, I guess there are no wrong answers when you're making predictions about the future. Who knows what will happen?

Anna: That's true. By the way, I'm going to work on my project later in the library. Do you want to join me? Maybe I can give you some positive ideas so your project isn't so negative!

Jason: Sure, why not?

UNIT 6 – The Big Screen

6b – Exercise 1 p. 48

Host: OK. So, the final round is a film trivia quiz. You are now just five questions away from winning the jackpot which today stands at £2,500. Are you ready?

Contestant: Yes, I am.

Student's Book Audioscripts

Host: Right, then here we go. *(dramatic music)* Question 1: when were the first Oscars awarded? Was it A 1929, B 1949 or C 1969?

Contestant: Oh, I know this one, it was A 1929.

Host: That's correct. Well done! Now question 2: what was George Lucas's dog named? Was it A Chewie, B Indiana or C Luke?

Contestant: Oh, dear. That's a tricky one. Well, they are all names of characters from his films. Luke is a strange name for a dog, so I don't think it's that. Chewie is a name you might call a dog, but I think I'll go for B Indiana.

Host: Ooh, so you're not sure. Have you just lost the round? … *(pause)* No you haven't, B is the correct answer!

Contestant: Phew! Hahaha. What a lucky guess!

Host: Yes. Well done. You're almost halfway. Just three more questions and you'll be taking home £2,500! Here's Question 3: which was the first film to be filmed in Iceland? Was it A *Land Ho!*, B *Noah* or C *Sons of the Soil*?

Contestant: Oh, my goodness! I have no clue. I'll have to guess … I'll say C *Sons of the Soil*.

Host: Oh, dear! You were doing so well … and you still are! What a lucky guess!

Contestant: Really? I don't believe it!

Host: Yes. You're so close now. Question 4: how many Oscars were won by the film *Jaws*? Was it A three, B none or C one?

Contestant: Well, I don't think it's none and I think it would have won more than just one because the acting was great and the music was great and the special effects were good too, so I say A three.

Host: Is it right? … *(pause)* Yes it is! Well done. Now, get this next question right and you'll be taking home £2,500! Are you ready?

Contestant: Yes, let's do it.

Host: Here goes question 5 for £2,500: which of these films wasn't directed by Steven Spielberg? Was it A *Hook*, B *The Post* or C *Good Time*? Take your time now.

Contestant: Well, I know he definitely directed *Hook* and I'm pretty sure he directed *The Post*. I haven't heard of *Good Time* so I'll say that one. C *Good Time*.

Host: Well, are you right? Is the answer C? … Yes it is! Congratulations! You've just won £2,500!

Contestant: I can't believe it! That's amazing! Thank you!

6c – Exercise 2 p. 50

1　**A:** Hurry up, Henry. It's nearly seven o'clock.
　　B: What's the hurry? It doesn't start until eight.
　　A: Yes, but we have to be there at half past seven. We're meeting Jane, remember?

2　**A:** Two tickets for *Robin Hood*, please.
　　B: Here you are. That'll be nine pounds seventy-five, please.
　　A: Really? I thought they were six fifty each.

　　B: Yes, but today it's buy one get one half price. So six fifty plus three twenty-five is nine seventy-five
　　A: OK. Great!

3　**A:** Do you fancy watching the new DIY show on Channel 5 tonight?
　　B: Not really. I'd rather watch the football match on ITV.
　　A: Didn't you hear? It was cancelled because of the weather. How about the film on ITV4?
　　B: OK then.

UNIT 7 – Narrow Escapes

7c – Exercise 3 p. 60

This is Michael Jones reporting from the scene of the wildfires in Australia. Nine hundred firefighters from the New South Wales Fire and Rescue Service are working to get the fires under control. A huge area of two thousand kilometres around the city of Sydney is affected.

The fires have destroyed over one hundred and fifty homes. Thousands of sheep have been killed and 500 square kilometres of land have been burnt. Residents in some areas have had no electricity for two days. No human lives have been lost but two firefighters had to be taken to hospital suffering from severe burns. One citizen also had head injuries when she fell over while running from the fire.

Fires in the Australian bush often start because of outdoor activities like barbecues and camping. But this year, high temperatures combined with strong winds are responsible. The police do not think that anyone started the fire on purpose. Weather forecasters say they expect some rain and thunderstorms at the weekend but not enough to put out the fires. "In fact, a lightning strike could cause more fires," said Commissioner David Owens. "We hope things will get better on Monday when heavier rainfall is expected."

7c – Exercise 10b p. 61

A strong earthquake struck Mexico City today at around 1 pm local time. The quake measured 7.1 on the Richter scale, making it the city's worst earthquake since 1985. At least 200 people have been seriously injured and thousands of people have lost their homes but thankfully there haven't been any reports of casualties so far. There has been lots of damage to property, including famous buildings and statues as well as valuable objects in the national museum. Fires have started due to electrical problems and public transport has stopped working. There is also a fear of gas leaks. Rescue teams and emergency services are working around the clock to search for survivors in the rubble, put out fires and treat the injured. "This is a national emergency," said the Mexican President, adding that other countries had been asked for their help. Food, medicines and tents are being sent to the area.

Student's Book Audioscripts

UNIT 8 – Learning & Earning

8c – Exercise 3 p. 68

Speaker 1

I think my job is very exciting. Sometimes, I do research in my office. Other times, I go out on ships to explore the ocean. I enjoy the variety, but the real thrill is studying the bottom of the sea. Swimming alongside a shark is pretty amazing, too! It can be cold, dark and wet down there, though. You do have to wear lots of heavy breathing equipment and there's always the risk of it not working properly!

Speaker 2

Of course, there are both advantages and disadvantages to doing my job. First, the hours are regular and the salary's fairly good. Also, I'm responsible for the books in the non-fiction section and I really enjoy answering readers' questions and helping them to find what they're looking for. Sometimes, they need help borrowing from the video section, too. But it can get boring on quiet afternoons, and there isn't really much chance of getting a promotion.

Speaker 3

I'm self-employed, so I don't have a boss to tell me what to do, which is great! And I don't have to worry if I open up the office half an hour late sometimes, too! In my job, customers want my advice but they all have different ideas. Some want a budget holiday while others want a luxury cruise. It's my job to make suggestions and help them decide what to book. That's the pleasant bit … but occasionally customers are rude or demanding – and that's when the job gets difficult!

Speaker 4

For me, work means working out! And when you're exercising all day, it's important to wear comfortable clothes. I buy them myself, and I always get good quality. You need to look professional, after all, in front of a class. I also give one-to-one instruction to clients. Sometimes I have to work long hours or at the weekend and you can injure yourself, too, if you aren't careful. But I work with a great team of people in the gym and it's quite a well-paid job.

8c – Exercise 10a p. 69

Good afternoon, everyone, and welcome to the college's Careers Open Day. As the first speaker, I've been asked to say a few words to students thinking of taking a degree in journalism. As a journalist myself, I'd like to share some of my experiences with you.

There's no doubt that being a journalist has some terrific advantages. In the first place, it's a great way to improve your knowledge about the world. If I hadn't become a journalist, I wouldn't have learnt all the things I know today! It's very important for journalists to thoroughly research every topic they write about, so I've read a lot of books and news reports in my career. A second advantage is that journalism can be exciting. You get to meet interesting people and even interview famous celebrities and politicians.

But if I said there were no drawbacks to being a journalist, I would be lying! For one thing, it's extremely stressful! For instance, journalists have to meet deadlines so that their stories are ready to print on time, and that's a major cause of stress. Also, journalists often work long, unsociable hours – sometimes at weekends and on public holidays.

So … now that you've heard a bit about the good and bad sides of the job, I hope that helps you make your decision. Many of the students who graduated in journalism from the college last year have already found jobs in top national newspapers. That's something to think about, isn't it?

UNIT 9 – Want to play?

9c – Exercise 3 p. 76

Terry: Welcome to Terry's Fitness Podcast, where I discuss common questions about keeping fit. You can also check out my blog at terrysfitnessblog@wordblog.com. The question today: is an individual sport or a team sport a better way to stay fit? I've asked a basketball coach and a jogging instructor to join me today and talk about it. First, team sports. Coach Johnson: what do they offer us?

Coach: Fun, first of all! Playing in a team is social. People make great friends, talk and laugh as well as play.

Terry: So you're more likely to continue.

Coach: Of course. Second, you're more likely to continue because you don't want to let the team down. It's related to the first point, but you're going to turn up to training or a match when you know your team is relying on you too.

Terry: That's very true. Now, can you tell me what the biggest disadvantage to playing a team sport is?

Coach: It takes a lot of work to organise. It's hard. For example, for basketball you need at least five people for a team, and another team to play against. Football even more.

Terry: I see. Now, over to our jogging instructor, Diane. Why would you recommend an individual sport?

Diana: It depends on the person, but if you're an independent person, they're more suitable. First of all, you choose when you train and for how long. If you want to go jogging right now, for example, you can be running in your neighbourhood within 15 minutes. You have complete independence.

Terry: Because you don't have to arrange it with anyone else, right?

Diane: Exactly. The other thing is, your success or failure is entirely up to you. It's your responsibility. Some people really respond to that.

Terry: Well, it certainly means that you can be very proud of your success. Now, any disadvantages?

Student's Book Audioscripts

Diana: Of course. It can be lonely. After all, it's just you taking part.

Terry: Right, yes. OK, so we'll talk in more depth in a moment, but now …

9c – Exercise 10 p. 77

Terry: Welcome to Terry's Fitness Podcast, where I discuss common questions about keeping fit. Remember, you can also check out my blog at terrysfitnessblog@wordblog. com. The question today: what are the benefits of hiring a personal trainer, and going to an exercise class? I've asked a personal trainer and an exercise class instructor in today to talk it out. First, personal trainer Michael Terrence, what do you offer us?

Michael: The most important thing is obviously individual attention, because everyone is different and has different needs. For example, if you're unfit, I can take things slowly, but if you're fitter, I can push you a bit harder. The second advantage a personal trainer gives you is encouragement, since they're next to you the whole time, not allowing you to give up. Just to have someone saying, "You can do it!" can make all the difference!

Terry: Yes, I can see how that would help. Now, turning to our exercise class instructor, Marsha Botham. What does an exercise class offer us, Marsha?

Marsha: The obvious thing is team spirit, I think. This is because when you're part of a team, you try harder. The second benefit, for me, is connected to the first. It's the friendship that develops between people in a regular class. This is important, as you are more likely to attend the class every week or twice a week if you know you're going to see some friendly faces when you get there.

Terry: Yes, that's certainly important to me …

UNIT 10 – Tech world

10c – Exercise 3 p. 86

Speaker 1

I spend quite a lot of time on social media. For me, it's a great way to find old schoolmates, and stay in touch with family members who live abroad. But I never let social media get in the way of the more important things in life. For example, I always make sure I've finished my reading for college before I sign into my accounts each evening.

Speaker 2

I'm a bit of a social media addict. I've got accounts with three different social media services and I spend a huge amount of my free time on them. My parents worry that social media is dangerous – that I'll give my personal information to a stranger or something – but I'm more worried about what it's doing to my exam scores. I really need to limit my time online.

Speaker 3

A lot of my friends have encouraged me to open a social media account, but I've always said no. I'm too busy at work to waste my time searching for old friends from primary school! And if you ask me, social media is quite unsafe. I mean, what if the person you're chatting to online isn't who they say they are? It's just not worth the risk.

Speaker 4

A lot of my friends think I'm addicted to social media, but they don't realise what I do when I sign into my accounts. You see, I don't spend my time chatting with old college friends – I actually use social media as part of my job. I own a small computer shop, and I regularly use social media to advertise new products and connect with my customers. It's really useful!

UNIT 11 – Food for thought

11c – Exercise 3 p. 94

Employee: Good afternoon, The Orchard. How can I help you?

Customer: Hello. I'd like to make a complaint about a meal I had at your restaurant on Tuesday evening – the 3rd of April.

Employee: Oh, I'm sorry to hear that. First, can I have your name, please?

Customer: Yes, it's Sally Bolton. That's B-O-L-T-O-N. The reservation was under my husband's name, though – Alfred.

Employee: OK, I see. And can I have your address, please?

Customer: It's 30 Victoria Road, Barton.

Employee: 13 Victoria Road.

Customer: No, no, it's 30, 3-0.

Employee: OK, got it. Now, a contact number, please?

Customer: Sure. My mobile is 0763232551 – that's 0763232551.

Employee: OK, now, what's the nature of your complaint?

Customer: Well, like I said, I had a meal with my husband at your restaurant on Tuesday evening. When we returned home, I checked the bill and realised that it included some items we hadn't ordered.

Employee: Oh, dear! What did you eat exactly?

Customer: We had the vegetable soup for our starter and I had the salmon with roasted vegetables for my main course. My husband had a steak with rice. We didn't have any dessert but you charged us for two pieces of chocolate cake and coffee after our meal.

Employee: Well, we're really sorry about this madam. I'm sad to hear that something like this happened. Could we offer you a free meal at the restaurant tomorrow evening?

Customer: OK, I'd appreciate that. I'll see you tomorrow evening, then.

Customer: OK, Mrs Bolton. Have a nice afternoon.

Student's Book Audioscripts

11c – Exercise 10a p. 95

A: Hello, Banquet Catering. How can I help?

B: Hi, my name's Harry Kemp from Gorton Manufacturing. I'm phoning to complain about the catering you provided yesterday evening for our office dinner.

A: Oh, I'm sorry to hear that. What was the problem exactly?

B: Well, where do I start? To begin with, the food wasn't here on time. You were supposed to be here at five but you turned up at six. That meant the meal was served one hour late.

A: Oh, perhaps there was heavy traffic at that time …

B: OK, but we were very disappointed by the quality of the food, too. In fact, it was very poor. For example, the chips were cold, and the chicken was very dry – it tasted like it was days old.

A: I'm shocked to hear that …

B: Also, there wasn't enough to eat. We paid for food for thirty people, but most of us went home hungry. At most, there was enough food for maybe ten people! The whole evening was a disaster and I'd like to know what you're going to do about it.

A: Oh, dear. I think you'd better talk to the manager. If you could hold the line, I'll put you straight through …

UNIT 12 – Earth, our home

12c – Exercise 2 p. 102

1   *A:* Look at all those plastic coffee cups and water bottles lying around. It's quite shocking!

    B: I know. You'd think there were no such things as recycling bins.

    A: And it's so unnecessary – most cafés let you bring in your own cups now and fill them up for you. But how did it all get there in the first place?

    B: Think about it! People were sitting here in a traffic jam like you and me; they finished their drink and then just threw their rubbish out of the window onto the side of the road!

2   Most people would agree that factories are not good for the environment, but what they may not realise is that they can actually be a direct danger to human health. Factories are responsible for half of all air and water pollution which cause all sorts of health problems. I'm not saying that we should close down factories completely. However, those that are in towns and cities should be moved to areas further out in the countryside …

3   *A:* Did you hear? There's a huge fire up in Yorkshire! I heard about it on the morning news. It's terrible. They're still trying to put it out and huge areas of forest have been destroyed.

B: How awful! Do they know what caused it?

A: They think someone had a barbecue and didn't put it out properly. And the lack of rain lately made it extra dangerous. They obviously didn't pay attention to what they were doing.

B: People like that make me so angry – they should have more respect for the natural environment!

4   *A:* I really don't think we do enough to help the environment, especially at home.

    B: Oh, I don't know. You never leave the computer plugged in if you're away from your desk and I always turn off the tap when I'm shaving.

    A: Yes, but we could do more! What about all those 'single-use' products we use, like plastic knives and forks? We mustn't buy throwaway items anymore – they're really bad for the environment!

    B: I guess you're right! We don't really need them anyway.

12c – Exercise 9a p. 103

Presenter: This week on *Environment Now* we've asked listeners to call in and say what they do to reduce plastic in their everyday lives. Caller One is on the line now. Hello, Adam. What's your answer to the problem?

Adam: Hello, Sarah. I always use my own shopping bag when I go shopping. That means I can use it again and again and avoid those awful plastic ones they give you in supermarkets. They cause shocking pollution! Saying no to plastic bags means a much cleaner environment.

Presenter: That's great, Adam. Thank you. Now, our next caller is Beth. Beth, hi!

Beth: Hi, Sarah. I really love your show and I'm pleased to share my favourite tip for reducing plastic!

Presenter: And what's that?

Beth: We shouldn't buy things sold in plastic. For example, plastic bottles of water are terrible for the environment. Whenever I go out, I take a glass bottle with me, just a small one so it's not too heavy! I just fill it up again when it's empty. And the great thing is you don't need to do any recycling! There's no waste at all – like, zero!

Presenter: Thank you for that, Beth! If anyone else would like to phone in with their suggestions, we're taking calls now on …

Formative Evaluation Chart

Name of game/activity: ....

Aim of game/activity: ....

Unit: .... Course: ....

Students' names:	Mark and comments
1	
2	
3	
4	
5	
6	
7	
8	
9	
10	
11	
12	
13	
14	
15	
16	
17	
18	
19	
20	
21	
22	
23	
24	
25	

Cumulative Evaluation

Student's Self Assessment Forms

CODE			
**** Excellent	***** Very Good**	**** OK**	*** Not Very Good**

Student's Self Assessment Form	**UNIT 1**
Go through Unit 1 and find examples of the following. Use the code to evaluate yourself.	
• use words/phrases related to character & appearance	
• use words/phrases related to clothes & accessories	
• understand texts related to character & appearance	
• listen to and understand dialogues related to clothes & accessories	
• express opinion politely	
• describe a person	
• decide what to wear	
• make suggestions – agree/disagree	
• identify diphthongs /eɪ/, /aɪ/, /ɔɪ/	
Go through the corrected writing tasks. Use the code to evaluate yourself.	
• write an article about an inspiring person with accurate spelling, punctuation and layout	
• link ideas using appropriate linkers (*also, and, as well, but, however, still, although*)	

CODE			
**** Excellent	*** Very Good	** OK	* Not Very Good

Student's Self Assessment Form   UNIT 2

Go through Unit 2 and find examples of the following. Use the code to evaluate yourself.

• use words/phrases related to types of books	
• use words/phrases related to feelings	
• understand texts related to books	
• relate the plot of a book & describe reactions	
• listen to and understand narrations related to feelings	
• narrate events	
• express sympathy	
• describe past habits/routines	
• narrate a story	
• use interjections to express feelings	
• present a book character	

Go through the corrected writing tasks. Use the code to evaluate yourself.

• write a paragraph to describe a book	
• write a story with accurate spelling, punctuation & layout	
• end a story using direct speech or a rhetorical question	

CODE			
**** Excellent	***** Very Good**	**** OK**	*** Not Very Good**

Student's Self Assessment Form   UNIT 3

Go through Unit 3 and find examples of the following. Use the code to evaluate yourself.

• use words/phrases related to travel & means of transport	
• use words/phrases related to parts of an airport	
• understand texts related to transport	
• listen to and understand dialogues related to transport	
• report lost luggage	
• identify silent letters	

Go through the corrected writing tasks. Use the code to evaluate yourself.

• write a comment on a blog about a trip	
• write an article describing a journey with accurate spelling, punctuation & layout	
• use the senses in narratives/descriptive articles	
• research and write about a symbol in a country	

CODE			
**** Excellent	*** Very Good	** OK	* Not Very Good

Student's Self Assessment Form

Values A – Public Speaking Skills A

Go through Values A – Public Speaking Skills A and find examples of the following. Use the code to evaluate yourself.

• identify purpose of text	
• understand texts related to people	
• express opinion	
• present a person	
• present a statue using a story	

CODE			
**** Excellent	***** Very Good**	**** OK**	*** Not Very Good**

Student's Self Assessment Form UNIT 4

Go through Unit 4 and find examples of the following. Use the code to evaluate yourself.

• use words/phrases related to stressful events	
• use words/phrases related to fears & physical reactions	
• understand texts related to stressful events	
• describe hopes, dreams and ambitions	
• listen to and understand a radio interview about fears & reactions	
• ask for/give advice	
• express opinion	
• identify /z/, /s/ sounds	

Go through the corrected writing tasks. Use the code to evaluate yourself.

• write an informal email asking for advice	
• write an informal email giving advice with accurate spelling, punctuation & layout	
• support advice with expected results	
• write a short text about a festival	

CODE			
**** Excellent	***** Very Good**	**** OK**	*** Not Very Good**

Student's Self Assessment Form   UNIT 5

Go through Unit 5 and find examples of the following. Use the code to evaluate yourself.

• use words/phrases related to cities of the future & predictions	
• understand texts related to predictions	
• make predictions	
• listen to and understand dialogues related to predictions	
• discuss future plans	
• design and present a city of the future	
• identify /uː/, /ʊ/ sounds	

Go through the corrected writing tasks. Use the code to evaluate yourself.

• write an essay making predictions with accurate spelling, punctuation & layout	
• introduce an essay with a statement or question	
• brainstorm for ideas	

CODE			
**** Excellent	*** Very Good	** OK	* Not Very Good

Student's Self Assessment Form

UNIT 6

Go through Unit 6 and find examples of the following. Use the code to evaluate yourself.

• use words/phrases related to types of films & TV programmes	
• use words/phrases related to types of music	
• understand texts related to films and music	
• express likes/dislikes	
• express preferences	
• listen to and understand dialogues related to films/TV	
• identify types of music	
• make a recommendation	
• recommend – criticise	
• express an opinion	
• identify /ʌ/, /æ/ sounds	

Go through the corrected writing tasks. Use the code to evaluate yourself.

• research and write a fact sheet about a film	
• write a quiz	
• write a film review with accurate spelling, punctuation & layout	
• use appropriate tenses in film reviews	
• brainstorm for ideas	
• prepare an advertising poster	

CODE			
**** Excellent	*** Very Good	** OK	* Not Very Good

Student's Self Assessment Form

Values B – Public Speaking Skills B

Go through Values B – Public Speaking Skills B and find examples of the following.
Use the code to evaluate yourself.

• predict content of text	
• give reasons	
• understand texts related to self-confidence	
• identify types of speeches	
• use cue cards to prepare for a speech	
• give a speech about a film director	

CODE			
**** **Excellent**	*** **Very Good**	** **OK**	* **Not Very Good**

Student's Self Assessment Form   UNIT 7

Go through Unit 7 and find examples of the following. Use the code to evaluate yourself.

• use words/phrases related to disasters	
• use words/phrases related to emergency services	
• understand texts related to disasters	
• recognise important points in a newspaper article	
• listen to and understand a news report	
• describe a rescue	
• call the emergency services	
• retell a story	
• give a presentation	
• identify /tʃ/, /dʒ/ sounds	

Go through the corrected writing tasks. Use the code to evaluate yourself.

• write a news report with accurate spelling, punctuation & layout	
• use formal impersonal style	
• brainstorm for ideas	
• research & write a short text about a disaster	
• make notes for a presentation	

CODE			
**** **Excellent**	*** **Very Good**	** **OK**	* **Not Very Good**

Student's Self Assessment Form   UNIT 8

Go through Unit 8 and find examples of the following. Use the code to evaluate yourself.

• use words/phrases related to work & jobs	
• use words/phrases related to work & education	
• understand texts related to work	
• make choices	
• express opinion based on a text	
• interview a person about their job	
• talk about one's job	
• listen to and understand monologues related to jobs	
• identify /uː/, /juː/ sounds	
• research and present a traditional job	

Go through the corrected writing tasks. Use the code to evaluate yourself.

• write a short text about one's job	
• write a for-and-against essay with accurate spelling, punctuation & layout	
• introduce main body paragraphs in essays with topic sentences	
• use formal style	

CODE			
**** Excellent	*** Very Good	** OK	* Not Very Good

Student's Self Assessment Form   UNIT 9

Go through Unit 9 and find examples of the following. Use the code to evaluate yourself.

• use words related to sports, equipment & places	
• understand texts related to sports	
• listen to and understand podcasts about sports & exercise	
• ask for information	
• present a sport & its rules	
• identify /eɪ/, /aɪ/ sounds	

Go through the corrected writing tasks. Use the code to evaluate yourself.

• write a blog entry about an extreme sport	
• write a blog entry about ways to get fit with accurate spelling, punctuation & layout	
• justify arguments with reasons	
• write a text about a sport & its rules	

CODE			
**** Excellent	*** Very Good	** OK	* Not Very Good

Student's Self Assessment Form

Values C – Public Speaking Skills C

**Go through Values C – Public Speaking Skills C and find examples of the following.
Use the code to evaluate yourself.**

• understand texts related to how to show appreciation	
• identify author's purpose	
• express opinion	
• use emotional language in public speaking	
• give a farewell speech	

CODE			
**** Excellent	*** Very Good	** OK	* Not Very Good

Student's Self Assessment Form   UNIT 10

Go through Unit 10 and find examples of the following. Use the code to evaluate yourself.

• use words/phrases related to chores	
• use words/phrases related to technology	
• use words/phrases related to digital communication	
• understand texts related to technology	
• listen to and understand monologues about social media	
• express opinion	
• give instructions	
• identify /əʊ/, /ɔː/ sounds	

Go through the corrected writing tasks. Use the code to evaluate yourself.

• write a comment for a blog expressing opinion	
• write an article giving an opinion using appropriate spelling, punctuation & layout	
• practise ways to start/end an article giving opinion	
• match viewpoints with reasons/examples	
• research and write an article about a museum	

CODE			
**** Excellent	*** Very Good	** OK	* Not Very Good

Student's Self Assessment Form   UNIT 11

Go through Unit 11 and find examples of the following. Use the code to evaluate yourself.	
• use words/phrases related to food, ways of cooking & tastes	
• use words/phrases related to customer complaints	
• understand texts related to food & food festivals	
• express opinion giving reasons	
• listen to and understand a telephone conversation about a complaint	
• make a complaint over the telephone	
• identify /ð/, /z/ sounds	
• research & present a food festival	

Go through the corrected writing tasks. Use the code to evaluate yourself.	
• research and write a paragraph about street food	
• write an online complaint form with accurate spelling, punctuation & layout	
• use formal language	

CODE			
**** Excellent	*** Very Good	** OK	* Not Very Good

Student's Self Assessment Form   UNIT 12

Go through Unit 12 and find examples of the following. Use the code to evaluate yourself.

• use words/phrases related to the environment	
• understand texts related to the environment	
• listen to and understand dialogues/monologues related to the environment	
• persuade sb to participate in an event (invite & ask for help, persuade)	
• research and present ways to reuse plastic bottles	
• identify /d/, /dʒ/ sounds	

Go through the corrected writing tasks. Use the code to evaluate yourself.

• write an article providing solutions to a problem with accurate spelling, punctuation & layout	
• link ideas	
• analyse a writing rubric	
• organise notes	
• research and write an article about an environmental organisation	

150 © Express Publishing PHOTOCOPIABLE

CODE			
**** Excellent	***** Very Good**	**** OK**	*** Not Very Good**

Student's Self Assessment Form

Values D – Public Speaking Skills D

Go through Values D – Public Speaking Skills D and find examples of the following. Use the code to evaluate yourself.

• understand texts related to caution	
• describe an experience	
• research & write a short text about hackers online	
• use persuasive approaches in public speaking	
• identify opening/closing techniques in a speech	
• give a talk about the right way to use social media	

Progress Report Cards

Progress Report Card

.... (name) can: **Unit 1**

	very well	OK	not very well
use words/phrases related to character & appearance			
use words/phrases related to clothes & accessories			
understand texts related to character & appearance			
listen to and understand dialogues related to clothes & accessories			
express opinion politely			
describe a person			
decide what to wear			
make suggestions – agree/disagree			
identify diphthongs \eɪ\, \aɪ\, \ɔɪ\			
write an article about an inspiring person with accurate spelling, punctuation and layout			
link ideas using appropriate linkers (*also, and, as well, but, however, still, although*)			

Progress Report Card

.... (name) can: **Unit 2**

	very well	OK	not very well
use words/phrases related to types of books			
use words/phrases related to feelings			
understand texts related to books			
relate the plot of a book & describe reactions			
listen to and understand narrations related to feelings			
narrate events			
express sympathy			
describe past habits/routines			
narrate a story			
use interjections to express feelings			
present a book character			
write a paragraph to describe a book			
write a story with accurate spelling, punctuation & layout			
end a story using direct speech or a rhetorical question			

Progress Report Card

.... (name) can: **Unit 3**

	very well	OK	not very well
use words/phrases related to travel & means of transport			
use words/phrases related to parts of an airport			
understand texts related to transport			
listen to understand dialogues related to transport			
report lost luggage			
identify silent letters			
write a comment on a blog about a trip			
write an article describing a journey with accurate spelling, punctuation & layout			
use the senses in narratives/descriptive articles			
research and write about a symbol in a country			

Progress Report Card

.... (name) can: **Values A – Public Speaking Skills A**

	very well	OK	not very well
identify purpose of text			
understand texts related to people			
express opinion			
present a person			
present a statue using a story			

Progress Report Card

.... (name) can: **Unit 4**

	very well	OK	not very well
use words/phrases related to stressful events			
use words/phrases related to fears & physical reactions			
understand texts related to stressful events			
describe hopes, dreams and ambitions			
listen to and understand a radio interview about fears & reactions			
ask for/give advice			
express opinion			
identify /z/, /s/ sounds			
write an informal email asking for advice			
write an informal email giving advice with accurate spelling, punctuation & layout			
support advice with expected results			
write a short text about a festival			

Progress Report Card

.... (name) can: **Unit 5**

	very well	OK	not very well
use words/phrases related to cities of the future & predictions			
understand texts related to predictions			
make predictions			
listen to and understand dialogues related to predictions			
discuss future plans			
design and present a city of the future			
identify /uː/, /ʊ/ sounds			
write an essay making predictions with accurate spelling, punctuation & layout			
introduce an essay with a statement or question			
brainstorm for ideas			

Progress Report Card

.... (name) can:	Unit 6		
	very well	OK	not very well
use words/phrases related to types of films & TV programmes			
use words/phrases related to types of music			
understand texts related to films and music			
express likes/dislikes			
express preferences			
listen to and understand dialogues related to films/TV			
identify types of music			
make a recommendation			
recommend – criticise			
express an opinion			
identify /ʌ/, /æ/ sounds			
research and write a fact sheet about a film			
write a quiz			
write a film review with accurate spelling, punctuation & layout			
use appropriate tenses in film reviews			
brainstorm for ideas			
prepare an advertising poster			

Progress Report Card

.... (name) can:	Values B – Public Speaking Skills B		
	very well	OK	not very well
predict content of text			
give reasons			
understand texts related to self-confidence			
identify types of speeches			
use cue cards to prepare for a speech			
give a speech about a film director			

Progress Report Card

.... (name) can:	very well	OK	not very well
Unit 7			
use words/phrases related to disasters			
use words/phrases related to emergency services			
understand texts related to disasters			
recognise important points in a newspaper article			
listen to and understand a news report			
describe a rescue			
call the emergency services			
retell a story			
give a presentation			
identify /tʃ/, /dʒ/ sounds			
write a news report with accurate spelling, punctuation & layout			
use formal impersonal style			
brainstorm for ideas			
research & write a short text about a disaster			
make notes for a presentation			

Progress Report Card

.... (name) can:	very well	OK	not very well
Unit 8			
use words/phrases related to work & jobs			
use words/phrases related to work & education			
understand texts related to work			
make choices			
express opinion based on a text			
interview a person about their job			
talk about one's job			
listen to and understand monologues related to jobs			
identify /uː/, /juː/ sounds			
research and present a traditional job			
write a short text about one's job			
write a for-and-against essay with accurate spelling, punctuation & layout			
introduce main body paragraphs in essays with topic sentences			
use formal style			

Progress Report Card

.... (name) can: **Unit 9**

	very well	OK	not very well
use words related to sports, equipment & places			
understand texts related to sports			
listen to and understand podcasts about sports & exercise			
ask for information			
present a sport & its rules			
identify /ei/, /ai/ sounds			
write a blog entry about an extreme sport			
write a blog entry about ways to get fit with accurate spelling, punctuation & layout			
justify arguments with reasons			
write a text about a sport & its rules			

Progress Report Card

.... (name) can: **Values C – Public Speaking Skills C**

	very well	OK	not very well
understand texts related to how to show appreciation			
identify author's purpose			
express opinion			
use emotional language in public speaking			
give a farewell speech			

Progress Report Card

.... (name) can:　　　　　　　　**Unit 10**

	very well	OK	not very well
use words/phrases related to chores			
use words/phrases related to technology			
use words/phrases related to digital communication			
understand texts related to technology			
listen to and understand monologues about social media			
express opinion			
give instructions			
identify /əʊ/, /ɔː/ sounds			
write a comment for a blog expressing opinion			
write an article giving an opinion using appropriate spelling, punctuation & layout			
practise ways to start/end an article giving opinion			
match viewpoints with reasons/examples			
research and write an article about a museum			

Progress Report Card

.... (name) can:　　　　　　　　**Unit 11**

	very well	OK	not very well
use words/phrases related to food, ways of cooking & tastes			
use words/phrases related to customer complaints			
understand texts related to food & food festivals			
express opinion giving reasons			
listen to and understand a telephone conversation about a complaint			
make a complaint over the telephone			
identify /ð/, /z/ sounds			
research & present a food festival			
research and write a paragraph about street food			
write an online complaint form with accurate spelling, punctuation & layout			
use formal language			

Progress Report Card

.... (name) can: **Unit 12**

	very well	OK	not very well
use words/phrases related to the environment			
understand texts related to the environment			
listen to and understand dialogues/monologues related to the environment			
persuade sb to participate in an event (invite & ask for help, persuade)			
research and present ways to reuse plastic bottles			
identify /d/ /dʒ/ sounds			
write an article providing solutions to a problem with accurate spelling, punctuation & layout			
link ideas			
analyse a writing rubric			
organise notes			
research and write an article about an environmental organisation			

Progress Report Card

.... (name) can: **Values D – Public Speaking Skills D**

	very well	OK	not very well
understand texts related to caution			
describe an experience			
research & write a short text about hackers online			
use persuasive approaches in public speaking			
identify opening/closing techniques in a speech			
give a talk about the right way to use social media			

Workbook Key

Unit 1

1a – Vocabulary

1
1	bushy	3	curved	5	elderly
2	hooked	4	chubby	6	bottom

2
1	honest	4	brave	7	sociable
2	jealous	5	calm	8	reliable
3	lazy	6	funny		

3
1	to	4	after	7	up
2	about	5	forward	8	to
3	to	6	for		

4
1	teenager	5	long	9	ears
2	thick	6	forehead	10	full
3	lip	7	early	11	eyes
4	forties	8	nose	12	eyebrows

5
1	kind	3	adventurous	5	patient
2	generous	4	charming	6	bossy

1b – Grammar

1
1	comes	4	is looking
2	Are they cleaning	5	catch
3	doesn't open	6	is meeting

2
1	smells	4	tastes
2	is seeing	5	are you thinking
3	looks	6	do not know

3
1	am visiting	6	doesn't like
2	lives	7	are going
3	works	8	am catching
4	loves	9	leaves
5	is thinking	10	Do you want

4
1	that	3	where	5	why
2	which	4	when	6	whose

5
1	whose	4	when	7	why
2	which	5	who	8	where
3	who	6	which		

In 2, 3 and 6, the relative can be omitted.

6
1. who loves basketball
2. whose trip was cancelled
3. who are talking to the bus driver
4. which is about Indian music
5. whose car broke down

1c
Vocabulary

1
1	pullovers	3	raincoats	5	blouses
2	polo shirts	4	waistcoats	6	jeans

2
1	dresses, womenswear	4	footwear, shoes
2	suits, menswear	5	tracksuits, sportswear
3	leather, accessories		

3
1	creative	3	attractive	5	responsible
2	reliable	4	famous		

Everyday English

4 1 goes with   2 fit   3 suits   4 match

5 1 b   2 b   3 b

6
1. My brown jacket and jeans.
2. You're probably right.
3. You look very smart in it.
4. I'm thinking of my brown ones.
5. It matches the suit perfectly.

Reading

7 1 T   2 F   3 T   4 F

8
1. James Bond has a charming side to his personality.
2. Lara Croft enjoys taking risks.
3. Lara Croft often explores ancient buildings.
4. Captain Jack Sparrow is a great sword fighter.

9 1 LC   2 JS   3 JB   4 JS   5 LC   6 JB

Unit 2

2a – Vocabulary

1
1	fantasy	3	health
2	biography	4	science fiction

2 **a)**
1	scary	4	complicated
2	impossible	5	full
3	exciting	6	easy

b)
1	horror	4	crime
2	science fiction	5	fantasy
3	action & adventure	6	comedy

3
1	out	3	down	5	up
2	at	4	about	6	at

4
1	settled	3	stay	5	take
2	break	4	solve	6	see

Workbook Key

5
1. bestseller
2. epic
3. main
4. stay
5. falling
6. arrives
7. rules
8. broken
9. missing
10. confusing
11. dull
12. powerful

2b – Grammar

1
1. was boarding, heard
2. visited, went
3. did you stop, walked
4. were watching, were making
5. got, locked, walked
6. wasn't studying, was playing

2
1. ~~Were~~ **Was** he working yesterday evening?
2. Molly didn't ~~went~~ **go** to the book fair.
3. Fran wasn't ~~had~~ **having** lunch when we saw her.
4. Jake was reading ~~when~~ **while** Sally was watching TV.
5. The sun was ~~shine~~ **shining** in the sky.
6. Did Harry and Amy ~~came~~ **come** to the cinema with you?

3
1. wasn't/was not snowing, left, began
2. was tidying, went out
3. was sleeping, was watching, hit
4. grabbed, was feeding
5. could not/couldn't, was blowing
6. Did you come across, were walking

4
1. used to have
2. used to/would take
3. Did Fred use to be
4. didn't use to/wouldn't wake up
5. used to/would jog
6. used to/would walk

5
1. used to go/would go/went
2. used to have/had
3. used to love/loved
4. didn't use to be/wasn't
5. used to bring/would bring/brought, used to visit/would visit/visited
6. used to visit/would visit/visited, went

6
1. Danny ~~would~~ **used to** live in Brighton when he was a child.
2. Did Ellie ~~used~~ **use** to go to school by bus?
3. I didn't use to ~~liking~~ **like** train journeys, but now I enjoy them.
4. Tom and Susie ~~use~~ **used** to go for long walks in the forest.
5. Where did Olly ~~would~~ **use to** go running when he lived in town?
6. ~~Does~~ **Did** Rachel use to have a part-time job when she was at university?

2c
Vocabulary

1
1. relieved
2. scared
3. amazed
4. annoyed
5. nervous

2
1. bored
2. embarrassed
3. miserable
4. confused
5. disappointed

3
1. confusing
2. depressing
3. terrified
4. worried
5. exciting
6. exhausted

Everyday English

4
1. c
2. b
3. a

5
1. a
2. a
3. a
4. b

6
1. You won't believe what happened to Max last week
2. What did he do
3. Did he manage to get some help
4. It was after midnight when he got home
5. Poor him
6. Oh man, that sounds like an awful weekend

Reading

7
1. D
2. B
3. C
4. A
5. B
6. D
7. B
8. A

8
1. D
2. B
3. C
4. A

9
1. B
2. A
3. C

Unit 3

3a – Vocabulary

1
1. foreign
2. boat
3. car
4. train
5. sled

2
1. slow
2. long
3. modern
4. huge
5. hot
6. amazing
7. cheap

3
1. do
2. go
3. take
4. go
5. take
6. make

4
1. by
2. on
3. into
4. in
5. over
6. at
7. in

5
1. trip
2. come
3. ride
4. platform
5. set up
6. whizzing

Workbook Key

3b – Vocabulary

1
1 hasn't booked
2 seen, –
3 just, the
4 been, –
5 the, for
6 has been trying, the

2
1 Has Mark ever been, the
2 has been preparing, –
3 Have you seen, the
4 have been taking, the
5 haven't had, –
6 has been skiing, the

3
1 have been
2 have been studying
3 have warned
4 have been rising
5 have already disappeared
6 have moved
7 has been increasing

4
1 hadn't eaten
2 Had Sophie locked
3 hadn't finished
4 had you been waiting

5
1 had been looking
2 had repainted
3 had already booked
4 had you been sitting

6
1 had
2 had arrived
3 –
4 had been standing
5 told
6 the
7 didn't inform
8 had been travelling
9 –
10 Have you had

3c
Vocabulary

1
1 customs
2 duty-free
3 check-in
4 passport control
5 departures

2
1 baggage reclaim
2 arrivals
3 information
4 check-in
5 customs

3
1 cloudy
2 historic
3 energetic
4 daily
5 romantic
6 dramatic
7 lovely
8 artistic

Everyday English

4
1 reclaim
2 flight
3 receipt
4 boarding
5 contact

5 1 d   2 c   3 b   4 a

6
1 Tania Walker. Flight SN 965 from Helsinki.
2 It's an expensive, brown, leather one with gold straps.
3 Did you lose it on the plane?
4 OK. Where are you staying?
5 Alright, Ms Walker, we'll have a look for your handbag.

Reading

7 1 F   2 DS   3 DS   4 T

8
1 around 5 million
2 the 4th century
3 get a better price
4 (a performance of) traditional Georgian dance.

9
1 narrow streets, colourful houses and small shops
2 glass and steel
3 spicy beef and lamb in dough
4 They leap around.

Skills Practice A (Units 1-3)
Reading

1 1 A   2 B   3 B   4 C   5 D

2
1 Bastille Day
2 islands
3 like a waistcoat
4 Mexico
5 hole

3 1 F   2 T   3 DS   4 F   5 T

Everyday English

4
1 b   3 a   5 d   7 c
2 g   4 f   6 h   8 e

5
1 b   3 a   5 b   7 a
2 b   4 b   6 b   8 b

6 1 C   2 E   3 G   4 A   5 D   6 H

Listening

7 1 C   2 E   3 B   4 D   5 F   6 A

8
1 Rose
2 3/three
3 Australia
4 The Agency
5 thriller

9 1 B   2 A   3 B   4 C   5 A

Writing

10 a) Name: Bethany Hamilton
Where from: Hawaii, USA
What famous for: one of the world's best surfers
Achievements: has won many competitions
Appearance: fit and attractive

Workbook Key

Character: brave and determined
Why inspiring: shows that anything is possible

b)
1. Bethany Hamilton
2. Hawaii, USA
3. one of the world's best surfers
4. has won many competitions
5. fit and attractive
6. brave and determined
7. shows that anything is possible

11 a)
1. summer   4. excited
2. bike ride   5. sunny
3. countryside

b) One summer afternoon, Brian set off for a bike ride in the countryside. He had a bottle of water, a snack and his mobile phone in his backpack, and felt very excited. It was hot and sunny.
After half an hour, he turned down a quieter road with empty fields of grass on both sides. He was really enjoying the peace and quiet, when he got a puncture in the front tire of his bike, and he lost control and fell, hurting his knee.
Somehow, he managed to drag himself off the road. He tried to call his dad, but the fall had broken his phone. Soon, he started to feel worried, because the road was very quiet. "How am I going to get out of here?" he wondered.
Finally, he saw a tractor coming. The farmer kindly drove Brian home in the tractor. He felt glad to be home safe and sound.

12 The Great Pyramid
I'm an Egyptian who lives in Cairo, but I only saw the Great Pyramid at Giza up close for the first time last summer! A friend of mine came for a visit from the UK, so we went by taxi – Giza is only 16 km from Cairo.
You don't realise how big the Great Pyramid is until you get up close. Each stone is nearly as high as a person, and it's nearly 150 metres tall! We spent three hours walking round on foot, our eyes and mouths wide open!
The best part was when we actually went inside the pyramid. It was a strange feeling, a bit like going back in time. It has woken a deep curiosity in me for all things ancient!
Anyone visiting Egypt must of course visit the Great Pyramid, but Egyptians should too. As the only Wonder of the Ancient World still standing, it's well worth it!

Revision (Units 1-3)

Vocabulary

1 A	6 A	11 A	16 D	21 B
2 C	7 C	12 C	17 A	22 C
3 D	8 D	13 A	18 D	23 A
4 B	9 B	14 B	19 B	24 D
5 C	10 C	15 A	20 C	25 A

Grammar

1 C	6 C	11 C	16 A	21 C
2 A	7 C	12 B	17 C	22 C
3 D	8 A	13 C	18 A	23 D
4 A	9 B	14 A	19 D	24 B
5 B	10 A	15 B	20 B	25 C

Unit 4

4a – Vocabulary

1 1 d   2 f   3 a   4 e   5 b   6 c

2
1. fundraising   3. think   5. cause
2. take   4. afford   6. proud

3
1. became   3. let   5. started
2. applied   4. stole   6. was

4
1 of   3 about   5 in   7 at   9 from
2 after   4 up   6 off   8 over

5
1. reasons   5. divorce   9. volunteer
2. miserable   6. promotion   10. causes
3. financial   7. pile up
4. Retiring   8. useful

4b – Grammar

1
1. will open   4. Are you going to play
2. is flying   5. will buy
3. starts, won't be   6. am meeting

2
1. leave   3. Will it be   5. will go out
2. starts   4. get   6. receives

3
1. Is it going to rain   4. leaves
2. is going   5. won't pass
3. will enjoy   6. aren't meeting

4 1 c   2 f   3 a   4 b   5 d   6 e

5
1. takes   3. don't face   5. apologise
2. will go   4. will be   6. visit

Workbook Key

6 1 If we **don't** leave the house now, we'll miss the start of the film.
2 I won't phone you unless there **is** a problem.
3 If I**'ll pass** my driving test, I'll take everyone out to celebrate.
4 Anna **won't** be able to go to university if she fails her exams.
5 Charlie won't get a job unless he **does** better in interviews.
6 Tracy won't be able to work full-time if she **has** a baby.

4c
Vocabulary

1 1 sweat   3 freezes   5 harm
   2 feel   4 face   6 stood

2 1 goes   4 avoid
   2 control   5 beat
   3 ran   6 shook/was shaking

3 1 disobey   4 disappeared
   2 rethink   5 misspell
   3 misunderstood   6 reuses

Everyday English

4 1 c   2 a   3 d   4 b

5 1 a   2 a   3 b

6 1 You look a bit worried
2 What do you mean
3 Do you have any advice
4 It might be a good idea to
5 By doing this
6 Another idea would be to
7 Thanks for the tips
8 My pleasure

Reading

7 A 3   B 4   C 1   D 2

8 1 A   2 B   3 C

9 1 The physical effects of aquaphobia are increased heartbeat, sweating, trouble breathing and feeling sick or dizzy.
2 Some people become aquaphobics because of a bad experience with water that has followed them throughout their lives.
3 Doctors show sufferers small amounts of water, then move on to bigger ones, until they eventually face rivers and oceans.

Unit 5

5a – Vocabulary

1 1 d   3 e   5 g   7 c
   2 f   4 b   6 a

2 1 3D-printed house   5 front door
   2 Solar windows   6 Charging stations
   3 Vertical farms   7 traffic jams
   4 Drone deliveries

3 1 increase   3 deliver   5 produce
   2 provide   4 improve   6 transport

4 1 into   4 in   7 off
   2 with   5 back   8 about
   3 across   6 within   9 round

5 1 crowded   4 reducing   7 green
   2 constructing   5 floating   8 bright
   3 take up   6 create

5b – Grammar

1 1 will be waking up   4 will be visiting
   2 will be taking   5 won't be staying
   3 Will ... be flying   6 will be enjoying

2 2 Will Pam be having a History lesson at 10:00 tomorrow morning?
No, she won't. She'll be having a Biology lesson.
3 Will Pam be eating lunch with her friends at 1:15 tomorrow afternoon?
Yes, she will.
4 Will Pam be having piano practice at 3:00 tomorrow afternoon?
No, she won't. She'll be studying in the library.
5 Will Pam be cooking dinner for her parents at 5:30 tomorrow afternoon?
No, she won't. She'll be having piano practice.

3 2 In ten years' time, Paul will have found a well-paid job.
3 In ten years' time, Paul won't have moved into a new house.
4 In ten years' time, Paul won't have bought an expensive car.
5 In ten years' time, Paul will have travelled to a lot of countries.
6 In ten years' time, Paul won't have started his own family.

4
1 will have sent
2 won't have completed
3 will have closed
4 will you have done
5 will have had
6 won't have finished

5
1 will be sailing
2 Will you have finished
3 will be meeting
4 won't have completed
5 will be performing
6 Will you be seeing

5c
Vocabulary

1
1 decrease
2 polluted
3 expensive
4 poverty
5 affordable
6 cures

2
1 advanced
2 levels
3 Space
4 regular
5 serious
6 electric

3
1 lengthen
2 activate
3 advertise
4 lessen
5 darkened
6 specialises

Everyday English

4 1 b   2 c   3 d   4 a

5 1 b   2 a   3 b

6
1 What are your plans for this summer
2 Haven't you heard
3 I'll be working in the local library
4 So what will your duties be there
5 How long will you be working there
6 How about your plans
7 Sounds like fun

Reading

7 1 C   2 D   3 E   4 A   5 B

8
1 walk / speak without the use of a computer
2 learn how to avoid the risks
3 didn't turn out so well

9 1 C   2 B   3 A

Unit 6

6a – Vocabulary

1
1 crime
2 fantasy
3 western
4 drama
5 sci-fi
6 action-adventure

2
1 boring
2 amusing
3 scary
4 funny

3
1 series
2 adventures
3 role
4 spectators
5 created
6 opera

4
1 away
2 on
3 at
4 in
5 in
6 up

5
1 queue
2 blockbuster
3 series
4 plays
5 proves
6 screen
7 effects
8 enjoyable
9 audiences
10 sequel

6b – Grammar

1
1 filmed
2 appeared
3 be released
4 being
5 being streamed

2
1 was saved, by
2 are created, with
3 will be written, by
4 has just been released by
5 had been stolen, by
6 be made, with

3
1 We hope the film festival this weekend will be attended by lots of people!
2 The festival is being opened by actress Nicole Hart.
3 Her films are loved by people all over the world.
4 Her first film was made in 1991.
5 A famous DJ has been hired for the opening ceremony.
6 Tickets can be booked online.

4
1 myself (emphatic)
2 herself (reflexive)
3 herself (reflexive)
4 ourselves (emphatic)
5 themselves (emphatic)
6 himself (reflexive)

5
1 ourselves (R)
2 herself (E)
3 itself (E)
4 themselves (R)
5 yourself (E)

6
1 was created by
2 cut himself
3 are being taught
4 had been opened
5 are made scarier with
6 was the film *Jaws* made

Workbook Key

6c
Vocabulary

1
1 reality show
2 game show
3 DIY programme
4 documentary
5 chat show

2
1 opera
2 talk
3 cookery
4 travel
5 sitcom

3
1 thrilling
2 amazing
3 imaginative
4 talented
5 wonderful

Everyday English

4   1 c   2 d   3 b   4 a

5   1 a   2 b   3 a   4 b

6
1 No, I haven't.
2 You really must see it.
3 What's it about, anyway?
4 Well, the special effects are amazing.
5 Tell me more!

Reading

7   1 A   2 C   3 B   4 A   5 A

8
1 ran successful businesses themselves
2 comes from the 'shark'
3 a show in Japan called *Tigers of Money*
4 what contestants featured on the show have been doing

9   1 F   2 T   3 T   4 T   5 F   6 F

Skills Practice B (Units 4-6)
Reading

1   A 4   B 3   C 5   D 1   E 2

2   1 C   2 B   3 A   4 C   5 D

3   1 F   2 DS   3 T   4 T   5 F

Everyday English

4
1 a
2 b
3 d
4 c
5 f
6 e
7 h
8 g

5
1 b   3 b   5 b   7 b
2 b   4 a   6 b   8 b

6   1 E   2 C   3 D   4 H   5 B   6 G

Listening

7
1 Time
2 Selves
3 health
4 Rose
5 5/five

8   1 Y   2 Y   3 Y   4 N   5 N   6 N

9   1 C   2 C   3 B   4 B   5 C

Writing

10
1 action – adventure
2 Otto Bathurst
3 21st November
4 Taron Egerton
5 classic
6 English King
7 cast
8 special effects

11 a)   1 c   2 P, b   3 P, a   4 N, d

b) Suggested answer

The Future of Education

What does the future hold for education? In my opinion, developments are generally positive, though there is a darker side.

In the first place, new technology will make learning more fun. For instance, VR devices will bring lessons to life. Another positive is that more online courses will be available for free. As a result, anybody will be able to learn skills and get qualifications.

On the other hand, there will be less face-to-face teaching. As a result, students will feel less motivated as they are learning from an e-teacher. Another negative is that students' writing skills will worsen. For instance, they will lose handwriting and spelling skills by typing on computers.

To sum up, I feel that we should be positive about the future of learning. After all, technology offers many more advantages than disadvantages.

12   Hi Kate,

Sorry to hear about your problem. I completely understand – public speaking was something I was terrified of for years. But I learnt how to deal with it, and so can you!

Firstly, why don't you practise in front of a mirror? This way, you'll see how you look to the audience, and you'll get more confident.

Also, make cue cards with the important points from your presentation on them. Have them in front of you as you do your presentation, and go through them one by one. This is so that you know what to say next even when your mind goes blank!

I know what you're going through, and I hope my tips help. Write and tell me how you get on.

Talk soon,
Maria

Revision (Units 4-6)

Vocabulary

1	B	6	D	11	D	16	C	21	B
2	D	7	B	12	A	17	C	22	C
3	A	8	C	13	A	18	B	23	D
4	C	9	B	14	D	19	D	24	C
5	C	10	B	15	B	20	A	25	A

Grammar

1	B	6	B	11	C	16	D	21	C
2	A	7	A	12	C	17	D	22	B
3	C	8	C	13	B	18	C	23	D
4	B	9	A	14	D	19	B	24	A
5	C	10	C	15	A	20	A	25	A

Unit 7

7a – Vocabulary

1
1 warning
2 international
3 gas
4 clean
5 heavy
6 flooded
7 strong
8 rescue

2
1 with
2 in
3 on
4 out
5 off
6 to

3
1 difficult
2 huge
3 real
4 dark
5 dangerous

4
1 fire
2 flood
3 thunderstorm
4 avalanche
5 earthquake
6 eruption

5
1 loud
2 rain
3 conditions
4 struck
5 supplies
6 calm
7 narrow
8 unhurt

6
1 international
2 shake
3 rescuers
4 trapped
5 spread
6 control
7 conditions
8 alive
9 injured
10 recovering
11 warning
12 calm

7b – Grammar

1
1 told, was
2 had been, that
3 her, previous
4 told, they, then
5 said, had

2
1 to check
2 I was
3 not to forget
4 to

3
1 said
2 had to
3 had just got
4 told
5 didn't have
6 if
7 going
8 agreed
9 had told
10 to take

4
1 Max asked me if/whether I had got home OK in the previous night's thunderstorm.
2 Paul said that they had been waiting for the ambulance for over an hour.
3 Harriet asked me/us if/whether I/we were volunteering to help clean up the beach that day.
4 Michael said that we wouldn't be able to cross the river in that weather.

5
1 apologised
2 informed
3 warned
4 agreed
5 offered

6
1 the earthquake had happened that
2 me if I had called
3 how he had taken
4 promised to bring his
5 advised us to get out
6 apologised for not calling

7c
Vocabulary

1
1 mountain rescue
2 ambulance
3 coastguard
4 fire

2
1 accident, mountain rescue service
2 letting, coastguard
3 trapped, cave rescue service
4 behaving, police
5 struck, ambulance service

3
1 responsible
2 careless
3 suitable
4 magical
5 accidental
6 terrible

Everyday English

4
1 operator
2 connect
3 emergency
4 calm
5 way

Workbook Key

5 1 b   2 a   3 a

6 1 I'll connect you now.
    2 Please help!
    3 I'm at 45 Carrington Close, Parkway.
    4 No, I'm all by myself.
    5 Will they be long?

Reading

7 1 C   2 B   3 D   4 A

8 1 F   2 F   3 T   4 F

9 1 B   2 C   3 A   4 D

Unit 8

8a – Vocabulary

1 1 wages   3 job   5 contract
    2 peak   4 position   6 shift

2 1 on   3 for   5 on   7 out
    2 for   4 out   6 from   8 at

3 1 breathing   3 pearl   5 poisonous
    2 freezing   4 outdoor   6 mountain

4 1 watch   3 win   5 spend
    2 hold   4 earn   6 work

5 1 carried   5 full-time
    2 overalls   6 earn
    3 risky   7 wages
    4 work   8 responsible

8b – Grammar

1 1 would   4 give
    2 had   5 didn't have
    3 were   6 had applied

2 1 worked   4 had had
    2 had got   5 earned
    3 hadn't missed

3 1 wishes he hadn't behaved
    2 you had got
    3 I wouldn't have got
    4 didn't eat so much
    5 you had met

4 1 didn't   3 shall   5 does
    2 isn't   4 will   6 did

5 1 Despite   4 Even though
    2 do   5 did
    3 didn't   6 In spite of the fact

6 1 have you   4 Despite   7 have we
    2 Although   5 shall we   8 Although
    3 is she   6 isn't it

8c
Vocabulary

1 1 c   2 e   3 d   4 b   5 a

2 1 course   3 qualifications   5 marks
    2 advanced   4 training

3 1 Actor(s)/Actress(es)   4 sailors
    2 Librarian   5 engineer
    3 receptionist   6 presenter

Everyday English

4 1 part   3 hours   5 responsible
    2 sounds   4 love

5 1 a   2 b   3 a

6 1 You've got a new job, haven't you?
    2 What do you do in the job?
    3 I also advise them on healthy eating.
    4 I earn around £100 a day.
    5 What qualifications did you need?

Reading

7 1 T   2 F   3 F   4 T

8 1 D   2 B   3 F   4 A

9 1 D   2 A   3 B

Unit 9

9a – Vocabulary

1 1 f   3 g   5 b   7 c
    2 d   4 e   6 a   8 h

2 1 racket, trainers   3 climbing   5 cricket
    2 stick   4 gloves   6 helmets

3 1 playing   4 face   7 goes
    2 winning   5 energy   8 take
    3 beat   6 go

Workbook Key

4
1	about	3	into	5	for	7	down
2	at	4	up	6	with	8	under

5
1	limit	4	mind	7	taste
2	experience	5	deal	8	risk
3	energy	6	situations		

9b – Grammar

1
1	playing	4	going
2	start	5	have been training
3	to go		

2
1 Mike can't have run in the race.
2 Don't you just love hiking in the forest?
3 Molly suggested joining the local gym to get fitter.
4 Are you looking forward to going swimming on holiday?
5 Coach let everyone finish training early yesterday.
6 Have you asked Zack to play in the football team?
7 Niall hates doing any exercise at all!
8 Do you really need to carry all that equipment?

3
1 having, to go
2 to play, to have enjoyed
3 climbing, to see
4 being, run
5 giving, join
6 to have come, have started

4
1	is	3	is	5	are
2	Are	4	is	6	Was

5
1	are, is	3	is, is	5	are, are
2	is, are	4	are, is		

6
1	want to go	4	would hate to
2	was made to train	5	should meet outside
3	is our favourite	6	to be climbing

9c – Vocabulary

1
1	badminton	4	sailing
2	baseball	5	windsurfing
3	ice skating	6	water skiing

2
1	pitch	3	fitness	5	course
2	track	4	team		

3
1	membership	5	neighbourhood
2	decision	6	difference
3	training	7	abilities
4	excitement	8	weakness

Everyday English

4
1	How much	3	How often
2	What	4	What time

5
1	b	2	b	3	b

6
Hello, what can I do for you?
Hi. Can you tell me how much membership of the leisure centre is?
It's £50 for a year.
What does that include?
You get full use of the gym and 25% off all classes.
Are there any dance classes?
Yes. They cost £5 a session.
How often are they?
They're very popular, so they're every night apart from Saturdays.
Great. Can I join today?
Of course. Just fill in this form, please.

Reading

7
1	E	2	C	3	A	4	B

8
1	T	2	T	3	F	4	F

9
1 a helmet, boots, a mallet, a ball and a horse
2 by scoring the most goals
3 the nomadic tribes of Asia
4 Lessons are not expensive.

Skills Practice C (Units 7-9)

Reading

1
1	C	2	D	3	A

2
1	B	2	A	3	C	4	A	5	C

3
1	A	2	D	3	A	4	A

Everyday English

4
1	f	3	a	5	g	7	b
2	d	4	e	6	c		

Workbook Key

5
1	a	3	b	5	b	7	a
2	b	4	a	6	b	8	a

6 1 F   2 D   3 B   4 E   5 G   6 C

Listening

7
1 flexibility
2 family
3 work
4 money
5 sociable
6 friends
7 work
8 time

8 1 B   2 C   3 A   4 E

9 1 B   2 C   3 A   4 D

Writing

10
1 avalanche
2 Zermatt
3 10:35 am
4 Matterhorn Ski Paradise
5 100,000 tonnes
6 21/twenty-one
7 emergency services
8 chalets
9 closed
10 government
11 protection walls
12 tourist

11 **Suggested answer**
Today, I want to write about the positives of working at home versus in an office.
There are certain advantages to working at home. First of all, you can choose to work whenever you want. That's especially important when you have a young family. Second, you don't have to travel to work. That means you save lots of time and money.
Working in an office has certain advantages. First, it's more sociable. After all, you meet your colleagues every day, and you can even become good friends with them. Also, when you work in an office, it's easier to focus on your work. For instance, in any office, you don't have the option to surf the Net or watch TV, so you don't waste time.
All in all, both working at home and working in an office have their advantages. You have to think very carefully about what suits you best.

12 **Suggested answers**
a) 1 can get help from staff
2 trainers usually available to give expert advice
3 very public places
4 shy people don't like to go to gyms

b) Gym or no gym?
Joining a gym may seem like an attractive route to fitness. What exactly are its advantages and disadvantages, however?

A gym has clear advantages. To begin with, gyms have a variety of equipment that members can use. For example, there are exercise bikes and machines you can use for different muscles. Besides this, users can get help from staff. This is because trainers are usually available in gyms to give expert advice.
However, exercising in gyms has its disadvantages. Firstly, gyms are often crowded at popular times. This means users need to wait for machines and this wastes time. In addition, gyms are very public places. Shy people, for example, do not enjoy exercising in places like this.
In conclusion, although there are good and bad points to going to a gym, I believe it is well worth doing. After all, fitness is the goal, and membership of a gym is the best route there.

Revision (Units 7-9)
Vocabulary

1	B	6	A	11	A	16	A	21	B
2	C	7	A	12	B	17	D	22	D
3	A	8	D	13	C	18	B	23	A
4	B	9	D	14	B	19	C	24	B
5	C	10	C	15	C	20	A	25	A

Grammar

1	C	6	C	11	C	16	A	21	C
2	A	7	D	12	C	17	C	22	B
3	D	8	A	13	A	18	B	23	D
4	B	9	C	14	D	19	B	24	B
5	B	10	D	15	B	20	A	25	D

Unit 10
10a – Vocabulary

1
1 do
2 mopping
3 serving
4 make
5 lay
6 doing

2
1 share
2 feed
3 does
4 waters
5 take
6 bring
7 cook
8 serve

3
1 with
2 to
3 across
4 over
5 along
6 between

4
1 trade
2 high-definition
3 designers
4 sale
5 device
6 cleaner
7 got
8 maid
9 machine
10 app

10b – Grammar

1
1	could	3	ought to	5	can
2	Could	4	can't	6	Shall

2
1	ought to	3	shouldn't	5	could
2	have to	4	mustn't	6	was able to

3
1	must	3	must	5	must
2	might	4	can't	6	must

4
1	may be doing	3	can't be online
2	must know	4	couldn't have downloaded

5
1	must be having	4	may be planning
2	can't be studying	5	must be
3	must know		

6
1 Do we have to/need to attend the lecture?
2 Can/Could/May I use your computer?/Am I allowed to use your computer?
3 We have to use this operating system at work.
4 We/You, etc. mustn't/can't make phone calls in the library.
5 John could/may/might be online right now.

10c Vocabulary

1
1	instant	3	mobile	5	video
2	social	4	blog	6	online

2
1	make	3	use	5	send
2	write	4	commented	6	create

3
1	easily	6	possibly
2	extremely	7	definitely
3	privately	8	strongly
4	automatically	9	happily
5	directly	10	quickly

Everyday English

4
1	a	2	a	3	b

5
1	hand	4	decide	7	what
2	set	5	enter	8	problem
3	click	6	exactly		

6
2 OK, that's easy. First, go to the social networking site you want to join. Then, click on 'Open a new account'.
3 OK, got it. Now what?
4 Now, you need to enter the information it asks for and create a username.
5 OK, give me a minute … I've done that. Then, I click on 'Create your account', right?

6 Yes, exactly. Now, you can search for friends and send them friend requests.
7 How do I do that?
8 You just need to click on the 'find a friend' icon and type in their names.
9 Is that all? Thanks for your help.
10 No problem.

Reading

7
1	A	2	C	3	D	4	E

8
1	F	2	T	3	T	4	T	5	F

9
1	C	2	C	3	D

Unit 11

11a – Vocabulary

1
1	baked	3	fried	5	roasted
2	grilled	4	boiled		

2
1	out	3	at	5	for
2	of	4	off	6	up

3
1	sour	2	spicy	3	sweet	4	salty

4
1	street	3	fried	5	dishes
2	vendor	4	travel	6	main

5
1	spicy	6	dessert
2	dough	7	soft
3	toppings	8	ignore
4	dish	9	Trust
5	fillings	10	nutritious

11b – Grammar

1
1	least	3	more	5	much
2	longer	4	a lot	6	well

2
1 The new cafe is the ~~more~~ **most** expensive one in the area.
2 I think that Dad is a ~~best~~ **better** cook than Mum.
3 This is the most delicious dessert ~~of~~ **in** the world!
4 It's the ~~noisier~~ **noisiest** coffee shop I've ever been to!
5 We should tip our waiter; he is a lot more ~~politest~~ **polite** than the one we had last time.

3
1	crowded as	6	spicier
2	drier	7	the hottest
3	the best	8	less quickly
4	less	9	the most delicious
5	larger	10	more slowly

Workbook Key

4
1 no 3 nobody 5 anywhere
2 something 4 anything 6 too much

5
1 How ~~much~~ **many** times have you eaten at this restaurant?
2 ~~Nothing~~ **Everything** is wonderful, thank you. We love it here!
3 Can you buy a couple of ~~jars~~ **cartons** of milk?
4 There are a ~~bit of~~ **few** different dishes on the menu.
5 I can't think of ~~something~~ **anything** to make for dinner.
6 Can I have ~~any~~ **some** more cake, please?

6
1 a couple, much
2 can, anything
3 any, a few
4 every, nowhere
5 bar, slice

11c
Vocabulary

1
1 date 2 change 3 receipt 4 refund

2
1 order 3 change 5 credit
2 bill 4 manager

3
1 uncomfortable 4 constantly
2 rudely 5 service
3 apologise 6 disappointed

Everyday English

4
1 b 2 a 3 c

5
1 replacement 3 charge
2 problem 4 receipt

6
1 Can I speak to the manager, please?
2 How can I help you?
3 Really? What seems to be the problem?
4 I'm sorry to hear that.
5 I was upset to find that the order was wrong.
6 That's very kind of you, thanks.

Reading

7
1 D 2 A 3 C 4 D 5 C 6 D

8
1 DS 2 T 3 DS 4 F 5 T

9
1 C 2 C 3 D

Unit 12

12a – Vocabulary

1
1 pollution 3 water 5 camp
2 fires 4 waste

2
1 rain 3 join 5 staff
2 cutting 4 rubbish

3
1 clean 3 eco-friendly 5 plastic
2 environmental 4 clear

4
1 off 2 in 3 out 4 on 5 of 6 in

5
1 waste 4 receive 7 break up
2 support 5 pick up 8 earn
3 go on 6 look after

12b – Grammar

1
1 have 3 cleaned 5 built
2 had 4 has had

2
1 My mother has the grass ~~to~~ **cut** once a week.
2 Should I have my fire alarm ~~testing~~ **tested** regularly?
3 I hear that Michael had his electric car ~~stole~~ **stolen** at the weekend.
4 ~~Do~~ **Did** you have vegetables planted in your garden yesterday?
5 They had their house alarm ~~install~~ **installed** by a professional.

3
1 We were having a compost bin made for us at 3 pm yesterday.
2 I will have these boxes taken to the recycling centre for me.
3 Laura is having her water heater repaired because it's using too much electricity.
4 You should have your shower replaced with one that saves water.
5 David had the wind turbines on his farm designed by an engineer.
6 Michael has had the tap water at his house examined.

4
1 so, since 2 so, both 3 every, such a

5
1 either 3 so 5 whole
2 in case 4 Neither

6
1 both Jake and Samantha are
2 is so polluted that
3 in case he wants
4 such a rainy day that

12c
Vocabulary

1
1 take 2 send 3 use 4 print 5 plant

Workbook Key

2
1 take 5 wrap 9 turn
2 driving 6 food 10 tap
3 buy 7 leave 11 plant
4 season 8 use

3
1 horrifying/horrible 4 packaging
2 universal 5 replace
3 Education 6 easily

Everyday English

4 1 b 2 b 3 a

5
1 Would you like to join us?
2 We're hoping you could help out.
3 Any help is welcome.
4 I'd be glad to give you a lift there.

6
1 We're hoping you could help out
2 Why don't I pick you up
3 I'd be glad to give you a lift there
4 any help is welcome

Reading

7 1 F 2 F 3 T 4 T 5 F

8
1 trees 5 electricity
2 eco-friendly 6 inspire
3 greenhouses 7 environment
4 water

9 1 A 2 B 3 D

Skills Practice D (Units 10-12)

Reading

1 1 B 2 C 3 D 4 A 5 D

2 1 T 2 F 3 T 4 DS 5 T

3 1 B 2 D 3 B

Everyday English

4
1 e 3 c 5 a 7 f
2 g 4 d 6 b

5
1 b 3 a 5 a 7 a
2 b 4 b 6 b 8 J

6
1 F 3 D 5 H 7 C
2 G 4 A 6 E 8 J

Listening

7
1 Jones 3 camera 5 742436521
2 GY750 4 replacement

8 1 D 2 A 3 E 4 B

9 1 A 2 C 3 B 4 A 5 C

Writing

10 The Earth is Not our Litter Bin!
These days, litter is a problem in many towns and cities around the world. Often this problem is caused by the lack of litter bins around the city. So, how can we solve this problem?
One useful solution is to install more litter bins. For instance, we could install them in parks and on busy streets. This way, we make it easy for people to get rid of their litter.
Another way to solve the problem could be to organise clean-up days. For example, schools could be encouraged to get their students to take part in one. By doing this, we would get people of all ages actively involved in solving the problem.
All in all, by taking action, I believe that we can solve this problem. As the saying goes, we need to "be a part of the solution, not part of the pollution!"

11 a) 1 c 2 a 3 b 4 d

b) No to Smartphones
There's no doubt that smartphones are great for many things. But are they making us smarter? I don't think so.
First of all, smartphones distract you from important tasks. For example, when you're trying to study, a message might come in that you have to answer. This means that you lose focus and can't concentrate properly.
Also, smartphones are very addictive. There are many things to do on them, like playing games, going on social media sites and sending texts. As a result, there is no time for things like study or work.
All in all, although smartphones are obviously great in some ways, we have to be careful. They can easily turn us into dummies, unable to think for ourselves.

12 I am writing to complain about a phone I bought from your shop on Monday 3rd September. It is the Powerplus GY750 model.
To begin with, when I opened the box, the charger was missing. What is more, when I tried to take pictures, I discovered that the camera was not working.

Workbook Key

All in all, I was very disappointed with this phone and believe that I am entitled to a replacement. You can contact me on 742436521. I look forward to your prompt reply.

Revision (Units 10-12)

Vocabulary

1	A	6	A	11	C	16	B	21	D
2	C	7	C	12	B	17	D	22	B
3	B	8	B	13	C	18	A	23	A
4	B	9	A	14	A	19	C	24	C
5	C	10	D	15	D	20	B	25	A

Grammar

1	B	6	D	11	D	16	C	21	C
2	D	7	B	12	B	17	B	22	B
3	C	8	C	13	A	18	A	23	C
4	A	9	A	14	B	19	D	24	D
5	A	10	B	15	C	20	D	25	D

Workbook Audioscripts

Skills Practice A

Exercise 7 p. 18

One afternoon last summer, I got the idea to go for a bike ride in the countryside. I packed a small backpack with a bottle of water, a snack and my mobile phone, and felt very excited as I rode out of my driveway and down the road. It was really hot and sunny – the perfect weather for a bike ride!

After cycling on the main road for half an hour, I decided to turn down a quieter road with empty fields of grass on both sides. I was really enjoying the peace and quiet, but then something awful happened. After I rode over a pothole in the road, I got a puncture in the front tyre of my bike, and I lost control. Suddenly, I fell off the bike and hurt my knee. I was in a lot of pain and couldn't walk.

Somehow, I managed to drag myself to the side of the road, and sat down against some rocks. I decided to call my dad to come and pick me up, but when I opened my backpack, I saw that my phone had broken when I fell! Soon, I started to feel really worried, because the road was very quiet. After thirty minutes, no cars had passed, and I was feeling extremely hot under the blazing sun. "How am I going to get out of here?" I wondered. Luckily, I had the bottle of water, which I drank very slowly and carefully.

Finally, after around an hour, I saw a tractor in the distance. I shouted as loudly as I could for help, and luckily the farmer who was driving it heard me. He kindly drove me all the way home in the tractor. My parents were very relieved when I arrived, because they had been waiting for me all afternoon. I felt really weak after being out in the sun all day, but I was glad to be home safe and sound.

Exercise 8 p. 18

A: Hi, Pam. Did you have a nice weekend?

B: Yes, it was great. On Saturday afternoon, I attended a really enjoyable book reading. It was in Book Worms, that new bookshop across from the post office in Rose Street.

A: Oh, I heard something about that. It was at 3 pm, wasn't it? I wanted to attend, too, but I had basketball practice at 3:30, so it wasn't possible. Anyway, what was it like?

B: It was great! My favourite author was giving the reading, so I really enjoyed it.

A: Oh, who is that? You like James Moloney, don't you – from Australia?

B: No, you've got the name wrong – it's James Phelan – but yes, he's Australian. I've read every book that he's ever written – ever since his first novel *Fox Hunt* came out in 2006.

A: So, was the reading from that book?

B: No, it was from his new novel, called *The Agency*. I bought a signed copy at the book reading and I've read it already. It's fantastic!

A: That's a strange title. Is it about a travel agency or something?

B: No, of course not! It's a thriller about a spy called Jed Walker. It's the fifth book in a series about that character, actually. All of them are great.

A: Well, maybe I should give them a try then. Could you lend me the first in the series sometime?

B: Yes, of course! It's called *The Spy*. I'll bring it around to your flat this evening. It's a novel that's impossible to put down!

Exercise 9 p. 18

A: Hi, David. I thought you were on holiday with your family in Spain?

B: Well, that was the plan, Lisa. But it didn't work out in the end. At least my parents are having a good time. I phoned them earlier today. They had just eaten breakfast by the pool, and they were getting ready to go on a sightseeing tour. I felt really jealous!

A: But, I don't understand. Weren't you supposed to go with them?

B: Yes, we had booked the holiday at the travel agency for three people, and I had gone to the airport and checked in my suitcase. But then I got a big shock at passport control.

A: Don't tell me that your passport had expired!

B: Yes, exactly! I went to the information desk to see if there was anything I could do, but there wasn't. My parents offered to stay, but I told them to go without me.

A: That's awful!

B: But that's not all! By the time my parents had flown out, it was midnight, so all the public transport had stopped. There was no bus or train, and even though Dad had left the car in an airport car park, he had taken the key with him! So, I had no choice but to pay £50 for a taxi home!

A: Oh, no! And you're home alone now?

B: Yes, it's just me and the cat! But I don't mind. I enjoy cooking for myself, and I do my own laundry. I have to admit, though, that the house has become really messy in the last few days!

A: And are you going to get a new passport soon?

B: Yes, I have to because I'm going to my cousin's wedding in Italy next month. So, I went to the passport office and applied this morning. The normal price is £85 but I paid £50 extra to receive the passport quicker – within 14 days.

A: So, that adds up to £135 – that's a lot of money.

B: I know. It's been a really expensive month for me!

Workbook Audioscripts

Exercise 11a p. 19

One afternoon last summer, I got the idea to go for a bike ride in the countryside. I packed a small backpack with a bottle of water, a snack and my mobile phone, and felt very excited as I rode out of my driveway and down the road. It was really hot and sunny – the perfect weather for a bike ride!

Skills Practice B

Exercise 7 p. 36

Welcome back. You've tuned to Exeter University Radio. Now, I've just received an email about a talk from a guest speaker that I want to tell you about. The guest speaker will be Stan Wright. He's the Professor of Future Studies at York University, but these days he's more famous for his YouTube channel – *The Wright Time*. On the channel, Professor Wright posts weekly videos about news events and how they will affect the future. These videos are very popular with people of all ages, so this talk will probably be attended by a lot of people.
Professor Wright is also a writer, and he's recently released a book called *Our Future Selves*. Some of you might have read his last book – *Our Future Travels* – which was about the future of travel. Well, this book mainly deals with the future of health – and that's what Professor Wright will be speaking about in his talk.
Now, information about the talk. Unlike most talks from guest speakers, which take place in the Pine Room, Professor Wright will be speaking in the Rose Room – probably because it will be able to fit a larger audience. The talk will take place on 5th November, and it will start at 5 pm and last for around an hour. Then, Professor Wright has promised to stay for another half hour for a question-and-answer session.
This event is open to anyone who's a student at Exeter University – but you need to show your student card to enter. Now, some sports news ...

Exercise 8 p. 36

A: I'm joined in the studio now by the filmmaker Katie Lombard. Katie's first film, *Cheesecake*, is in cinemas now. First, Katie, congratulations on the film. It seems to be doing very well at the box office, doesn't it?
B: Yes, already half a million people have watched it – and that's just in five days!
A: Well, I saw it yesterday, too, and I really loved it. The reviews in the newspapers haven't been so positive, though. How can you explain that?
B: Yes, I've heard about that – and it doesn't surprise me. I think it's because of the type of film I've made. I tried to make an entertaining film that doesn't force you to think too much. Reviewers don't usually like films like that.
A: I see. And as well as directing, I believe that you wrote the film, too. Is that right?

B: Yes, that's true. In fact, I even acted in the film, though I didn't have any lines. Blink and you'll miss me!
A: Oh, I had no idea! Now, for people who haven't seen the film yet, can you give us a summary of the plot?
B: Sure. Basically, *Cheesecake* is an action film about a young woman who works as a waitress in a restaurant. One day, she gets an offer to become a spy, and her life changes forever.
A: And before you go Katie, a lot of people online have been wondering whether there will be a sequel. Is there any chance of a *Cheesecake 2*?
B: Maybe in the future, but it won't be my next project. I've already started writing a sci-fi film, which will be shot early next year. It doesn't have a title yet, but the main cast has been chosen. It'll be completely different to *Cheesecake* – that's for sure.
A: Katie, thanks for speaking to us today! That's Katie Lombard, whose film, *Cheesecake*, is in cinemas now.

Exercise 9 p. 36

1 **A:** Hi, Lisa. I didn't expect to see you here. Weren't you supposed to fly to Italy yesterday to give a presentation for your company?
   B: Yes, I was, but I didn't go in the end. I just couldn't force myself to get on board.
   A: What do you mean? Do you have a fear of flying?
   B: No, it was the weather. Whenever there's a storm, I can't even go outside – so there was no way I was going up in a plane!

2 **A:** Look at this, Alan. They're going to set up a cinema screen in the park and show films there all this week. Do you fancy going one evening?
   B: Not really, Joe. I'd like to watch a film this week, but not outdoors. It's quite chilly in the evenings.
   A: How about at the indoor cinema near my house, then? We could watch a thriller there at 9 pm tonight.
   B: That sounds better. And it would be more fun than watching a DVD at home.

3 **A:** Welcome back to the show. We're talking about the world in 2050. Our next caller is Ned from Shropshire. What are your thoughts, Ned?
   B: Hi, Lucy. Well, first, I disagree with your last caller – the man who talked about vacuum tube trains. I don't think we'll be using them – it would be far too expensive to make the lines.
   A: What about electric cars, then?
   B: That's something that's very likely – but not flying cars like another caller mentioned.
   A: Yes, we'll probably have to wait a little longer for them!

Workbook Audioscripts

4   *A:* You'll never guess who I met today, Rachael – my favourite actor, Christian Bale!

B: You've got to be kidding me, Stan! Did he come into the café where you work?

A: No, I actually saw him during my break. I was in a bookshop buying a novel – and there he was standing in the line behind me!

B: Are you sure it was him?

A: Yes, he was wearing a baseball cap and scarf, but it was definitely him.

B: Wow, I wonder what he was doing here.

5   *A:* Suzy, shouldn't you be getting ready for your interview now? It's almost 11 o'clock.

B: Don't worry, Mum – it's not until half twelve – I've got plenty of time to get ready. I'm really nervous about it, though. I'm sure I'll make a big mistake.

A: Well, I think you should be more worried about getting there on time. There's sometimes a lot of traffic in the city centre around noon.

B: OK, Mum, I'll start getting ready now.

Skills Practice C

Exercise 7 p. 54

Wendy: Welcome to Wendy's work podcast. Now, today, my guest is a good friend of mine, Max Cane. I first met Max when we were both working together in an office, but five years ago, he quit that job, and found a job where he can work at home. And that's exactly what we're going to discuss today – the positives of working at home versus in an office. Max, thanks for joining me.

Max: My pleasure, Wendy.

Wendy: So, Max, what are some of the advantages of working at home?

Max: Let's see. For one, there's more flexibility. Basically, I can choose to work whenever I want. That's great, especially when you have a young family.

Wendy: I see. What else?

Max: Another big advantage is that I don't have to travel to work. I don't need to drive or take public transport twice a day, so that saves me lots of time and money.

Wendy: But what about offices? I still work in an office, and I've got to say that an advantage is it's more sociable. You meet your colleagues every day, and you can even become good friends with them.

Max: That's right. It's something I miss. Plus, when you work in an office, it's easier to focus on your work. For instance, in an office, you don't have the option to surf the Net or watch TV, so you don't waste time, like I often do at home!

Wendy: That's true. Some interesting points there, Max, and I'll be writing a post about this topic on my blog later. You can check it out at wendywork@wordblog.com.

Exercise 8 p. 54

Speaker 1

I was on my way home from basketball practice one day when I saw black smoke coming out a building. Without thinking twice, I called 999 on my mobile. Soon, a fire engine arrived ... but by that time the smoke had gone. A family had just been burning some wood in the fireplace! One fireman told me not to worry about it – that it was good that I hadn't ignored it – but I felt terribly embarrassed.

Speaker 2

Last week, I was walking through the park when I saw a jogger breathing heavily. Then, he fell to the ground holding his heart. Luckily, I knew exactly what to do, and gave the man CPR while I shouted at a passer-by to call for an ambulance. The paramedics said that I had saved the man's life – and my picture even appeared in the newspaper! I'm just glad that I did that first-aid course last year!

Speaker 3

One afternoon last summer, I rowed my dad's small boat off the coast to go fishing. When I left the port, the sun was shining, but soon after, the sky turned black and a strong wind started blowing. I was out at sea in a storm! I immediately called the coastguard with my mobile phone, and in minutes a helicopter arrived to rescue me. I felt very silly that I hadn't read the weather forecast, though. I definitely won't make that mistake again.

Speaker 4

Last month, I travelled to Japan to take part in a martial arts competition. The day after I arrived, I was on a packed bus when, suddenly, the other passengers stopped talking and looked very serious. Then, the bus stopped and everyone got off. It turned out that there had been a small earthquake! Soon, the emergency services arrived and checked that everyone was OK. I guess, because I'd never experienced one before, I just thought it was a bumpy road!

Exercise 9 p. 54

Welcome back to the News Show on Shropshire FM. Now, some sports news. Yesterday, a record crowd of over 3,000 people turned out to see the Shropshire Football Women's Senior Cup Final between Dawley and Ludlow at Shrewsbury Stadium. As always, this was the final game of the season, so each team wanted to end the year on a high and lift the cup. Going into the final, both teams hadn't lost a game all season, including a one-one draw when they played each other in the league. So it was anyone's guess who would win.

The match itself was supposed to start at 3 pm, but the stadium's old clock showed 3:30 at kick-off. And unlike the men's final last weekend, when heavy traffic outside the stadium caused a delay, the reason was a heavy shower just before kick-off. So, referee Jenny Purcell wisely decided to let the rain pass before play got under way.

177

Workbook Audioscripts

The game itself was very tense. Neither team had many chances, and at half-time it was still zero-zero. Then, with just ten minutes to go in the second-half, Dawley scored the winning goal. And it was one to remember – from the Dawley goalkeeper! Rachael Cross, who had scored once before this season, scored directly from a free-kick close to the Ludlow goal. There was certainly nothing that the Ludlow players could do about it!

After the game, some Ludlow fans were angry about the performance of the referee, but Ludlow coach, Greta Moore, had no complaints. "I'm disappointed by the result, but I have nothing bad to say about the ref, or my players. They gave everything out there today, and I'm very proud of them." Also, Moore said that she looked forward to coaching the team again the following season. Now, let's get back to the main story of the day …

Skills Practice D

Exercise 7 p. 72

A: Hello, Fun Phones. This is Steven speaking. How can I help you?

B: Hi, my name's Sarah Jones. I'm calling to complain about a phone I bought at your shop earlier this week – on Monday the 3rd of September, to be exact.

A: Oh, I'm sorry to hear that. What model did you get?

B: It was a Powerplus phone – not the GY700, but the model after that, which came out this year. I can't think of the number right now.

A: OK, it must be the 750, then. What's the problem with the phone exactly?

B: Well, where do I start? In the first place, the box didn't include a charger, so I had to borrow my brother's to charge the phone. Then, when I turned it on, the camera was broken. I wasn't able to take any photos at all.

A: I'm shocked to hear that … I really can't explain what happened, but I apologise for the inconvenience that this has caused. What I can do is offer you a replacement, or you can get your money back, too, of course.

B: Well, I had chosen this phone because I thought it suited me perfectly, so I'd like to get another one, please. I just hope nothing goes wrong with it, too, though!

A: I'm sure there won't be any problems. Just come into the shop with the receipt and we'll take care of you. Oh, and can I have a contact number in case we need to get in touch with you?

B: Sure. It's 742-436521. I might come in this afternoon, then. Thanks for your help.

A: My pleasure, and apologies once again.

Exercise 8 p. 72

Speaker 1

I live in a city that has a lot of factories, and unfortunately, they pump large amounts of smoke into the sky. It means that we suffer a lot from smog. In fact, a lot of people wear face masks when they walk outside! There's hope for the future, though. We've got a very active environmental group here that's trying to get factories to install filters on their chimneys. Soon enough, I think they'll succeed – and that'll mean cleaner air for everyone.

Speaker 2

I live beside a large forest, and every day, I see huge lorries racing past my house loaded with trees that have been cut down. Unfortunately, the forest where I played as a child is slowly disappearing because of companies cutting it down. And there's not much I can do to stop them. I tried to form an environmental group to fight the companies, but I didn't get any support from my neighbours. That was really disappointing.

Speaker 3

We've got a litter problem in my city, and it's getting worse. It's hard to blame ordinary people, though. I think people try to put their litter in a bin, but because there are so few of them, they get full very quickly. Then, soon enough, litter falls out of these full bins and gets blown around by the wind. It's obvious whose fault this is, but the people in charge of this city haven't done anything to solve the problem!

Speaker 4

I read in the newspaper recently that there's a water pollution problem in the rivers and lakes around my city. In fact, a local environmental group has been protesting outside some of the factories in the suburbs. I think they're wasting their time, though. These factories are only interested in making money. We should be putting pressure on the government to change the laws. That's the only way to make them clean up their act.

Exercise 9 p. 72

1   When it comes to chicken, I think everyone has a different opinion. In the restaurant where I work, for example, one of our most popular dishes is roasted chicken with potatoes. And some people even order boiled chicken, sometimes. But if you ask me, nothing beats fried chicken! I know it's not very healthy, which is why I don't prepare it very often, but I really love it.

2   **A:** Excuse me. I bought this toaster yesterday, but it doesn't work.

　　B: Oh, I'm sorry to hear that, sir. Just give me your receipt and I'll give you a replacement.

　　A: Actually, I'd like a cash refund, please.

B: Hmm, but I see on your receipt that you bought it with a credit card. So, I'll have to put the money back on that.

A: OK, I suppose that works, too.

3   **A:** Peter, we need to talk about something. I hate to bring this up, but I've noticed that the rubbish hasn't been taken out for three days now.

     B: But Ken, the rubbish is Brian's job, isn't it? I'm cooking dinner this week, aren't I?

     A: But we changed the list last week, remember?

     B: Oh, now I remember ... and you have to do the vacuuming, right? Sorry, Ken, my mistake.

4   **A:** Hey, Frank. What's that poster you're sticking up about?

     B: It's about an event the environmental club is organising. We had a lot of success with our event last month about litter, and now we want to do something about the city's factories.

     A: Is it about the water pollution they're causing?

     B: No, we're more worried about the smoke they're pumping into the air. It's a huge problem and something's got to be done about it.

5   Last year, before I got a smartphone, I mainly sent text messages to my friends, but now that I own a smartphone, I usually use an instant messaging service. It's great because as long as you can find a Wi-Fi signal, it doesn't cost you a penny! Even my parents have accounts, so I use it to contact them when I'm out. Come to think of it, I can't remember the last time I made a call using my phone!

Grammar Book Key

Unit 1

1

+ -s	takes, eats, drives, boils
-ss, -sh, -ch, -x, -o, + -es	crashes, does, passes, teaches
vowel + -y + -s	buys, plays, lays, stays
consonant + -y → -ies	tidies, cries, flies, fries

2

+ -ing	drinking, applying, growing, repairing
-ie → -y + -ing	tying, dying
-e → -ing	giving, living, typing
double consonant + -ing	running, sitting, beginning

3
2	scores	6	departs
3	is driving	7	doesn't teach
4	cycles	8	Does water boil
5	Are they playing		

4
2	Do the Allens live	7	aren't/are not using
3	is painting	8	are you always
4	is doing		complaining
5	isn't/is not going	9	doesn't/does not work
6	does your flight leave	10	is becoming

5
2	'm/am staying	6	're/are planning
3	's/is	7	serves
4	's/is raining	8	'm/am arriving
5	're/are going	9	gets

6
2	'm/am making	6	're/are going
3	Do you eat	7	lives
4	eat	8	Are you taking
5	Are you spending	9	're/are spending

7
2	A	5	C	8	A	11	A
3	B	6	B	9	B	12	C
4	B	7	B	10	C		

8
2	smells	5	doesn't/does not believe
3	enjoy	6	'm/am thinking, Do you want
4	has		

9
1	2	isn't	3	's/is playing
2	1	are you going	3	prefers
	2	want		
3	1	're/are having	3	aren't
	2	Are you coming	4	're/are returning

4
1	do you usually have	3	eat
2	have		

5
1	do you think	4	Are you wearing
2	Do you like	5	don't/do not think
3	looks	6	'm/am saving

10
2 The children occasionally eat junk food.
3 They have never been abroad.
4 Do David and Sarah always do their homework before dinner?
5 I rarely see my sister because she lives so far away.
6 Emily seldom cooks dinner for herself.

11
2	who	5	whose	8	which
3	who	6	which	9	which
4	who	7	whose	10	who

12
2	why	5	where	8	where
3	when	6	why	9	when
4	where	7	when	10	when

13
2	whose	5	who's	8	who's
3	whose	6	who's	9	who's
4	whose	7	whose	10	whose

14
2 The Vikings were warriors who lived in Scandinavia.
3 Elephants are mammals which can eat about 225 kilos of grass in one day.
4 Alfred Hitchcock was a film director who made a lot of successful films.
5 Clare is an accountant who works for my father.
6 Bob is a photographer whose studio is located in the city centre.
7 Anne works for a large firm which produces cosmetics.
8 *Green World* is a magazine which sells millions of copies all over the world.
9 I live in a village which is very peaceful and quiet.
10 That is the man whose son is a professional basketball player.

15
2 That's the island which they discovered an ancient city on.
That's the island that they discovered an ancient city on.
That's the island they discovered an ancient city on.
That's the island where they discovered an ancient city.

3 That's the woman whom I worked for.
That's the woman I worked for.
That's the woman who I worked for.

4 That's the boat which we sailed around the world in.
That's the boat we sailed around the world in.
That's the boat that we sailed around the world in.

5   That's the film which my uncle stars in.
    That's the film my uncle stars in.
    That's the film that my uncle stars in.

16 2 A   4 B   6 A   8 C   10 B
        3 A   5 C   7 B   9 C

17 2 who, ND (cannot be omitted – put commas after
           Manuel and after bakery)
        3 when/that, D (can be omitted – no commas)
        4 which, ND (cannot be omitted – put commas after
           playroom and after redecorated)
        5 why, D (can be omitted – no commas)
        6 who, ND (cannot be omitted – put commas after
           Tom and after abroad)
        7 when, ND (cannot be omitted – put a comma after year)
        8 who, D (can be omitted – no commas)
        9 whose, D (cannot be omitted – no commas)
       10 whom, D (cannot be omitted – no commas)

18 2 My office, which is very big, is on the first floor. My
           office, which is on the first floor, is very big. (ND,
           cannot be omitted – put commas)
        3 Mark, who writes poems in his free time, works in
           the library. Mark, who works in the library, writes
           poems in his free time. (ND, cannot be omitted – put
           commas)
        4 The café where we had lunch serves delicious food.
           (D, cannot be omitted – no commas)
        5 I'll never forget the day when I got my master's
           degree. (D, can be omitted – no commas)

Unit 2

1 2 came, ate, went (actions which happened
          immediately one after the other in the past)
       3 read (past habit)
       4 arrived, turned on, started (actions which happened
          immediately one after the other in the past)
       5 Did you see (an action which happened at a definite
          time in the past)
       6 didn't wear (a past action which won't take place
          again)
       7 walked (past habit)
       8 bought (an action which happened at a definite
          time in the past)

2 2 went
       3 was eating, rang
       4 took, was
       5 was having, gave
       6 didn't meet
       7 Did Robert tell
       8 wasn't studying, was playing

9   got, locked, headed
10   were standing, were trying

3 2 flew   8 were driving
       3 was waiting   9 started
       4 was complaining   10 was pouring
       5 Didn't it take   11 Did you stay
       6 did you do   12 spent
       7 took

4 2 saw   7 lost
       3 was standing   8 hit
       4 happened   9 Was the boy cycling
       5 was riding   10 Did anyone else see
       6 drove

5 2 A: What were you doing when the car crashed?
          B: I was walking down the street.
          A: What did you do?
          B: I called the police.

       3 A: What were you doing when the film star arrived?
          B: I was waiting in the queue.
          A: What did you do?
          B: I asked for an autograph.

       4 A: What were you doing when the earthquake hit?
          B: I was sleeping in my bed.
          A: What did you do?
          B: I dived under a table.

       5 A: What were you doing when the roof collapsed?
          B: I was watering the plants in the garden.
          A: What did you do?
          B: I phoned my father.

       6 A: What were you doing when the kitchen flooded?
          B: I was cleaning the house.
          A: What did you do?
          B: I rang my neighbour.

6 2 was leaving, heard (leaving the house is the longer
          action)
       3 saw, were driving (driving down the deserted street
          is the longer action)
       4 started, were waiting (waiting at the bus stop is the
          longer action)
       5 was writing, went out (writing a letter is the longer
          action)
       6 was tidying, found (tidying his room is the longer
          action)
       7 was cycling, got (cycling to work is the longer action)

Grammar Book Key

7 A
2 was pouring
3 arrived
4 took off
5 hung
6 walked
7 fed
8 was making
9 heard

B
1 were having
2 rang
3 got up
4 opened
5 came
6 were driving
7 had
8 was
9 came

8
3 She didn't use to live on a boat.
4 They used to have beards.
5 She didn't use to grow her own vegetables.
6 They used to watch TV every day.
7 He didn't use to go to the theatre once a week.
8 She didn't use to know how to use a computer.

9
2 Is, used to
3 used to/would
4 is used to
5 used to
6 used to/would
7 'm/am getting used to
8 are used to
9 got used to
10 used to

10
2 isn't used to
3 would often travel
4 was keeping
5 looked
6 get used to
7 used to have
8 would go

11
2 walking
3 living
4 read
5 go
6 wearing
7 have
8 drinking

12
2 tiring
3 confusing
4 relaxed
5 annoyed
6 frightening
7 interesting
8 amazed
9 charming
10 excited

13
2 boring
3 amusing
4 thrilled
5 shocked
6 embarrassing
7 frightened
8 exhausting

14
2 were very bored by
3 get used to driving
4 are used to walking
5 used to have long hair

15
2 past
3 through
4 towards
5 behind
6 from
7 to
8 down
9 over

Unit 3

1
2 have they known
3 Have you seen, haven't/have not seen
4 Has Mike ridden
5 Have you booked, have printed
6 has changed

2
2 Have, been
3 has gone
4 have been
5 has, been
6 has gone
7 has, gone
8 has gone
9 has been
10 have been

3
2 have been chatting
3 has been using
4 has been looking

4
2 still
3 before
4 for
5 already
6 never
7 since
8 yet
9 ever
10 lately

5
2 Have you seen, have been looking for
3 Did you have, was
4 Have you been cooking, have just started
5 have you been, have been calling, was working, didn't hear
6 were you doing, began, was driving
7 has been repairing
8 Have you finished
9 did Amy break, was running, slipped, fell
10 Have you met, introduced

6
2 had written
3 reached, had left
4 had lost
5 had gone
6 enjoyed, had already been
7 had visited
8 had finished, took
9 hung up, hadn't taken
10 had set, overslept

7
2 had written
3 had fully recovered
4 had been studying
5 had already learnt
6 had been crying
7 had been waiting
8 had got away
9 had been digging
10 had become

8
2 had been working
3 had been searching
4 had been shopping

9
2 had already eaten
3 Had Peter finished
4 had been working
5 had they been cycling
6 had almost completed
7 had never been

Grammar Book Key

10 A 2 had been travelling   4 was
        3 had forgotten

    B 1 hadn't relaxed   4 had studied
        2 was   5 didn't feel
        3 was

    C 1 was   4 noticed
        2 was sitting   5 were trembling
        3 was putting on   6 had been waiting

11 2 A   7 one
     3 some, an, a   8 One
     4 a   9 a
     5 one   10 one
     6 one

12 1 one   5 a, –
     2 –, an, the   6 an, the, one
     3 –, the, an, the   7 an, an, the, the
     4 a, ones, the, the   8 the, The

13 **(Suggested Answers)**

    2 A: … an Indian restaurant
       B: Yes, there's one near my house and I eat there
          once a month.
    3 A: … tennis
       B: No, but I can play football.
    4 A: the USA
       B: I wouldn't move to the USA, but I'd like to travel
          around both North and South America.
    5 A: … dinner
       B: I usually have something light, like a green salad
          and some fish or chicken.
    6 A: a helicopter
       B: No, I've only travelled by plane.

14 2 one   5 ones   8 a
     3 the   6 an   9 –
     4 –   7 one   10 a

15 2 C   3 C   4 B   5 A   6 B

16 2 The Italians
     3 the Museum of Modern Art
     4 the saxophone
     5 the morning
     6 chess
     7 dinner
     8 Japanese
     9 the elderly
   10 The Grays
   11 the baker's
   12 the Star

   13 South America
   14 the sun
   15 The Prime Minister
   16 Princess Anne
   17 the Himalayas
   18 bed
   19 the first
   20 Lake Geneva
   21 Leicester Square
   22 May Day
   23 The *Mary Rose*
   24 Santorini
   25 The United Nations

17 2 –   9 –   16 –
     3 the   10 the   17 –, –
     4 –   11 the   18 –, –
     5 –   12 the   19 –, the
     6 –   13 –, –   20 the
     7 the   14 –, the, –
     8 –   15 the, the, the

18 1 –, a, the   4 the, an, the
     2 the, the, the   5 –, the, a
     3 a, a

Revision A (Units 1-3)

1 1 look
    2 haven't/have not been sleeping
    3 are you walking
    4 crawl
    5 Has Jake finished
    6 's/is looking
    7 hasn't/has not apologised
    8 's/is smelling
    9 does this bag belong
   10 Have you been exercising

2 1 escaped
    2 had fallen
    3 didn't/did not travel
    4 had been driving
    5 lost
    6 had you been waiting
    7 were you doing
    8 had set
    9 had never flown
   10 didn't/did not study

Grammar Book Key

3
1. since
2. at the moment
3. always
4. for
5. in
6. yet
7. already
8. ago
9. seldom
10. when

4
1. Owen bought a new tablet whose screen is 12 inches.
2. This is the reason why she has to move house.
3. We always eat fresh vegetables which we grow in our garden.
4. The police are talking to a woman who witnessed the accident.
5. Penny will never forget the day when her son took his first steps.
6. We stayed at a hotel where there were excellent facilities.
7. My father, whose name is Nigel, is the manager of the hotel.

5
| 1 | A | 3 | C | 5 | B | 7 | A | 9 | B | 11 | C |
| 2 | D | 4 | A | 6 | A | 8 | C | 10 | A | 12 | C |

6
1. have
2. has
3. have
4. the
5. being
6. his
7. in
8. like

7
1. has been cooking
2. who I interviewed owns a
3. since you met
4. we had a barbecue
5. after she had brushed
6. get used to driving
7. doesn't have/does not have
8. usually plays

Unit 4

1
2. are/'re going to wake
3. will/'ll make
4. will/'ll have
5. will find
6. is/'s going to fall
7. will have
8. Is Alex going to come
9. am/'m going to paint

2
2. won't/will not take
3. aren't/are not travelling
4. won't/will not pass
5. are you doing
6. am/'m visiting
7. am/'m spending
8. will/'ll see

3 a
- She's going to throw a party to welcome the new students.
- She's going to invite artists from all over the world to give lectures.
- She isn't going to organise an arts and crafts workshop for local kids.
- She isn't going to take the new students on a tour of the city's museums.

b
- She's giving an interview to *Art World* magazine on 2nd June.
- She's having dinner with local artists on 25th June.
- She's leaving for a sailing trip on 12th July.
- She's meeting the new students at the airport on 20th August.

4
2. is going to hand
3. won't come
4. closes
5. will throw
6. is Dad coming
7. will win
8. will get
9. won't give
10. is going to be

5
2. am/'m going to apply/am/'m applying
3. will/'ll make
4. am/'m coming
5. Are you doing/Are you going to do

6
1. get
2. drink, won't/will not be able to
3. boils, heat
4. go, will/'ll feel

7
2. comes
3. try
4. work
5. Will Greg post
6. drive
7. doesn't/does not water

8
2. d If you go to India, you can admire the Taj Mahal.
3. c If you go to France, you can walk under the Arc de Triomphe.
4. b If you go to Greece, you can visit the Parthenon.

9
2. unless
3. If
4. When
5. unless
6. When
7. unless
8. if

10
2. If I pass my exams, I'll go to university.
3. If I do well in university, I'll get a degree.
4. If I get a degree, I'll get a good job.
5. If I get a good job, I'll have a lot of money.
6. If I have a lot of money, I'll live in a nice house.

11
2. will
3. will
4. will
5. ✓
6. will
7. ✓
8. will
9. ✓
10. ✓

12
2. A: When will you visit Aunt Bessy?
   B: I'll visit Aunt Bessy as soon as I finish/'ve finished the shopping.

Grammar Book Key

3 A: When will you have a haircut?
   B: I'll have a haircut before I go away for the weekend.
4 A: When will you vacuum the carpet?
   B: I'll vacuum the carpet when I get home from work.

13 2 a   3 f   4 b   5 c   6 d

14 2 until   5 before   8 before
     3 once   6 as   9 when
     4 while   7 After   10 Since

15 2 After   5 Since   8 until
     3 By the time   6 By   9 as
     4 before   7 after   10 By the time

Unit 5

1 2 b future continuous
   3 a future continuous
   4 c future continuous

2 2 This time next month, I will be skiing with my friends.
   3 At two o'clock next Monday, I will be meeting Mr Brown.
   4 This time tomorrow, we will be moving house.

3 2 will/'ll be seeing   5 will/'ll be putting up
   3 will/'ll ask   6 will/'ll be sitting
   4 will/'ll probably be

4 2 will/'ll give
   3 will/'ll turn on
   4 will/'ll be sailing
   5 Will you be going
   6 will/'ll be seeing, will/'ll tell

5 2 Sarah will have travelled all over the world by the time she's thirty years old.
   3 Martin will have directed a successful film by the time he's thirty years old.
   4 Alice will have joined a famous dance company by the time she's thirty years old.
   5 Matthew and Sonia will have become famous actors by the time they're thirty years old.
   6 Miranda will have started working in a big hospital by the time she's thirty years old.

6 2 until   5 by
   3 by   6 by the time
   4 until, by then

7 2 b   3 b   4 a   5 b   6 a

8 2 will/'ll have finished
   3 will/'ll snow
   4 Will you be going
   5 will/'ll wake
   6 will be
   7 will/'ll be babysitting
   8 won't/will not have tidied

9 2 will/'ll have completed   7 will be taking
   3 will/'ll be skiing   8 will/'ll do
   4 will/'ll pick up   9 am/'m going to buy
   5 will have finished   10 will invite
   6 get

10 2 'll/will be   6 'll/will have
   3 'll/will probably swim   7 'll/will be going
   4 will/'ll go   8 'll/will be
   5 'll/will come   9 'll/will have arrived

Unit 6

1 2 have already been watered
   3 is being painted
   4 had already been collected
   5 could not/couldn't be read
   6 was being cut
   7 is washed
   8 had been broken
   9 would be sold
   10 was invited

2 3 A lovely picture has been painted by Sue.
   4 It cannot be changed.
   5 A letter has to be posted by Melanie.
   6 A fantastic puppet was made by Bob.
   7 It cannot be changed.
   8 The fish bowl is being cleaned by Joseph.

3 2 with   7 by   12 with
   3 by   8 with   13 by
   4 with   9 by   14 with
   5 with   10 with   15 by
   6 by   11 by

4 2 All the money in the till was stolen (by the thief).
   3 Who has this poem been written by?
   4 When will the annual dance be held?
   5 The Eiffel Tower is visited by many tourists every year.
   6 Was the parcel given to Susie?
   7 That table needs to be moved.
   8 Have the invitations been sent out by Victoria?

Grammar Book Key

5 2 had been painted
3 's/is being repaired
4 was given
5 was made
6 'll/will be developed
7 were handed
8 was still being fixed
9 had been fully booked
10 must be fed
11 is being built, will be opened
12 is/has been trapped
14 were flooded
15 will the report be finished

6 2 A sports centre will be opened by the town mayor tomorrow.
3 An elderly couple were rescued from a burning house last night.
4 A decision about new speeding fines has already been made./A decision has already been made about new speeding fines.

7 A ... To build the waiting room, the Carltons had imported red brick from England. The President himself opened the station in 1896. That year, a steam locomotive visited Rosemary Hills for the first time. It was pumping clouds of white smoke and giving out such loud whistles that all the townspeople could hear it.

B A man who broke into the National Bank is being looked for by the police. The wires of the alarm were cut and then the bank's city centre branch was broken into some time late last night. £500,000 was stolen from the bank. The city centre is being searched by the police as the thief may still be in the area.

8 2 e Where were the 2004 Summer Olympic Games held?
The 2004 Summer Olympic Games were held in Athens.
3 a Who was the telescope invented by?
The telescope was invented by Galileo.
4 f When was *Zootopia* released?
Zootopia was released in 2016.
5 h Where is the Colosseum located?
The Colosseum is located in Rome.
6 g When was Vivaldi's *Four Seasons* first performed?
Vivaldi's *Four Seasons* was first performed in 1725.
7 b Where was chocolate first made?
Chocolate was first made in South America.
8 c Who was penicillin discovered by?
Penicillin was discovered by Alexander Fleming.

9 2 Were you given
3 was introduced
4 was shown
5 had been repainted
6 have you been given
7 was asked to submit
8 will be told
9 taken
10 allowed to go

10 2 A village north of Montreal was buried by/under ten metres of snow.
3 Three people have been pulled out from under the rubble by rescue workers.
4 Many houses in the area are destroyed by violent winds each year.
5 Hundreds of acres of forest will be burnt.
6 Tents are being sent to shelter people because their houses have been swept away by the water.

11 2 ... A small window had been left open by an employee. We are told that the men climbed in through the window. £2,500 worth of toys were stolen. The men have not been found (by the police) yet.

12 2 became
3 were
4 were invented
5 are used
6 are
7 are combined
8 is put
9 (is) refrigerated
10 are added
11 is packaged
12 is frozen
13 love
14 is
15 is topped

13 (Suggested Answer)
How Paper is Recycled
1 Paper is taken from rubbish bins and put into large recycling containers.
2 The paper is taken to a recycling plant where it is separated into different types.
3 The paper is then washed with soapy water to remove coloured inks and glue.
4 Next, the paper is mixed with water to create a thick substance.
5 This thick mixture is spread on large rollers and made into large thin sheets.
6 The paper is left to dry and then it is rolled up ready to be cut and sent back to printers.
7 There, different paper products can be created, such as cardboard, office paper, books and newspapers.

14 2 ourselves
3 yourself
4 themselves
5 myself
6 himself
7 herself
8 ourselves
9 myself
10 yourselves

Grammar Book Key

15 2 himself 4 herself 6 herself
3 themselves 5 himself

16 2 A 3 C 4 C 5 A

17 2 made ourselves 4 design, (by) herself
3 cut myself 5 poured himself

18 2 like 6 as 10 as 13 like
3 as 7 like 11 like 14 like
4 as 8 like 12 as 15 as
5 like 9 as

Revision B (Units 1-6)

1 1 are using 5 have been
2 Have you heard 6 feel
3 are you feeling 7 have been working
4 takes

2 1 had booked 5 had been waiting
2 attended 6 were watching
3 Did he go 7 hasn't got used to
4 used to work

3 1 arrives
2 will come
3 aren't/are not going (to go)
4 is Dad going to come/is Dad coming
5 isn't/is not going to rain
6 will be
7 will/'ll throw

4 1 will/'ll be swimming 5 will have organised
2 will/'ll finish 6 won't/will not be
3 won't/will not have read sleeping
4 Will you be meeting 7 will/'ll collect

5 1 follow 4 doesn't/does not finish
2 will you take 5 lift
3 get/will/'ll get

6 1 The new film will be directed by a famous director.
2 Rob was given a part in the play./A part in the play was given to Rob (by the producer).
3 Has the application been approved by Mr Finn yet?
4 The lecture must be given in German by Terry.
5 Who was the damage caused by?

7 1 c 2 e 3 a 4 d 5 b

8 1 before 3 since 5 after
2 during 4 while

9 1 A 3 D 5 B 7 C
2 C 4 A 6 A

10 1 ago 4 the (prison) 7 have 10 gone
2 had 5 not 8 for
3 be 6 will 9 got

11 1 have not/haven't been to a
2 was found under
3 which is next to
4 long ago did they buy
5 unless you come
6 was made to pay
7 is being sent to
8 was congratulated by

Unit 7

1 2 said 6 asked 10 tell
3 told 7 tell 11 tell
4 asked 8 ask 12 tell
5 said 9 said

2 2 He said (that) he had never caught such a big fish before.
3 She told her mum (that) she would help her with the gardening.
4 He told Paul (that) he could find a lot of information on the Internet.
5 He said (that) he was/had been digging the garden all morning.

3 2 Mr Bradley says (that) Mr and Mrs Wilson have gone on holiday.
3 Lynn said (that) she was going to the dentist then/at the time.
4 John said (that) Jamie had never seen a dolphin before.
5 He said (that) he would order a pizza.
6 The teacher said (that) the sun rises/rose in the east.
7 Gregory said (that) there had been a big flood in that area the year before/the previous year.

4 2 He says (that) he got a letter from Joanne this morning.
3 He told us (that) there's/was a bus strike tomorrow/the following day.
4 He said (that) he was going to the airport to pick up James.
5 They told her (that) they all spoke French fluently.
6 She told me (that) if she had more time, she would volunteer for the emergency services.
7 He said (that) he had been reading the novel for a month.

Grammar Book Key

5
2. Josh asked me where I was going on holiday that year.
3. Helen asked what time the match started.
4. Jill asked if/whether John went/had gone to the gym the previous night/the night before.
5. Philip asked me why I was laughing.
6. Peter asked how long it took me to walk home from there.
7. Lesley asked Sara if/whether she would lend her some money.
8. The old lady asked her husband who that man was.
9. Paul asked them/us why they/we had packed such big suitcases.
10. Sheila asked me when I would visit my parents.

6
2. She asked if/whether it came in blue.
3. She asked if/whether they could order one for her.
4. She asked how much it cost.
5. She asked if/whether she could try it on.
6. She asked if/whether there were any shoes to match.
7. She asked if/whether she could pay by credit card.
8. She asked when their new stock would come in.

7
2. … what that person's name is
3. … what time the last bus leaves
4. … how long the flight to Rome takes
5. … how much this dress costs
6. … why the train was delayed

8
2. He asked her to open the door.
3. Georgia told me not to let the dog out.
4. She told him not to go away.
5. The police officer ordered them to get out of the car.
6. She told them not to touch the wires.
7. She suggested that I (should) buy some new safety equipment.
8. Tom suggested visiting Thailand the following year.

9
2	begged	5	accused	8	offered
3	invited	6	threatened	9	admitted
4	denied	7	complained		

10
2. My sister allowed me to borrow her laptop for my presentation.
3. She reminded me to call John.
4. Rick agreed to pick Susan up at the station.
5. She promised to call/that she would call me as soon as she arrived.
6. He explained to his mother how to install the program.
7. He wondered when help would arrive.
8. She refused to buy her daughter such an expensive watch.

9. She boasted that no one had worked as hard as her.
10. Mary apologised to Jane for not coming/not having come to the meeting.
11. The sergeant ordered the soldiers to do a hundred sit-ups.
12. Leo accused me of breaking/having broken the lamp.
13. He instructed us/them to put on our/their safety helmets immediately.

11
2. She wondered what she could do/what to do.
3. He insisted on my/me accepting a little gift.
4. Amy exclaimed that it was a shocking disaster.
5. They encouraged/urged us to donate generously.
6. He informed them that the ambulance was on its way.
7. She claimed that she had been/was nowhere near the scene of the crime./She claimed to have been nowhere near the scene of the crime.

12
Reporter: What were you doing when the earthquake struck?
Mrs Smith: I was at home doing the housework. I wasn't very frightened. We live in a strong building.
Reporter: Lots of your neighbours' homes were damaged.
Mrs Smith: That's true. I feel lucky to have escaped.

Unit 8

1
2 a	3 d	4 b

2
If he hadn't forgotten to pack his sleeping bag, he wouldn't have slept on the cold, hard ground.
If he had taken some insect repellent, he wouldn't have been bitten by mosquitoes.
If it hadn't rained on Sunday, he wouldn't have left early.

3
2	were – Type 2	5	had known – Type 3
3	had finished – Type 3	6	would drive – Type 2
4	would open – Type 2		

4
2. If she knew how to sew, she would make her own clothes.
3. If Tom had a bicycle, he would cycle to work every day.
4. If they had left on time, they wouldn't have missed the train back home.

5
1. weren't
2. were, would call
3. had practised, would have passed
4. had taken, would have been
5. had remembered, could have made

6 **(Suggested Answers)**

2 … I would go to the shopping mall.
3 … he could/would understand what they were saying.
4 … she wouldn't have had to sit/take them again.
5 … he could/would stay there for the summer.
6 … I wouldn't have been late for my appointment.
7 … I wouldn't have become rich.
8 … he would have gone with them.

7
2 I wish/If only I had (got) a motorcycle.
3 I wish/If only I were/was brave enough to try bungee jumping.
4 I wish/If only you would stop complaining.
5 I wish/If only I hadn't/had not missed the plane to Lisbon.
6 I wish/If only the weather would improve.
7 I wish/If only I had called my grandfather last night.
8 I wish/If only I had gone to university.

8
2	hadn't/had not forgotten	8	had followed
3	were/was	9	hadn't/had not
4	hadn't/had not eaten		cheated
5	had	10	had called
6	had brought	11	would not make
7	would tell	12	would come

9
2 I wish I had more customers. If I had more customers, I would hire a shop assistant.
3 I wish I had known the answers. If I had known the answers, I would have been able to pass the exam last week.
4 I wish I had had some help yesterday. If I had had some help, I would have finished more quickly.

10
2	will you	8	isn't he
3	did he	9	shall we
4	won't you	10	haven't you
5	isn't she	11	are you
6	didn't he	12	isn't it
7	have they	13	won't you

11
2	shall we	7	doesn't he
3	hasn't she	8	don't you
4	do you	9	am I
5	will you	10	are we
6	did they		

12
2	is she, she isn't	6	isn't it, it is
3	do they, they don't	7	is he, he isn't
4	haven't you, I have	8	isn't there, there is
5	do they, they don't	9	didn't they, they did

13
2	isn't he	7	isn't she
3	didn't she	8	won't he
4	aren't they	9	do you
5	haven't you	10	isn't it
6	doesn't he		

14
2	Nevertheless	4	Despite
3	but	5	On the other hand

15
2 … Damian is tall, his brother is rather short.
3 … he is injured, Mason will play in this week's match.
4 … fact that he is experienced, Michael can't find a job.
5 … the professor's lecture was interesting, it was long.

16
2 Even though the film lasted for three hours, nobody was bored.
The film lasted for three hours, yet nobody was bored.
3 Sophie looked everywhere for her missing ring. Nevertheless, she didn't find it.
In spite of looking/having looked everywhere for her missing ring, Sophie didn't find it.
4 Edward Norton is my favourite actor. However, I haven't seen his latest film yet.
Although Edward Norton is my favourite actor, I haven't seen his latest film yet.

Unit 9

1
2	(to) be believed	6	(to) to have been ironing
3	(to) be talking	7	(to) have slept
4	(to) arrive	8	(to) have been made
5	(to) have cleaned		

2
2	being made	6	having worn
3	taking	7	finishing
4	having eaten	8	having worked
5	working		

3
2	a/b	6	a	10	b	14	b	18	a
3	c	7	c	11	c	15	b/c	19	c
4	b	8	a	12	a	16	a	20	b
5	a/c	9	a	13	c	17	a		

4
2	(to) having robbed/ robbing	6	to have improved
3	to have done	7	to speak
4	to buy	8	to be working, to finish
5	stay	9	living, living
		10	clean

5
2	to inform	5	taking	8	talking
3	watching	6	to find	9	to drink
4	to add	7	to water	10	going

Grammar Book Key

6
2 Swimming
3 wait
4 drive
5 to stay
6 going
7 to catch
8 fishing
9 go
10 doing
11 not to cook
12 to find
13 eat
14 to revisit

7
1
2 make
3 teaching
4 painting
5 writing

2
1 help
2 to open
3 to do
4 be

3
1 to do
2 seeing
3 going
4 to stay
5 order

4
1 talking
2 to change

5
1 to go
2 to hear

6
1 to speak
2 to start

8
2 to buy
3 to wear
4 To tell
5 wearing
6 suit
7 looking
8 to spend
9 to pay
10 like
11 to try

9
2 to buy
3 inviting
4 joining
5 to sign
6 tell
7 have read

10
2 too tired
3 strong enough
4 too cloudy
5 tall enough
6 too busy

11
2 b
3 f
4 a
5 g
6 d
7 c

12
2 The road was too slippery for her to drive.
3 Mark isn't fit enough/is too unfit to take part in the competition.
4 The water is too cold for them to swim in.
5 Megan sings well enough to be a member of the local rock band.
6 It's too dark for me to see./It isn't/is not bright enough for me to see.
7 The earrings were too expensive/were not cheap enough for her to buy.
8 He is smart enough to solve the Maths problem.
9 These potatoes are too hot/not cold enough for me to eat.
10 The steak was too tough/wasn't tender enough for him to cut.
11 It's hot enough (for me) to go to the beach.
12 The article was too difficult/wasn't/was not easy enough for them to understand.

13
2 pouches
3 oxen
4 combs
5 swimming pools
6 lice
7 photos
8 berries
9 feet
10 knives
11 notebooks
12 glasses
13 potatoes
14 roofs
15 toys

14
2 is
3 Is
4 are
5 are
6 are
7 are
8 is
9 is
10 is

15
2 are
3 is
4 have
5 are
6 is
7 are
8 has

16
2 knowledge
3 is
4 is
5 are
6 are
7 advice
8 is
9 information
10 sisters-in-law

REVISION C (UNITS 1-9)

1
1 often rains
2 Have you been studying
3 used to have
4 are going to trip
5 Has Carol visited
6 opens
7 rains
8 Will you have finished
9 didn't tell
10 has gone

2
1 'll/will love
2 would have seen
3 would go
4 rains
5 formed
6 hadn't/had not gone
7 told

3
1 *Guernica* was painted by Picasso.
2 Philip was sent an invitation by Tony./ An invitation was sent to Philip by Tony.
3 I was bought two presents for my birthday./Two presents were bought for me for my birthday.
4 Who was the window broken by?
5 The actor is being asked questions.

4
1 Jennifer said (that) they would probably sell their house.
2 Mum said (that) she had baked a cake for the children.
3 Bill asked me if/whether he could borrow my jacket.
4 Dad reminded Jake to lock the front door.
5 Emma refused to tell me what (had) happened.
6 Meg asked her who her favourite actor was.
7 He apologised for not telling/having told me the whole truth.
8 She accused the boy of stealing/having stolen her bag.

5
1 I wish I hadn't broken my sister's new tablet.
2 If only my computer wasn't/was not/weren't/were not so slow.
3 I wish I could join you on holiday.
4 I wish I had the chance to work abroad.
5 If only I hadn't/had not argued with my best friend yesterday.
6 If only you wouldn't/would not talk so much.

6
1	doesn't	4	haven't	7	will
2	isn't	5	aren't		
3	will	6	do		

7
1	to find	4	Bargaining	7	to go
2	to take	5	travel		
3	work	6	walking		

8
1	D	3	A	5	B	7	B	9	C
2	B	4	A	6	C	8	B	10	D

9
1	was	3	will	5	it	7	to
2	for	4	be	6	have		

10
1 not to be late
2 were too small for
3 she had studied for
4 wish I had been at
5 unless you get
6 apologised for being/having been
7 I hadn't/had not lied
8 were you, I would/'d put

Unit 10

1
2	had to	5	needn't
3	mustn't	6	needs
4	should	7	have delivered

2
2	mustn't	6	doesn't have to
3	have to	7	mustn't
4	must	8	needn't
5	don't have		

3
2	mustn't/can't	5	needn't
3	don't need to/needn't	6	must/has to
4	can't	7	have to

4
2	can	4	wasn't
3	Could	5	May

5
2	A	3	B	4	A	5	C	6	A

6
2	Could	5	needn't, can	8	shall, can
3	ought to	6	didn't need to		
4	could, might	7	should, might		

7
2	a	4	b	6	a	8	a	10	b
3	b	5	b	7	a	9	a		

8
2	i	4	k	6	d	8	g	10	e
3	f	5	a	7	b	9	j	11	h

9
2 You should/ought to exercise regularly.
3 The teacher told me I had to/needed to organise my study time.
4 Sally couldn't/could not read when she was five.
5 You can't/cannot/mustn't/must not walk on the grass.
6 Would you like to watch the match tonight?
7 Laura could/may/might have asked for a pay rise.
8 Sia could/may/might take up cooking lessons.

10
2 You should ask your teacher to help you with your project.
3 You mustn't enter this area.
4 Ian may have gone to work early.
5 Shall I read you a story?
6 The children were able to do the puzzle even though it was difficult.
7 Rita needn't go to school because it's Sunday.
8 Can I take this chair?
9 Would you hold this box for me, please?
10 Shall we go for a picnic this weekend?

11
2 should/ought to
3 can't/cannot
4 could/may/might
5 needs/has
6 couldn't/could not/wasn't/was not able to
7 mustn't/must not/can't/cannot
8 can/may

12
2	A	5	A	8	C	11	B	14	C
3	A	6	B	9	A	12	A	15	B
4	C	7	B	10	C	13	A		

13
2	can't	7	may/might/must
3	must/may/might	8	must
4	can't	9	must
5	must	10	must
6	may/might		

14
2	have arrived	7	have burnt down
3	live/be living	8	have hurt
4	be	9	be
5	have had	10	have gone
6	have finished		

Grammar Book Key

15 (Suggested Answers)

  2 may/might/   4 must   7 may/might/could
      could   5 must   8 can't
  3 can't   6 must

16 2 f He can't have graduated from university because he hasn't got a degree.

     3 a They must have been cooking because the kitchen smells wonderful.

     4 c They can't be back from their holiday because no one's at home.

     5 b They must have had a good time at the event because they stayed until ten o'clock.

     6 e He can't have paid the bill because the telephone has been cut off.

17 3 She must have overslept.

     4 She can't have taken her umbrella.

     5 They must have had a good holiday.

     6 He must have stayed at the office late.

     7 He must be upstairs.

     8 They must have eaten dinner.

     9 She must be hungry.

    10 She can't have written that letter.

18 2 … can't have gone sailing because it's too stormy today.

     3 … may/might/could be afraid of heights if you feel dizzy on the roller coaster.

     4 … may/might/could have a social phobia as she doesn't feel comfortable around people.

     5 … must be seeing the doctor today because he's in a lot of pain.

     6 … can't be scared of spiders as she's got three pet spiders.

Unit 11

1

Comparative	Superlative
lovelier	the loveliest
more	the most
worse	the worst
healthier	the healthiest
more amazing	the most amazing
more intelligent	the most intelligent
longer	the longest
more expensive	the most expensive
bigger	the biggest

2 2 than   4 the, of   6 the, in
    3 than   5 the, in   7 the, in

3 2 more interesting   6 younger
    3 the most successful   7 the quietest/
    4 the most popular   the most quiet
    5 the worst   8 further/farther

4 2 biggest   5 as/so difficult
    3 the most amazing   6 the best
    4 more impressive   7 the most convenient

5 • The maid service at the King Hotel is as good as/the same as the maid service at the Rose Hotel.

    • The room service at the Rose Hotel is faster than the room service at the King Hotel.
      The room service at the King Hotel is not as/so fast as the room service at the Rose Hotel.
      The room service at the King Hotel is less fast than the room service at the Rose Hotel.

    • The prices at the King Hotel are more expensive than the prices at the Rose Hotel.
      The prices at the Rose Hotel are not as/so expensive as the prices at the King Hotel.
      The prices at the Rose Hotel are less expensive than the prices at the King Hotel.

    • The location of the Rose Hotel is more convenient than the location of the King Hotel.
      The location of the King Hotel is not as/so convenient as the location of the Rose Hotel.
      The location of the King Hotel is less convenient than the location of the Rose Hotel.

6 2 faster   the fastest
    3 earlier   the earliest
    4 worse   the worst
    5 more   the most

7 2 the worst   5 further/farther
    3 less   6 more often
    4 better   7 more easily

8 2 three times   5 More   8 very
    3 too   6 the same   9 to win
    4 far   7 harder   10 half

9 2 more/less often   5 more carefully
    3 more loudly   6 colder
    4 further   7 less serious

10 2 a   6 are   10 is   14 are
    3 some   7 are   11 a   15 is
    4 is   8 is   12 are
    5 is   9 some 13 is

Grammar Book Key

11
2	a glass of	7	a bottle of
3	a bowl of	8	a can of
4	a slice/piece of	9	a piece/slice of
5	a loaf of	10	a jar of
6	a cup of		

12
2	no	6	anything	10	no
3	anywhere	7	anyone	11	someone
4	no one	8	some	12	some
5	Somebody	9	everywhere		

13
2	some	5	nothing	8	everyone/
3	no	6	something		everybody
4	any	7	some		

14
2	any	5	any	8	some
3	some	6	a lot of		
4	much	7	a few		

15 2 a little   3 a little   4 a few   5 a few

16
2	All of	4	a bit of	6	several
3	too much	5	Both	7	enough

17
2	How many	7	How many	12	How much
3	How much	8	How much	13	How much
4	How many	9	How many	14	How many
5	How much	10	How much	15	How much
6	How much	11	How many	16	How much

18
2	much	5	how many	8	How much
3	How many	6	many		
4	How much	7	much		

Unit 12

1
2	in order to	7	in order not to
3	so that	8	for
4	so that	9	so that
5	in case	10	so as not
6	to		

2
2 We should all volunteer to patrol our forests to protect them from fires.
3 The government has introduced stricter traffic laws to reduce road accidents.
4 She spent the summer in Rome to improve her Italian.
5 Bob called his brother to tell him about his new job.
6 Kirsten went to the gift shop to buy a present for her friend.

3
2 g A: Should I take a penknife with me?
   B: Yes. Take a penknife so that you can/in order to/to open canned food.

3 a A: Should I take a sleeping bag with me?
   B: Yes. Take a sleeping bag so that you can/in order to/to sleep in it.
4 b A: Should I take a tent with me?
   B: Yes. Take a tent so that you can/in order to/to stay in it.
5 h A: Should I take a radio with me?
   B: Yes. Take a radio so that you can/in order to/to listen to the weather forecast.
6 c A: Should I take a torch with me?
   B: Yes. Take a torch so that you can/in order to/to see in the dark.
7 d A: Should I take insect repellent with me?
   B: Yes. Take insect repellent so that you won't/so as not/in order not to be/to avoid being bitten by mosquitoes.
8 f A: Should I take a compass with me?
   B: Yes. Take a compass so that you can/in order to/to find your way.

4
2 She circled the day on her calendar to prevent her from missing the appointment.
3 She bought a phone card in order to make some phone calls.
4 He wrote down the address in order not to forget it.
5 Pierre is taking cookery classes with a view to becoming a chef.
6 He is learning karate so that he will be able to/can defend himself.
7 We went to the butcher's for some meat.
8 She went to bed at ten o'clock in order not to wake up late the next morning.
9 Ann is working hard so that she can finish/will finish/finishes her report on time.
10 I'll pack a lot of warm clothes in case the weather turns cold.
11 Sue called her best friend to tell her the great news.
12 He bought a second-hand car to avoid spending too much money.

5
2	Since	7	the reason for
3	because of	8	As
4	the reason why	9	due to
5	due to the fact that	10	on account of
6	for	11	Now

6
2 She went to bed since she was tired./Since she was tired, she went to bed.
3 His manager gave him a warning because of his lateness./Because of his lateness, his manager gave him a warning.
4 I can't come with you as I have to help my mum with the chores./As I have to help my mum with the chores, I can't come with you.

193

Grammar Book Key

5   The reason why he changed jobs was (the fact) that he had been offered a better salary./The fact that he had been offered a better salary was the reason why he changed jobs.
6   I drove to work because it was raining./Because it was raining, I drove to work.

7   2   such a   4   so   6   so
        3   such   5   such a

8   2   The girls are such good friends that they have never argued about anything.
        3   It was such a long film that my little sister fell asleep in the cinema.
        4   Rita did so much gardening this morning that she feels tired now.
        5   Pam missed her flight and, as a result, she was late for the conference.
        6   There were so few people at the event that it finished early./There were few people at the event, so it finished early.
        7   The information is confidential and, therefore, only a few people know about it.
        8   So many people signed up for French lessons that they hired an extra teacher./Many people signed up for French lessons, so they hired an extra teacher.
        9   Lynn had so many clothes that she gave some of them away./Lynn had many clothes, so she gave some away.

9   2   every   5   Neither   8   every
        3   Both   6   either   9   every
        4   None   7   another   10 each

10 1   neither   5   Both, neither
        2   None   6   All
        3   Both   7   Both, neither
        4   All

11 2   both   6   Both   10 Every
        3   whole   7   all   11 Either
        4   Neither   8   None   12 whole
        5   none   9   Neither

12 2   are having   6   have, had
        3   had   7   have
        4   is having/will have 8   have
        5   was having

13 2   Gary had his motorcycle stolen from outside the shop.
        3   The Smiths had their basement flooded by heavy rain.

4   Ann had her favourite dress torn by her friend.
5   Thomas had his CD player broken by his little brother.
6   Mary had her window smashed by a ball.
7   Charles had his car damaged by a falling tree.

14 2   She has her nails painted by a manicurist.
        3   She has her shopping done by her housekeeper.
        4   She has her telephone answered by her secretary.
        5   She has her letters typed by her secretary.
        6   She has her appointments made by her secretary.
        7   She has fresh flowers delivered to her office every morning by the florist.
        8   She has her house cleaned by a cleaner.

15 2   Will Henry have a mechanic fix his car?
        3   Margaret got her sister to join a gym.
        4   William made me take him to his football practice.
        5   Paula will have the furniture shop deliver her new sofa on Monday.
        6   Tim got his roommate to do the dishes.

16 2   Mark has had the garden tidied.
        3   He wants to have his telephone fixed.
        4   Pat has the windows cleaned every week.
        5   Can you have those boxes moved?
        6   When will Dan have his sofa delivered?
        7   There's no point having our tickets booked (by the travel agent).
        8   Howard should have the package delivered.
        9   When will you have the car serviced?
        10 Have the curtains made for you.
        11 Alison has had her skirt shortened.
        12 Doug will have some bills paid for him (by the bank).
        13 Jeremy had been having the car repaired (by the mechanic) all day yesterday.

REVISION D (UNITS 1-12)

1   1   be meeting   6   had landed
        2   was speeding   7   took
        3   smell   8   is having
        4   will   9   rarely takes
        5   used to   10 Haven't you received

2   1   living   3   to listen   5   give
        2   to fit   4   running

3   1   You needn't finish the project today.
        2   Would you like me to make you some hot chocolate?
        3   You must pay the speeding ticket.
        4   In the end, he was able to escape the burning building.
        5   He can't be hungry. He's just had lunch!

Grammar Book Key

4
1. an, some/a
2. some, a
3. a, an
4. a, some

5
1. book
2. would have found
3. went
4. get
5. are

6
1. Helen told James (that) he could ask Kevin for advice.
2. She said (that) Laura was always late.
3. Lisa asked me if/whether I would send her the email.
4. The policeman ordered them to put their hands up.
5. He told me (that) he would need my help the next/following day.

7
1. anywhere
2. some
3. anything
4. Every
5. Anyone

8
1. has her nails done
2. will have/is having her album released
3. is having his temperature taken
4. had the carpets hoovered
5. have had their house broken

9
1. the easiest
2. as tall
3. slimmer than
4. the fittest
5. faster than/as fast as
6. more successful than
7. thinner
8. less

10
1. the
2. much
3. been
4. The
5. still
6. so
7. to

11
1. A
2. C
3. D
4. A
5. B
6. B
7. A
8. A
9. C
10. D

12
1. must have finished typing
2. a photographer to take my
3. it been since they moved
4. until he has
5. too much

WORD FORMATION

1
1. talented
2. entertaining
3. glamorous
4. numerous
5. messy
6. funny
7. wonderful

2
1. producer
2. charming
3. caring
4. interesting
5. restless
6. skilful/skilled

3
1. marvellous
2. excellent
3. comfortable
4. impressed
5. organised
6. helpful
7. active
8. enjoyable

4
1. amazing
2. fantastic
3. tasty
4. spicy
5. sandy
6. delightful

5
1. heavily
2. widely
3. tragically
4. possibly
5. immediately
6. truly

6
1. uncomplicated
2. illogical
3. disqualified
4. uninterested
5. unrealistic
6. informal
7. immature
8. impersonal
9. incorrect
10. irregular

7
1. students
2. typist
3. tourists
4. accountant
5. electrician

8
1. famous
2. beautiful
3. interested
4. impressive
5. valuable
6. impossible
7. successful
8. attractive

9
1. difficulty
2. importance
3. independence
4. popularity
5. happiness
6. safety
7. shyness

10
1. unpredictable
2. dishonest
3. illegal
4. impolite
5. inappropriate
6. disapprove

11
1. fascinating
2. actor
3. finally
4. dramatic
5. nervous
6. luckily
7. monorail

12
1. reliable
2. affordable
3. stylish
4. reasonable

13
1. dangerous
2. rewarding
3. unusual
4. trainee
5. demanding
6. risky
7. bored
8. promising
9. certainly
10. disadvantage

14
1. adventurous
2. exceptional
3. natural
4. inspiring
5. interesting
6. sensational
7. experienced
8. educational
9. delightful
10. expensive
11. enjoyable
12. information

15
1. attractive
2. sunny
3. peaceful
4. relaxed
5. traditional
6. hungry

16
1. usually
2. rocky
3. extremely
4. lovely
5. divers
6. expensive

17
1. stormy
2. hunters
3. historical
4. slowly
5. mysterious
6. silence
7. frightening
8. darkness
9. scared
10. loudly

Grammar Book Key

18
1 actor
2 singer
3 drummer
4 designer
5 painter
6 editor
7 employee
8 lawyer

19
1 gifted
2 teacher
3 successful
4 recognised
5 unhappy
6 easily

20
1 different
2 probably
3 exciting
4 useful
5 imagination
6 drivers
7 reliable
8 advanced
9 illness
10 researchers

PHRASAL VERBS

1
1 up
2 after
3 forward to
4 for
5 after
6 for
7 up
8 forward to

2
1 out
2 up
3 down
4 into
5 up
6 out
7 up
8 into

3
1 out of
2 over
3 after
4 into
5 over
6 out of
7 after
8 into

4
1 up
2 up
3 off
4 off
5 after
6 up
7 off
8 over

5
1 across
2 into
3 back
4 round/over
5 into
6 across
7 round/over
8 across

6
1 up
2 away
3 in
4 away
5 up
6 back
7 in
8 in

7
1 out
2 on
3 up
4 off
5 on
6 up
7 out
8 off

8
1 out
2 on
3 out
4 out
5 on
6 off
7 on
8 out

9
1 down
2 into
3 down
4 on
5 into
6 on
7 down
8 up

10
1 on
2 across
3 over
4 by
5 along/on
6 across
7 over
8 along/on

11
1 away from
2 on
3 off
4 out
5 off
6 out
7 on
8 up

12
1 out
2 off
3 out
4 on
5 off
6 on
7 off
8 off

REVISION: PHRASAL VERBS

1
1 C
2 B
3 B
4 A
5 C
6 B
7 C
8 D
9 C
10 B

2
1 across
2 on
3 down
4 back
5 up
6 up
7 down
8 on
9 into
10 along/on

3
1 look after
2 broke out
3 take up
4 turn into
5 taken over
6 Put on
7 put off
8 broke down
9 put up
10 broken into

PREPOSITIONS OF PLACE & TIME

1
1 against
2 in
3 opposite
4 among
5 near
6 around
7 next to
8 under
9 below
10 outside
11 above
12 behind
13 on
14 between

2
1 B
2 C
3 A
4 C
5 A
6 C
7 A
8 B
9 A
10 A
11 C
12 A
13 B
14 C
15 B

3
1 on
2 at, in
3 in
4 –, on
5 –, on
6 on
7 in, at
8 in, on
9 in
10 at, –, on
11 in, –
12 at, at
13 at, in
14 –, on

VERBS, ADJECTIVES, NOUNS WITH PREPOSITIONS

1
1 with
2 of
3 of
4 on
5 in
6 between
7 with
8 about
9 to
10 on
11 about
12 at
13 to
14 for
15 at
16 of
17 with
18 about
19 about
20 at

2
1 for
2 for
3 from
4 to
5 in
6 of
7 from
8 for
9 of
10 to
11 about
12 in
13 for/from
14 about
15 for
16 into
17 for
18 for
19 with
20 of

Grammar Book Key

3
1	C	3	A	5	B	7	B	9	C
2	A	4	A	6	A	8	B	10	B

4
1	at, in, on	4	in, by, on	7	on, by
2	on, by	5	for, at, for, in	8	on, in
3	on, on, in	6	for, on, under		

REVISION

1
1	of	9	At	17	by
2	with	10	with	18	with
3	about	11	under	19	of
4	To	12	for	20	with
5	in	13	by	21	By
6	in	14	to	22	from
7	about	15	On	23	of
8	from	16	for		

2
1	in	4	on	7	to
2	for	5	To	8	into
3	out of	6	by		

3
1	g	3	e	5	f	7	j	9	b
2	d	4	h	6	i	8	c	10	a

4
1	in	5	at/by	9	on
2	to	6	of	10	into
3	by	7	of	11	for
4	by/with	8	to	12	from

5
1	B	4	B	7	D	10	C	13	B
2	D	5	C	8	A	11	C	14	C
3	B	6	C	9	D	12	B	15	C

Progress Tests Key

Progress Test A (Units 1-3)

1	B	6	B	11	A	16	D
2	B	7	C	12	C	17	B
3	C	8	A	13	D	18	B
4	A	9	D	14	D	19	C
5	C	10	D	15	D	20	C

Progress Test B (Units 4-6)

1	B	6	C	11	C	16	D
2	B	7	A	12	C	17	C
3	A	8	A	13	C	18	B
4	D	9	D	14	A	19	C
5	B	10	D	15	B	20	A

Progress Test C (Units 1-6)

1	B	6	B	11	C	16	A
2	A	7	C	12	A	17	C
3	C	8	D	13	D	18	D
4	A	9	B	14	A	19	D
5	C	10	B	15	B	20	B

Progress Test D (Units 7-9)

1	D	6	B	11	C	16	D
2	B	7	C	12	A	17	B
3	B	8	B	13	B	18	A
4	C	9	C	14	C	19	A
5	A	10	D	15	C	20	C

Progress Test E (Units 10-12)

1	B	6	D	11	B	16	C
2	C	7	B	12	A	17	B
3	C	8	C	13	A	18	D
4	A	9	C	14	D	19	D
5	A	10	C	15	A	20	B

Progress Test F (Units 1-12)

1	C	6	B	11	C	16	B
2	A	7	C	12	A	17	B
3	B	8	C	13	D	18	C
4	B	9	B	14	D	19	C
5	A	10	A	15	C	20	B